Clinical Rehabilitation Assessment and Hearing Impairment:

A Guide to Quality Assurance

Larry G. Stewart

Editor

Arkansas Rehabilitation Research and Training Center
on Deafness and Hearing Impairment
University of Arkansas

1986

This publication was made possible in part through research and training center grant No. G008103980-RT-31 from the National Institute of Handicapped Research, United States Office of Education.

FOREWORD

This book is the University of Arkansas' Rehabilitation Research and Training Center on Deafness and Hearing Impairment (RT-31) response to the need for developing guidelines for quality assurance in the assessment of hearing-impaired persons in vocational rehabilitation. The purpose of this book, developed under the leadership of Dr. Larry Stewart, is to provide a handbook for rehabilitation, education and other service providers on information related to assessment procedures, techniques, and issues in the psychological, psychiatric, neuropsychological, vocational, and related areas of evaluation of hearing-impaired persons. The rationale for this approach is that presently there is no single reference book available to counselors with hearing-impaired persons to guide them in the planning and selection of specific assessment services for their clients, or to guide the counselor in assessing the quality of such reports after they are completed.

Procuring rehabilitation assessments of high quality for hearing-impaired persons is fundamental to a valid and reliable determination of capabilities, potentials, and needs. Because counselors frequently have had little training and experience in assessing the quality of specialized rehabilitation assessment reports, it becomes important that they have a resource to guide them in selecting specialized assessments and in evaluating the quality of each.

Stewart, in developing this book with invited contributors, has organized the individual chapters in this book to address the following questions: When should a specialized assessment be used? What does the counselor tell the client about the assessment? How does the counselor locate a qualified examiner? What information does the counselor give the examiner prior to the assessment? What should be included in a specific specialized assessment, and what should the counselor expect in the written report? How is the report discussed with the client? The intent is to encourage the counselor to develop expectations and standards with respect to such assessments, and apply this knowledge in daily practice with hearing-impaired individuals.

In this context, Stewart's concepts of "quality assurance", manifested in the counselor assuming an active, informed, and central role in the assessment of hearing-impaired clients, are most useful. The counselor is provided simple, clear, and straightforward information about how to identify, select, procure, and monitor quality assessment services for clients. This contrasts with much of the work in psychology, education, and rehabilitation, which actively maintains barriers between the disciplines and their respective functions.

Stewart has articulated not only a conceptual framework by which the field can strive for quality assurances in the assessment of hearing-impaired persons, but also provides counselors with information they can use to guide those efforts. Quality assurance for the rehabilitation assessment of hearing-impaired persons is not simply a useful concept. It is the preferred approach, for it is based upon the principle of practicing that which we wish to effect.

In summary, Stewart's effort to articulate the means by which the field can translate implicit principles into applied practice represents a significant contribution to the deafness rehabilitation literature. Its statement is clear and straightforward. It should be read by all those counselors, educators, psychologists, evaluators, and others who are concerned with the translation of their cooperative efforts in assessments into tangible human benefits for hearing-impaired clients.

Douglas Watson
Director
Arkansas Rehabilitation
    Research and Training Center
    on Deafness and Hearing
    Impairment
University of Arkansas

iii

PREFACE

The roots of **Clinical Rehabilitation Assessment and Hearing Impairment: A Guide to Quality Assurance,** in a sense, can be traced back to the time I first started to work with deaf children and young adults as a teacher, fresh out of Gallaudet College. At that time, I was assigned to teach a group of 14 deaf, multiply handicapped children ranging from 13 to 18 years of age. All of these children had in the past functioned poorly in school for reasons no one seemed to understand clearly since diagnostic services were practically nonexistent at the time. As I commenced teaching, or rather, trying to, I found my efforts often ineffectual and, worse, the children became bored, restless, and frustrated, exhibiting various forms of learning, emotional, and behavioral disturbances. Unfortunately, the attitude among most of the professional staff at the school and indeed in deaf education generally, toward these children was, essentially, that they were "problem" children, "stubborn", "troublemakers", and in need of "discipline from a strong male deaf teacher". As a result, I received little guidance in meeting the real needs of these children. As time passed, I began to see that these children had special problems that interfered with their growth and development. The real problem was not in the children but in the lack of diagnostic and teaching/treatment methodologies. However, curriculum guides, diagnostic procedures, and teaching materials for these special children were years in the future.

Later on, this belief was reinforced further when I worked as a rehabilitation counselor. Many times I received diagnostic reports on the deaf persons I served—medical, ophthalmological, otological, psychological, social work, and vocational, for example—that were superficial, incomplete, and, at times, misleading, erroneous or even damaging to the client. There were many excellent assessments and reports, but the proportion of inadequate diagnostic studies was large enough to represent a major concern. I can remember one physician who typically conducted a general medical assessment in 15 minutes, and, in the psychological assessment area, I received more than one psychological report of several pages consisting of complex, jargon-riddled psychodynamic interpretations based on only one projective personality test, with no recommendations.

It is difficult for general practitioners in the various disciplines to examine deaf individuals properly due to communication and other related factors. However, as the state-of-the-art has advanced in medicine, psychiatry, psychology, and other fields, we continue to see too many instances where deaf individuals in education, rehabilitation, and mental health treatment settings do not benefit fully from these advances. We continue to encounter deaf children and young adults who are victims of no diagnostic services, of poor diagnostic services, or of erroneous diagnostic services. Fortunately, there are enough quality diagnostic services now available to deaf persons to convince us that there is no valid reason why such services cannot become the rule rather than the exception.

Today, there are many excellent publications on assessment methods, procedures, and instruments for use with deaf persons. These, however, are addressed to professionals who are in the process of learning how to provide such diagnostic services themselves, or are so general in nature that the reader gains only a global understanding of assessment processes. There appear to be few publications intended for *users* of diagnostic reports, particularly in the areas of psychological, psychiatric, and vocational assessment. As a result, many counselors, teachers, program coordinators, independent living training specialists, speech and language pathologists, and others who are daily involved with deaf children, adults, and their families possess only a marginal understanding of diagnostic procedures and the use of diagnostic results that come from diagnosticians from other disciplines. Under such circumstances, diagnostic studies become mere formalities, with the diagnostic results made available only to a few who may not even understand the report due to jargon, lack of specificity, and general unfamiliarity.

Clinical Rehabilitation Assessment and Hearing Impairment: A Guide to Quality Assurance is intended primarily for professionals who receive and need the information contained in clinical assessment reports—counselors, teachers, therapists, and case coordinators. Its purpose is to inform these service providers of the nature and scope of general and specialist psychometric, psychological, psychiatric, and vocational assessments, and to help them develop skills in using diagnostic resources. The book, however, should also be of value to diagnosticians themselves. It is hoped that through this book, the reader will develop expectations and standards with respect to such assessments, and apply this new knowledge in daily practice with deaf individuals.

This book was made possible through research and training center grant No. G008103980-RT-31 from the National Institute of Handicapped Research.

Many individuals were instrumental in shaping the development of this book, and much appreciation is due to them. First and foremost are the deaf children and adults I have been privileged to serve over the years, including the 14 deaf, multiply disabled children who first brought my attention to the need. I also wish to thank Dr. John F. McGowan of the University of Missouri and Dr. David W. Smith of the University of Arizona for their many contributions to my professional development. Special appreciation is also due to my friend and colleague, Dr. Douglas Watson, who encouraged me in the development of this book and who was a helpful reviewer along the way. A debt of gratitude is owed to Mrs. Sandra Pledger, who typed and retyped numerous drafts of the book manuscript. And, I wish to thank Ms. Susan Adams and Ms. Susan Wootton, who assisted in editing portions of this book, and Dr. Glenn Anderson, who provided valuable input as well as encouragement along the way.

Much time, effort, and care were devoted to the preparation of the individual chapters in this book, and a special note of appreciation is extended to each one of the contributors and to their families.

Finally, I would like to express my deep appreciation to the members of my family for their understanding and support during the preparation of this book.

Larry Gene Stewart

February, 1986
Little Rock, Arkansas

ABOUT THE EDITOR
AND CONTRIBUTORS

Dr. Michael D. Bullis is currently Project Director for the National Deaf Blind Center and Assistant Research Professor for the Division of Oregon State System of Higher Education, Teaching Research Division, Monmouth. A graduate of Purdue University, Dr. Bullis received his Master of Science degree in education counseling from the same institution and his Ph.D. in Special Education and Rehabilitation from the University of Oregon. He brings to the field ten years of experience in various capacities of service delivery in rehabilitation including rehabilitation counselor, work adjustment supervisor and, most recently, research associate with the University of Arkansas Rehabilitation Research and Training Center on Deafness and Hearing Impairment. His professional and research interests include: rehabilitation/habilitation of handicapped persons, interpersonal competence, problem solving and decision making as well as assessment, statistics and research design.

Dr. A. Barry Critchfield is currently an educational psychologist and Supervisor of Counseling and Guidance Services at the California School for the Deaf at Fremont. He received his Ph.D. in Educational Psychology from Brigham Young University in 1982, and has a Master's in Education, Administration and Supervision from California State University, Northridge, under the National Leadership Training Program in the Area of the Deaf. Dr. Critchfield served for four years as a counselor at Crossroads Rehabilitation Center in Indianapolis in a program for severely handicapped deaf adults, and has had extensive experience in psychological, vocational, and educational testing of deaf persons. He has authored numerous articles on the subject of testing hearing-impaired persons.

Dr. Asa J. DeMatteo is a psychologist on the staff at the University of California Center on Deafness in San Francisco where he provides assessment, therapeutic, and consultation services to a deaf clinical population. He completed his doctoral work in clinical psychology at the University of Alabama and his predoctoral internship at the San Francisco Veterans Administration Medical Center. Dr. DeMatteo has also completed postdoctoral work in neuropsychology at the SFVAMC under Dr. Amy Wisniewski. His undergraduate work was in psychology and psycholinguistics, and, in addition to holding a Master's degree in theoretical linguistics, he spent three years in the doctoral program in linguistics at the University of California, Berkeley, where his research was in the area of American Sign Language. Dr. DeMatteo has worked in several rehabilitation settings providing clinical services to deaf individuals while in Alabama, and his current clinical and research interests are in strategic family therapies and neuropsychological assessment with deaf populations.

Bernard M. Gerber, M.D. is Clinical Assistant Professor, Department of Psychiatry, Baylor College of Medicine, Houston, and is in the private practice of general psychiatry. During 1976–1978 Dr. Gerber was the Director of Mental Health Services for Deaf Persons, Department of Mental Health, Commonwealth of Massachusetts, involved in the development of the first mental health services programs for deaf people in Massachusetts. He has also served on the Mental Health Advisory Committee of the National Association of the Deaf and in a variety of other national, state, and local organizations serving deaf people. His clinical practice includes evaluation and treatment of deaf persons, as well as consultation to rehabilitation, school, and community agencies and groups in the area of deafness and mental health.

Dr. S. Margaret Lee is a clinical psychologist working at the University of California Center on Deafness in San Francisco. She provides evaluation and treatment to deaf adults, deaf children, and their families. Dr. Lee has worked with deaf persons for the past 13 years. She has presented at numerous workshops on issues related to mental health and deafness, and co-authored, with Hilde Schlesinger, M.D., a chapter on sensory disabilities in the 1980 *Annual Review of Rehabilitation*. Dr. Lee obtained her doctorate from the California School of Professional Psychology in Berkeley in 1978. Her dissertation examined issues in mother-child interaction with deaf children. Dr. Lee's current research interests include psychological and neuropsychological assessment of deaf individuals, play therapy with deaf children, and the application of ego psychology to the development of deaf children.

Paula A. Marut is currently a reasearch associate at the University of Arkansas Rehabilitation Research and Training Center on Deafness and Hearing Impairment. Ms. Marut received her Bachelor of Science degree in elementary education/ hearing impairment from Bloomsburg State College and her Master's degree in rehabilitation counseling with the hearing-impaired from New York University. Her professional experience includes that of psychometrist for the Comprehensive Evaluation and Training Center in Cambridge, MA and as psychometrist/evaluator for Delaware Elwyn Institute's program for deaf individuals. In addition to her position with RT-31, Ms. Marut teaches sign language for the University of Arkansas at Little Rock in the Interpreter Training Program. Her professional interests include assessment of deaf individuals and applications of microcomputers in the rehabilitation setting.

Dr. Forrest C. Orr is currently on the staff of the University of California Center on Deafness in San Francisco, providing mental health services to deaf individuals and their families. He also has a part-time private practice in Berkeley. Dr. Orr received his Bachelor's and Master's degrees from the University of Illinois, and his Ph.D. degree in psychology from the University of Missouri. He has taught psychology at Blackburn College, California State University in Chico, Washington University, and the University of California. He has also worked as a clinical psychologist in a variety of clinical settings, including many years in private practice, hospitals, and rehabilitation settings. He is currently interested in the psychology of deafness, and is doing psychological evaluation and psychotherapy with deaf individuals. Dr. Orr holds a diploma in clinical psychology from the American Board of Professional Psychology.

Dr. David A. Pritchard is currently Supervising Forensics Psychologist at Rogers Hall, the forensic unit of the Arkansas State Hospital, Arkansas Division of Mental Health, Little Rock. He also serves as director of a special project to provide community mental health services to deaf persons and their families. Dr. Pritchard obtained his B.A. in psychology from The Creighton University in Omaha, Nebraska, and his M.A. and Ph.D. degrees were obtained in clinical psychology at Indiana University. He has had extensive clinical experience in a number of mental health settings, and has taught in the psychology departments at Indiana University, North Texas State University, and the University of Mississippi. Dr. Pritchard is a diplomate in the Academy of Forensic Psychology and the American Board of Forensic Psychology. He has published numerous articles and presented in the speciality area of forensic psychology. His current interests are in the areas of forensic psychology and mental health services for deaf persons and their families.

Dr. Lois A. Shafqat is currently the Director of the Disabled Students Program at Golden West College in Huntington Beach, California. Since 1972 she has worked with hearing-impaired people over the educational spectrum from preschool through college age. Her interest in appropriate assessment tools for the disabled population led to the pioneering of the first translation of a paper and pencil test into American Sign Language on videotape. Dr. Shafqat obtained her B.S. degree in psychology from the University of Tennessee, her Master's in psychology from Chapman College in Orange, California, and her Ph.D. in psychology from U.S. International University in San Diego, California.

John W. Shiels is Administrative Coordinator of Rehabilitation at the Hearing, Speech and Deafness Center in Seattle, a comprehensive rehabilitation program for deaf adults, where he has worked for many years as a vocational evaluator. A former Gallaudet student, he has a Master's degree in rehabilitation counseling. Mr. Shiels is currently chairperson of the Washington State Department of Social and Human Services Advisory Committee on Deafness, and is also a member of the State Vocational Rehabilitation advisory committee. He has published several articles and made numerous presentations in his speciality area.

Dr. Larry G. Stewart is currently Associate Professor of Rehabilitation, Arkansas Rehabilitation Research and Training Center on Deafness and Hearing Impairment, Little Rock. A graduate of Gallaudet College, Dr. Stewart received his Master's degree in rehabilitation counseling from the University of Missouri, and his Ed.D. degree in rehabilitation from the University of Arizona. A licensed counseling psychologist, Dr. Stewart's career has included teaching, clinical services, administration, graduate education, and research in the areas of education and rehabilitation of deaf persons. He has directed national projects focusing on the rehabilitation of multiply disabled deaf children and adults. In addition to serving as a consultant to federal and state agencies, for many years he has performed psychological assessments with deaf individuals for rehabilitation agencies, schools for deaf children, and the justice system, and has taught at the University of Arizona, University of Arkansas, and New York University. A past president and former board member of the American Deafness and Rehabilitation Association, he has authored many publications in the field of deafness and has presented at conferences and workshops throughout the country. Dr. Stewart's current interests include clinical assessment, research, and writing in the area of psychology and rehabilitation.

Dr. Patricia M. Sullivan is presently Coordinator of Psychological Services at The Boys Town National Institute for Communication Disorders in Children, Omaha, Nebraska. She received her doctorate in psychology from the University of Iowa. Dr. Sullivan is an assistant professor in the Department of Human Communication at The Creighton University Medical School and is a member of the Nebraska Commission for the Hearing-Impaired. She is a specialist in psychological practices with deaf persons and has worked in a residential school for the deaf and as a provider of clinical psychological services to deaf children and adults.

Dr. David P. Yandell is presently in independent practice in the Phoenix, Arizona area. He completed his Ph.D. degree at Arizona State University in 1973, and later that year studied with Dr. Stewart at the University of Arizona in providing psychological services to deaf persons. Dr. Yandell founded the Counseling Center for the Hearing-Impaired in Phoenix in 1978, and in July 1982 the program became a part of Good Samaritan Medical Center, with Dr. Yandell remaining director until 1984. He has been a psychologist and chief psychologist with the Arizona Department of Vocational Rehabilitation, and has served as Director of Training for the Department of Psychology at Good Samaritan Medical Center. He is a member of the National Register of Health Services Providers in Psychology and a past president of the Arizona State Psychological Association, Maricopa Society of Clinical Psychologists, and the Central Arizona Rehabilitation Association.

Dr. Amy M. Wisniewski is Chief of the Neuropsychology and Assessment Units at the San Francisco Veterans Administration Medical Center. In addition to administrative responsibilities, she directs the postdoctoral training program in neuropsychology and provides assessment, treatment and consultation services to brain-injured veterans and their families. She is a member of the Senior Core Faculty at the Pacific Graduate School of Psychology and adjunct faculty in the Psychology Department of San Francisco State University. Her research and clinical interests include investigation of neuropsychological dysfunction associated with endocrine and metabolic disorders and exposure to environmental toxins. Her most recent project involves development of neuropsychological assessment procedures for clinical use with deaf individuals.

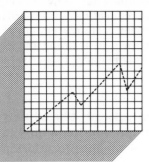

Introduction

Larry G. Stewart

Clinical Rehabilitation Assessment and Hearing Impairment: A Guide to Quality Assurance presents descriptions of processes and procedures typically used among specialist examiners who serve deaf persons in the areas of psychology, psychiatry, and vocational evaluation. It is intended to acquaint consumers, or users, of diagnostic reports with specific types of clinical assessments conducted with deaf persons in educational, rehabilitation, and mental health settings. Professionals who typically receive and read clinical diagnostic reports often do not have adequate information on the nature and scope of such assessments, and this makes it difficult for them to know when to request these assessments, what to anticipate from them, and what to do if a particular assessment does not provide needed information.

A reading of this book, hopefully, will lead to three primary results. One, service providers will learn of the types of information that *can* be obtained on a deaf student or client through the kinds of assessments discussed in the chapters that follow. Second, service providers will become knowledgeable concerning the kinds of information that *should* be included in each type of assessment. And, third, service providers will have illustrative examples of each type of assessment report that can be used as a model against which they may compare and contrast diagnostic reports they receive from diagnosticians who serve their students and clients. In this manner, it is hoped that these typical *users of assessment results*—teachers, counselors, instructors, supervisors, coordinators, therapists—will be enabled to more confidently approach the tasks of seeking properly qualified diagnosticians, providing diagnosticians with feedback on the usefulness of their reports, and working with diagnosticians to reach higher levels of effectiveness in the provision of diagnostic and treatment services to deaf individuals and their families.

What is clinical assessment? Woody (1980) defines it as follows:

Clinical assessment is a set of processes and procedures for human services professionals. It is inherent in all professional functions, be it the reaction in the initial contact with a prospective patient, the decision to accept or reject a patient, the services to be offered and the techniques to be used, the decision to terminate treatment, or the impression of the treatment's efficiency and relevance to treating other patients.

. . . clinical assessment focuses on the individual; that is, for the most part it is *idiographic*, as opposed to *nomothetic*.

(p.xxxi)

Diagnostic studies in education and other human service settings have become increasingly critical program components in recent years due to new statutes and regulations. Public Law 94-142, the Education of All Handicapped Children Act (20 U.S.C., Section 1401), mandates a free, *appropriate* public education for all handicapped children. In the U.S. Department of Education's regulations for the Rehabilitation Act of 1973, Title V, Section 504 (29 U.S.C., Section 794), public schools are required to provide a free, *appropriate* public education to qualified handicapped children regardless of the nature of their handicap. Section 504 also prohibits discrimination against handicapped persons in postsecondary education and in health care and social services. The Developmentally Disabled Assistance and Bill of Rights Act (42 U.S.C., Section 6000) mandates *appropriate* treatment, services, and habilitation for developmentally disabled persons in a setting that is least restrictive of personal liberty.

The determination of what is "appropriate" for a given child or adult in any program of services rests squarely on effective diagnostic services. Under P.L. 94-142, schools must devise an Individualized Education Plan for each handicapped child, and this written plan must *identify and assess* the child's disability, establish long- and short-term learning goals, and state which services the school must provide to help the child achieve them (National Center for Law and the Deaf, 1984, pp. 29–30). Similarly, appropriate services for disabled persons are mandated through the State/Federal Vocational Rehabilitation program, and an Individualized Written Rehabilitation Plan (IWRP) is required in each case. Indeed, as McGowan and Porter (1967) stated long ago:

> The rehabilitation process is a planned, orderly sequence of services related to the total needs of the handicapped individual. It is a process built around both the problems of a handicapped individual and the attempts of the vocational rehabilitation counselor to help solve these problems . . .
>
> (p. 51)

Thus, assessment procedures are of fundamental importance in the process of determining the needs of deaf children and adults. Unfortunately, the mystique that often surrounds the special knowledges and methods of specialists leads to poor or otherwise ineffectual communication between the specialist and those professionals who serve on an interdisciplinary team. The assessment by the specialist may have little meaning to those who read the assessment report unless there is good understanding and interaction among them.

Over the years, while working in a variety of educational, rehabilitation, and mental health settings, first as a consumer or user (teacher, counselor) of diagnostic reports and later as an examiner (psychologist), I have been impressed by several barriers that seem to inhibit effective diagnostic studies and the application of the results in student and client service activities. One of the main barriers lies with users of diagnostic reports. Too often, they are unaware of what to expect, and even demand, from a particular diagnostic study. This ultimately stands in the way of their objectively assessing the quality of a particular diagnostic report.

A second barrier is found in the fact that too many times the user of the report is in "awe" of the perceived special status of the diagnostician, and this may prevent questioning of the assessment report. This is unfortunate, because all diagnostic studies are for the benefit of the examinee and those who are affected by related recommendations. A healthy attitude to be fostered in overcoming this barrier is that users of diagnostic reports have a right, and an obligation, to communicate openly with assessment specialists in pursuit of the best possible services for the individual client or student. Examiners are not omnipotent, nor are they infallible. They are certainly not prophets or seers. As Thorne (1961) stated:

> Judgments concerning clinical matters can be made by anyone. Such *lay opinions* have only the weight of the level of intelligence, education, and experience of the person making them. It always remains to be demonstrated whether specialty training and experience make possible judgments of higher validity than lay opinions.
>
> (p. 7)

In short, the assessment specialist has the responsibility of demonstrating his or her ability to perform and report helpful diagnostic information; position or title in itself does not automatically confer expertise.

Examiners do have special knowledges and skills, but often the feedback potentially available from users of assessment reports can help the examiner produce better results.

A third barrier observed is that users of diagnostic reports are often unaware of their obligation to be discriminating about their choice of diagnostician. Users have the responsibility to actively search for those who are best qualified to render the desired service. Yet, a view often expressed is that a psychiatrist is a psychiatrist, a psychologist is a psychologist, and a vocational evaluator is a vocational evaluator, so all should be able to provide basically similar services! The truth is that diagnosticians in every discipline will be found to vary to greater or lesser extent in terms of training, knowledge, skills, area of specialization, attitudes, and perspective. Some will have more competence in conducting actual assessments, less skill in providing a written report, while with others these abilities will be reversed. Consequently, it becomes a responsibility of the assessment report user to be aware of such variations and to search for and find those examiners who are best able to provide quality assessments as well as helpful reports. At times, users of diagnostic reports will even need to become involved in assisting an examiner to become better able to provide the information that is needed.

A fourth barrier consists of the fact that on many occasions examiners are not informed of specific information needed from an assessment. This occurs when the person making the assessment referral does not provide the examiner with specific questions to be answered by the examination. This makes it very difficult for the examiner to meet the service provider's unstated expectations. It is incumbent upon the person making a referral to inform the examiner of specific needs from a given assessment.

Assessment specialists sometimes contribute to the barriers that lead to inefficacy of assessment procedures and results. They sometimes use professional jargon in their reports, and this clouds rather than clarifies the diagnostic findings. At times examiners literally bury nuggets of priceless diagnostic information among pages of irrelevant information, and at other times they write such brief reports that vital information is lost. There are also occasions when examiners assume that their style of written expression is sufficiently explanatory, whereas in reality it strikes the report reader as overly-generalized, complex, or even intellectually intimidating. Recommendations based on diagnostic findings sometimes are stated in terms that are meaningless to the teacher or counselor who must plan specific treatment activities. A recommendation such as "The client needs to enhance her self-esteem through programmatic activities" is hardly something a teacher can use when faced with a student who is constantly engaging in attention-getting activities. The examiner needs to be more specific, using clear language.

None of these barriers need to exist. Effective communication and awareness of one another's role and function are desirable goals for diagnosticians and those who use their services, and these are attainable when the goal is pursued with mutual respect and confidence.

This book is oriented primarily toward assessment of teenagers and adults rather than children. However, the *principles* exemplified throughout the chapters to follow are equally applicable in all service settings and at all age levels. These chapters also address the barriers that often inhibit diagnostic studies of deaf individuals. The authors of the individual chapters are skilled, experienced clinicians in their area of specialization, and they have presented their remarks from the vantage point of extensive experience in working with deaf persons and their families. The authors have attempted to describe what they do during an assessment and why they do it, and to present an example of their own work in the form of an assessment report.

Some professionals prefer to use the word "evaluation" rather than "assessment" to describe their work, while others prefer the word "examination". In the chapters that follow, no attempt has been made to differentiate between these words and they are used interchangeably.

The reader will note certain themes and concepts repeated in two or more of the chapters. It is instructive for the reader to search for and to note these, for they reflect important philosophical and professional beliefs held by experienced examiners who have worked with hundreds of deaf persons and their families. At the same time, the differences among the authors are equally important; they reflect the broad horizons yet to be explored in the area of deafness and the behavioral sciences.

Chapter I describes the psychometric assessment, with special attention given to the psychometric assessment of deaf persons. A sample psychometric assessment report at the end of the chapter presents a model for such an assessment.

Chapter II presents one perspective toward the psychological assessment. The nature and scope of the assessment are described, and a discussion is presented concerning special aspects of examining deaf persons. A sample psychological report is included to provide the reader with an illustration of the points covered in the chapter.

A second perspective on the psychological evaluation is provided in Chapter III. This chapter will enable the reader to gain insight into how two different examiners approach the task of conducting a psychological assessment. A comparison of the sample report from Chapter III with the one from Chapter II will add to the reader's understanding of this type of assessment when conducted with two individuals whose needs are quite different.

Chapter IV discusses the characteristics and assessment of students in transition. The concept of "students in transition" is a new one which promises to hold important implications for the field in the years ahead. An illustrative report demonstrates how a psychological evaluation differs with this type of examinee.

Chapter V introduces the neuropsychological assessment and its application with a deaf person. This is a specialty evaluation which is expected to be used more and more in the area of deafness in the years ahead. An illustrative report concludes the chapter.

Chapter VI describes the forensic psychological evaluation, which, like the neuropsychological evaluation, is a relatively new type of specialty assessment in the area of deafness. Its application with deaf persons is discussed, and a sample assessment report is provided.

Chapter VII presents a description of the psychiatric assessment and its use with deaf persons. An illustrative psychiatric assessment report on a deaf client of Vocational Rehabilitation is also presented.

The vocational assessment is described in Chapter VIII. The special considerations in assessing a deaf person are presented and a sample report concludes the chapter.

Chapter IX consists of a review of prior research studies on the use of vocational evaluation recommendations in actual service settings, and reports on a similar study recently completed with deaf clients. The implications of the findings are discussed, including the potential ramifications with all types of diagnostic assessments.

Chapter X discusses the problem of testing deaf individuals whose native language is American Sign Language and who have limited English language skills. An innovative adaptation of one personality test for use with deaf persons is described, and a sample report based on this adaptation is presented.

As mentioned previously, this book is intended to assist the consumer or user of clinical assessment results to understand selected types of assessment procedures in their application with deaf persons. The realization of this goal should contribute to improved quality assurance in services for the deaf community.

References

Developmentally Disabled Assistance and Bill of Rights Act, 42 U.S. Code, Section 6000.

McGowan, J. & Porter, T. (1967). *An introduction to the vocational rehabilitation process.* Washington, D.C.: U.S. Department of Health, Education, and Welfare.

National Center for the Law and the Deaf (1984). *Legal rights of hearing-impaired people.* Washington, D.C.: Gallaudet College Press.

Public Law 94-142, The Education of All Handicapped Children Act, 20 U.S. Code Section 1401.

Rehabilitation Act of 1973, Title V, Section 504, 29 U.S. Code, Section 794.

Thorne, F. C. (1961). *Clinical judgment: A study of clinical error.* Brandon, VT: Journal of Clinical Psychology.

Woody, R. H. (1980). Introduction: A conceptual framework for clinical assessment. In R. Woody (Ed.), *Encyclopedia of clinical assessment, Volume 1,* (pp. xxx-x1). San Francisco: Jossey-Bass.

Clinical Rehabilitation Assessment and Hearing Impairment: A Guide to Quality Assurance
Larry G. Stewart
Editor

		Page
Foreword	Douglas Watson	iii
Preface	Editor	v
Contributors		vii
Introduction	Larry G. Stewart	xi
Table of Contents		xv
Chapter I:	Psychometric Assessment *A. Barry Critchfield*	1
Chapter II:	Psychological Assessment: One Perspective *Larry G. Stewart*	9
Chapter III:	Psychological Assessment: Another Perspective *David P. Yandell*	27
Chapter IV:	Characteristics and Assessment of Students in Transition *Patricia M. Sullivan*	37
Chapter V:	Neuropsychological Assessment *Amy M. Wisniewski, Asa J. DeMatteo, Forrest C. Orr & S. Margaret Lee*	49
Chapter VI:	Forensic Psychological Assessment *Larry G. Stewart & David A. Pritchard*	71
Chapter VII:	Psychiatric Assessment *Bernard M. Gerber*	87
Chapter VIII:	Vocational Assessment *John W. Shiels*	95
Chapter IX:	Evaluation Recommendations and Rehabilitation Outcomes *Michael D. Bullis & Paula A. Marut*	111
Chapter X:	Innovations in Assessment Strategies: One Approach *Lois A. Shafqat*	119
Indices:	Author and Subject	131

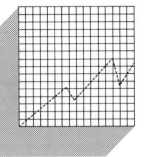

CHAPTER I

Psychometric Assessment

A. Barry Critchfield

Introduction

This chapter describes the nature and process of the psychometric assessment with hearing-impaired persons. Through a study of this chapter, readers will be able to recognize the components of such an assessment procedure and to ascertain the quality of assessment reports they have the opportunity to read. Samples of psychometric assessment reports are also included.

Psychometric Testing of Vocational Clients

Psychometric testing is performed in an effort to compare a particular client with a population of persons on any number of various individual attributes. It generally deals with such areas as individual intelligence, visual/motor coordination, academic achievement, communication skill, vocational aptitude, adaptive functioning and personal/vocational interest. Such testing assumes that there is a normal distribution of certain characteristics within a population and that these characteristics can be identified through standard testing practices. This type of testing is usually performed early in the evaluation period, to get a global picture of individual strengths and weaknesses in relevant areas, and may be repeated during the course of an education or training period to assess any significant improvements or deteriorations.

Essential to an understanding of psychometric practice is an awareness of certain basic statistical constructs, including population, sample, normal, valid, and reliable. For the purposes of this presentation, a population is defined as the entire group of all individuals in a given category, i.e., deaf persons in South Carolina; female basketball players in the N.B.A. The term, sample, refers to any subgroup of a population and, for statistical reliability purposes, a random sample must be drawn so as to accurately reflect the makeup of the entire population from which it is selected. For any of the factors being measured on a psychometric evaluation (reading, vocational interest, etc.), an assumption is made that, over the entire population, a "normal" distribution of high to low scores occurs. That is, some persons are measured as extremely high in a particular attribute, and others are found to be significantly low in that area, with the majority of scores falling between these two extremes and the largest number being exactly halfway between these two poles. When measuring any of the attributes described above, objective tests are used. For a test to be statistically useful, it must, in fact, measure what it purports to measure (validity), and it must also be consistent in measuring those attributes across the entire population (reliablity).

A key element of the psychometric evaluation process is the concept that objective measures offer the opportunity to assess a person, independent of such factors as background, handicapping conditions, personality differences or other variables. While these issues are all of great significance in the final synthesis of test data, at this point in the evaluation the goal is to analyze a large number of factors independent of one another, to get an overall listing of strengths and weaknesses. Once a test score is obtained, it is desirable to compare this score with those of other similar persons. This is accomplished through the use of *normative data*, which are the collected scores of a representative sample of the population. Thus, a valid psychometric assessment reveals a person's strengths and weaknesses in comparison with a normative population.

Controversy prevails over the issue of the choice of the normative group with which to compare deaf children and adults. Is it better, for example, to compare a hearing-impaired person with other hearing-impaired individuals or with the general population? This is an issue which has long divided evaluators, and one to which a simple solution is not available. There are appropriate times for both kinds of comparisons, and the decision as to which norm group to use should be carefully considered in light of the numerous factors impinging upon each client. Specific reasons for the choice of a particular norm group should be clearly stated. It should be noted here that very few reliable norms for the deaf are available for most tests and it is the belief of this author that, unless a valid reason exists for the alternative, the larger population norms should be utilized. For example, since the information being solicited from the psychometric assessment in rehabilitation is predominantly vocational in its nature, and since the client will usually be competing with the general population in the work environment, how that person compares with the general population is usually of greater importance than how the person compares with other hearing-impaired individuals.

One feature that separates a psychometric assessment from a psychological evaluation is the factor of *interpretation*. The purpose of a psychometric assessment is to arrive at objective test scores which allow comparisons, rather than interpretations of the meaning of the test results.

In requesting a psychometric assessment, it is important for the counselor or case coordinator and the psychometrist to understand what is desired. Much dissatisfaction and misunderstanding between professionals can be attributed to the simple issue of a referral question. Referring professionals have a responsibility to ASK for specific answers prior to the actual assessment. Specifics should be employed, such as "What is this person's reading level, IQ, and manual dexterity?", rather than, "What is this person's vocational potential?"

Another important concept is that the psychometric assessment should identify strengths as well as weaknesses in clients. Each client is a unique individual, and will be different in many ways from others. It should be expected that a psychometric evaluation will provide some identification of both positive and negative areas of performance *for the individual*.

The kinds of tests involved in a psychometric assessment may include measures of intelligence, psychomotor functioning, academic achievement, communication skills, vocational aptitude, adaptive functioning and personal/vocational interest. In addition, objective tests of personality are sometimes used. The overriding feature of all these tests, however, is their reliance on normative test scores rather than on the subjective impression of a particular examiner.

Interpreter services are being utilized more and more today, and while this is a significant step forward, it must be recognized that is only a stopgap measure in the provision of quality evaluation services. Interpreters by training and by professional ethical practice are unable to provide opinions or input in the evaluation process—their purpose is purely communicative.

It should be pointed out that many psychometric tests are not directly validated based upon educational and vocational performance. It has been noted that some individuals are able to perform extremely well in the classroom or on the job, despite weak test scores, while others who do relatively well on objective assessments do not always possess the necessary traits to be immediately successful educationally and vocationally. This, then, points out an important consideration—the appropriate use of test results. The psychometrist *reports* test results only, and it is up to the user of the report to apply the results.

The expected result of a psychometric assessment is a listing of test scores, with an explanation (if appropriate) as to their statistical meanings. With reasonably valid test scores in hand, a qualified counselor may be able to assist a deaf client in outlining realistic goals and objectives. Caution needs to be exercised, however, in limiting the degree of test interpretation to that which the counselor is legally and ethically prepared to substantiate.

Content of the Psychometric Evaluation

Referral Information. Here, the report states the purpose of psychometric testing. This purpose must be stated by the professional who made the referral.

Background Information. While the psychometric assessment is probably one of the most objective of all evaluations, it is important to provide the examiner with enough background information from which a reliable and valid assessment can be developed. The psychometrist needs to know such information as communication skills, educational background, hearing loss, medical problems, and the reason for referral. In addition, if prior psychological evaluations have been performed, these should be shared with the examiner unless there is a specific reason for not doing so. See the forms at the end of this chapter for examples of the types of background information which can be of great assistance to the evaluator.

Client Interview. The interview is an important step in the psychometric testing process. It is here that the psychometrist becomes familiar with the client's communication style and skills. This interview allows the psychometrist an opportunity to get an impression as to the direction and depth of formal testing, and also enables the psychometrist to establish rapport and develop a healthy relationship with the deaf client. The psychometrist should be willing to take enough time for these purposes.

A thorough explanation about the upcoming experience may be required if this has not happened previously, and experience has shown that many, if not most, deaf rehabilitation clients have not been adequately apprised of the testing procedures, or what impact the results may have on future vocational directions.

Tests. The issue of appropriate tests to administer to deaf persons has been covered extensively in psychological literature. Persons unfamiliar with the testing of hearing-impaired clients should become aware of the constraints imposed by such testing, and limit test selection to such tests as those considered appropriate by experienced deafness professionals (Levine, 1981; Sullivan and Vernon, 1979; Watson, 1976; Zieziula, 1982).

As with the testing of any client, individual factors such as educational background, multiple handicaps, vocational goals and personality variables must be considered when testing deaf subjects. In addition, such issues as degree of hearing loss, age at onset of hearing loss, communication mode and cultural factors are also of great significance when preparing to assess deaf persons.

Regarding appropriate test selection, Zieziula (1982) offers the following:

> There are four major questions that must be asked when choosing a test for a hearing-impaired person:
>
>> —Does the test consist of verbal test items or performance items?
>> —Do instructions for the test require verbal communication?
>> —Do any test items discriminate against an individual with an auditory impairment?
>> —Are hearing-impaired people included in the normative sample provided by the test developer?

With the above criteria in mind, the following tests are recommended as useful in psychometric assessment of deaf persons, but should not be considered as the only alternatives available:

(a) *Intelligence tests*
Wechsler Adult Intelligence Scale—Revised
Wechsler Intelligence Scale for Children—Revised
Hiskey-Nebraska Test of Learning Aptitude
Raven's Progressive Matrices
Leiter International Performance Scale
Revised Beta Examination

(b) *Achievement tests*
Gates-MacGinitie Reading Tests
Key Math Diagnostic Arithmetic Test
Stanford Achievement Test—Special Edition for Hearing-Impaired Students
Wide Range Achievement Test—Arithmetic Section only
Metropolitan Achievement Test
Peabody Individual Achievement Test—Using modified instructions
Adult Basic Learning Examination

(c) *Interest tests*
Wide Range Interest Opinion Test

(d) *Communication skills test*
Illinois Test of Psycholinguistic Abilities
Manual Communication Proficiency Test (Craig, 1969)

(e) *Visual perception tests*
Bender Visual Motor Gestalt Test
Graham-Kendall Memory-for-Designs Test
Motor-Free Visual Perception Test
Dvorine Color Plates

(f) *Vocational aptitude tests*
Purdue Pegboard
Minnesota Rate of Manipulation Tests
Revised Minnesota Paper Form Board Test
Crawford Small Parts Dexterity Test

Summary. The summary section of the evaluation provides an opportunity to summarize the test data.

Recommendations. As a logical development from the summary, recommendations should be specific and brief, with emphasis on specific test or observational data. As with other sections, the temptation to offer opinions and conjectures should be avoided in psychometric evaluation. In the case of vocationally-oriented assessments, recommendations which are related to specific jobs or training programs can be helpful to referring counselors. Should more in-depth testing be required, this also would be appropriately included here.

Evaluation Procedures with Deaf Clients

In administering psychometric tests to deaf persons, the procedures which are followed with other kinds of testing of deaf persons apply. Basically,

3

these concerns can be summarized by stating that procedures should not discriminate against deaf persons because of their handicapping conditions. Since deafness is a communication handicap, testing procedures should reflect an awareness of this limitation. Reading is usually an area of significant weakness for deaf persons, and any procedure which involves reading as a part of the test is highly suspect (unless reading itself is being tested). Usually, performance is a better measure of ability than verbal skill. Tests which permit the demonstration of instructions are usually better than those which rely on verbal directions. When normative data are available which include a hearing-impaired sample, one can feel more confident as to the appropriateness of a particular instrument. For a more indepth treatment of the testing issues and procedures, the reader is encouraged to consult the references which appear at the end of this chapter.

Deaf persons who have received a primarily oral education may be unable to benefit from traditional sign language testing programs. Such persons may require much more individual attention, and the use of oral interpreters is an alternative, should the person require this service. It should not be felt that, because a person has had an oral education, reading skills will be adequate. Indeed, many orally educated deaf persons exhibit the same reading deficits which other deaf persons experience.

People who are hard of hearing may also present unique testing difficulties. While their speech and language competencies may appear to be adequate, they often become masters at disguising misunderstandings, and an effective evaluator needs to be sensitive to the dynamics of this situation. Often, skills at diplomacy are required to help the individual recognize areas of misunderstanding, while maintaining interest and motivation. It is not uncommon to find persons (particularly the elderly) unwilling to accept their loss of hearing, and sometimes an evaluator can be an effective intermediary in assisting such persons to seek amplification or other types of assistance.

Answers to Questions

1. When is it appropriate to refer to a person for psychometric evaluation?

Psychometric testing is useful whenever *objective* indicators are needed regarding a student's or client's level of intelligence, academic performance, vocational aptitudes and interests, personality, and other relevant performance areas. Educational, vocational, and mental health placement and progress monitoring are facilitated through *appropriate* use of psychometric testing. Such testing is particularly useful for eligibility determination and initial program placement.

2. Is it appropriate to discuss test results with clients?

Both the psychometrist and the counselor should be willing to discuss in-depth, to the level of the client's capabilities, the test results and their implications. Often a client is able to provide valuable insight into test performance, and where unusual scores are noted, they should be discussed with the person involved. Aside from the fact that, legally, clients have access to records, ethics dictate that people have a right to an understanding of themselves. Where potentially damaging results may be obtained, these need to be considered carefully, and presented appropriately to the people involved.

Sample Vocational/Psychometric Assessment

Following is a sample psychometric assessment report with a vocational emphasis which is intended to illustrate a number of the criteria presented in this chapter. Through a careful study of the data contained in this report, it is expected that the reader will develop skills at evaluating the quality of reports received from actual assessment practitioners.

CLIENT: J __ R __   DATE(S) OF TESTING
                                       XXXXXXXXXX
                                       BIRTHDATE:
                                       XXXXXXXXXXX

DIAGNOSIS: Congenital hearing loss (severe)
                      Mild cerebral palsy (upper extremeties)

REFERRED BY: XXXXXXXXXXXX

EDUCATION: Junior High level—discontinued State
                     Residential School in 9th Grade.

Background Information

J. comes from a family of eight children, although not all are his natural siblings. He states that his family relationships have been good, and that he gets along well with his parents and siblings. Communication at home is entirely oral.

J. views himself as "hard of hearing" and this evaluator would tend to agree with this categorization. He has relatively good speech skills and is able to converse freely without sign language. His sign skills, however, are good and he relies on signs to augment his oral communication abilities.

J.'s attitude toward his education is quite negative. He states that he prefers work to school because he often was in trouble at school. His favorite class was gym, and he expressed a consistent dislike for all the rest of the subjects he took.

J. has previously worked as a laborer with an animal science lab, and at a sideshow at the State Fair. He has also worked with his father. J. reports his vocational goals to be: gas station attendant; dish washer; State Fair employee (the latter was unclear to both J. and the interviewer).

J. gives the overall impression of being a cheerful, happy-go-lucky teenager. He seems to be somewhat immature in his world-view, and needs the opportunity to develop personal and vocational skills.

Behavioral Observations

Public Image:	J. is short in stature, with a pleasant and cheerful disposition.
Motivation:	Responds to positive reinforcement, but seems to have an external locus of control.
Social Behavior:	J. seems to make friends easily, but is easily manipulated by other persons.

During testing, J. was cooperative and seemed to try hard. He appeared to understand instructions clearly, especially when signs were used along with voice for the instructional process.

Test Results

Wechsler Adult Intelligence Scale—Revised

Performance IQ	78
Picture Completion	8
Picture Arrangement	6
Block Design	4
Object Assembly	6
Digit Symbol	6

Bender Visual Motor Gestalt Test—
  Koppitz Score 5
Wide Range Interest Opinion Test
  —No significant positive interests manifest
  —Significant negative interest in Literary, Mechanical areas
Minnesota Rate of Manipulation—First percentile
Purdue Pegboard—First percentile
Differential Aptitude—Mechanical Reasoning Test—90th percentile
Gates MacGinitie Reading Test—

Vocabulary	1.7
Comprehension	1.4

Wide Range Achievement Test
  Arithmetic—Grade level 3.6

Summary

Academics appear to be an area of significant weakness for J., both in terms of his interest and ability. There are indicators of possible neurological dysfunction. J.'s coordination difficulties likely hampered his performance on many of the manipulation tests, and it is apparent that he is unable to perform at high levels of expectation when faced with limitations of time. While the quality of many of his test results was acceptable, his performance was significantly impaired because of his cerebral palsy condition. J.'s vocational goals do not appear to be well organized at this point in his life. He responds well to positive reinforcement, and is also highly motivated by the prospect of earning money for his efforts.

Recommendations

1. Work Adjustment Training in a program which is able to meet the specific needs of a multiply handicapped hearing-impaired young man, for a period of at least 6 months.
2. A physical/occupational therapy evaluation to determine whether J. can benefit from therapy.
3. Personal/vocational adjustment counseling to help J. set realistic vocational goals and deal with immature behavior.

It has been a pleasure working with this young man. If further information is required, feel free to contact me at any time.

_____
Psychometrist

SAMPLE BACKGROUND INFORMATION/INTERVIEW FORM

IDENTIFYING DATA:

Name _____ S.S. # ____-__-_____

Address _____

_____

Age _____ Date of Birth _____ Place of Birth _____

Referred by _____ Auth. # _____

Description

Race _____   Build _____   Height _____   Weight _____

Complexion _____   Scars _____   Eyes _____   Hair _____

Appearance _____

Physical

Unusual Birth _____

Illnesses & Handicaps _____

Exercise Program _____   Medication _____   Alcohol _____

Drugs _____ Smoke _____

In care of: Doctor _____ Counselor _____

BASIC MEDICAL

Secondary disabilities _____

Physical limitations _____

Dental report _____

Family medical history _____

Personal medical history _____

VISUAL ASSESSMENT

Type of problem, if any: Refractive errors:

Myopia _____

Hyperopia _____

Astigmatism _____

Structural anomalise _____

Infectious diseases _____

Muscle function _____

Ushers _____

Severity of the problem _____

Vocational implications _____

Correctable? _____

Corrective lenses? _____   Correct the anomaly? _____

Copies of: Opthalmological _____   Optical _____

AUDIOLOGICAL-HEARING

Type of Loss: Conductive   _____

Sensory neural   _____

Progressive/stable   _____

Recruitment   _____

Balance problems   _____

Prognosis   _____

Severity of impairment _____

Age at onset _____   Severity at onset _____

Etiology _____

Hearing aid: Type _____

Age first fitted _____

Type of training _____

Aided hearing level _____

6

Regularity of use _____

Copies of: Most recent audiogram _____   Otological _____

CLIENT PLANS

Problems _____

_____

_____

FAMILY HISTORY

	Age	Years Ed.	Occupation	Deaf?
Father ___				
Mother ___				
Sisters ___				
Brothers ___				

Placement in family _____   Living arrangement _____

Marital status of parents _____   Step or foster _____

Communication at home? (quality and mode) _____

_____

Marital status: _____

Spouse: _____

Children: _____

EDUCATION AND TRAINING

Highest grade completed _____   School _____   Year ____

Type of School _____   Voc/Academic? _____

Training programs _____

Class best liked _____   Class least liked _____   GPA ____

Achievement difficulties _____

VOCATIONAL HISTORY

Current job _____   How long? _____

Prior employment _____

Jobs most enjoyed _____   Least _____

Vocational goal _____   In 5 years _____

Financial support _____

SOCIAL AND ACTIVITIES

Member of clubs/special groups _____

Visit relatives? _____

Hobbies, interests? _____

INTERVIEW NOTES

_____

_____

_____

_____

_____

References

Craig, W. R. (Ed.). (1969). *Improved vocational, technical and academic opportunities for deaf people: Research component.* Pittsburgh: University of Pittsburgh.

Levine, E. S. (1976). Psychological evaluation of the deaf client. In B. Bolton (Ed.), *Handbook of measurement and evaluation in rehabilitation.* Baltimore: University Park Press.

Levine, E. S. (1981). *The ecology of early deafness.* New York: Columbia University Press.

Sullivan, P. M., & Vernon, M. (1979). Psychological assessment of hearing-impaired children. *School Psychology Digest, 8*(3), 271–290.

Watson, D. (Ed.). (1976). *Deaf evaluation and adjustment feasibility.* New York: New York University (Deafness Research and Training Center).

Zieziula, F. (Ed.), (1982). *Assessment of hearing-impaired people: A guide for selecting psychological, educational, and vocational tests.* Washington, D.C.: Gallaudet College Press.

CHAPTER II

Psychological Assessment: One Perspective

Larry G. Stewart

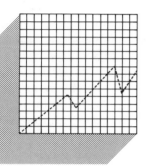

Introduction

The State/Federal program of Vocational Rehabilitation has the goal of restoring the handicapped individual to the fullest physical, mental, social, vocational, and economic usefulness of which he or she is capable (McGowan, 1969, p. 111). Toward the realization of this goal, the Vocational Rehabilitation counselor uses the diagnostic information available to guide the client in arriving at sound decisions concerning strengths, limitations, and needs in areas which are important in achieving effective employment and independent living adjustment. Rehabilitation services planning then proceeds from these decisions. From this vantage point, diagnostic services may rightfully be considered vital, indispensable components of the Vocational Rehabilitation process.

The goals of educational and mental health programs for the disabled differ in substantial ways from those of Vocational Rehabilitation. Yet, all share the goal of assisting the disabled individual to realize his or her potential.

The diagnostic phase in all human services programs consists essentially of gathering, interpreting, and integrating significant information about the client. The nature and extent of this process varies with each client. Some will require relatively limited, one-time-only assistance, (such as the purchase of a hearing aid); others will need quite extensive, long-term assistance in many areas of functioning (for example, physical restoration services, mobility training, attendance at college, and

on-going physical therapy during training). Clearly, diagnostic studies will be very different in each case. As a rule, clients will have varied medical, psychological, social, vocational, educational, economic, psychiatric, and/or social services needs. Hence, the diagnostic process can be expected to respond to the circumstances of the individual client. This process, however, always provides an opportunity for the counselor and the handicapped person to identify and to prioritize each rehabilitation need. The counselor or other services coordinator has a primary role in ensuring that diagnostic studies are used in appropriate ways.

The psychological evaluation is one of the diagnostic studies having the potential to assist the handicapped person. Through this type of evaluation, important information can be obtained concerning learning potentials, academic and vocational aptitudes, current functional skills in reading and writing, vocational interests and preferences, interpersonal relations skills, communication skills, personal adjustment, attitudes toward self, mental health status, and environmental conditions. This information can then be helpful in answering such client questions as "Can I be successful in a four year college with a major in mechanical engineering?"; "Can I read well enough to succeed in a community college major of computer programming?"; "Should I work with people or with things?"; "Will I be able to tolerate the competitive stresses involved in a sales career?"; "Do I need to have help with my feelings of anxiety and nervousness?"; and, "What can I do about all the

9

pressures I feel at school?" Many counselor questions can also be answered, such as "Does this client have a learning disability?"; "Is the client's previously diagnosed mental disorder in remission?"; "Does this client have a mental disorder which will preclude competitive employment and/or independent living?"; and, "Has substance abuse affected this client's intellectual functioning?" The psychologist's *interpretations* of the data from the psychological evaluation can contribute substantially to answering these and many other questions impacting upon educational and rehabilitation planning.

Persons who are handicapped by deafness or other types of serious hearing impairment present special needs in the diagnostic process. Clearly, these individuals have the same need for accurate diagnostic services that other handicapped persons have. However, serious hearing loss, particularly deafness, often creates communication barriers that can sharply curtail the effectiveness of diagnosticians since much of the data in diagnostic studies are obtained through communication between the examiner and the examinee. This is particularly true for the psychological evaluation, which is heavily dependent on examiner-client communication. Additionally, the psychological evaluation typically involves standardized and clinical tests having items presented through written and spoken language that is often beyond the deaf client's receptive abilities and/or comprehension level. There are methods and procedures for overcoming these barriers to an effective diagnostic study of the deaf individual in most cases, however (see, for example, Levine, 1960 & 1981). When an effective assessment is accomplished, the results can be valuable to the client and the counselor in planning specific goals and services.

Effectiveness in selecting diagnostic studies and in using the results in casework practices is a crucial consideration for service providers. An understanding of various kinds of such evaluation procedures contributes to this goal. This particular chapter presents an orientation to the psychological evaluation, with special emphasis given to its use with deaf persons. Included are summaries of the nature and scope of this evaluation and the special considerations that are important in evaluating deaf persons. Questions concerning the psychological evaluation frequently asked by service providers are answered, including when to make a referral for the evaluation, locating a qualified examiner, what the examiner needs to know prior to the evaluation, and preparing the client for the evaluation. Information is also provided concerning considerations in evaluating the quality of a psychological evaluation report, and in presenting the findings to the client. A sample psychological evaluation concludes the chapter. The reader should note that the chapter addresses what can appropriately be called *the general psychological evaluation*; other chapters deal with more specialized psychological evaluations which are frequently appropriate for some clients.

Nature and Scope of the Psychological Evaluation

The term "psychological evaluation" is a common one in the human services professions. It refers to an evaluation that is used in a wide variety of settings for purposes that include program eligibility determination, identification of problems and needs, selection of services to be provided, monitoring of progress toward individual goals, and evaluating the quality of services and programs. Psychological evaluations are conducted by psychologists in such diverse settings as community general hospitals, government- and privately-sponsored hospitals for the mentally ill, community mental health clinics, governmental rehabilitation agencies, educational settings of every kind, Veterans' hospitals, vocational services agencies, private consulting firms, and independent private practice offices. This widespread use of psychological evaluations tends to create the general impression that the evaluation is essentially one procedure. This is not the case, however. In actual practice, there are many types of psychological evaluations, ranging from brief screening assessments conducted on a group basis to intensive, specialized evaluations focusing upon a specific mental illness or another condition. Even one psychologist may vary in the type of evaluation conducted on the same individual within two different service settings. For example, evaluating an individual for Social Security disability status determination is quite different from evaluating this same individual for treatment services planning within a residential mental health center, and psychological assessments conducted in a school setting will be different from those conducted in a rehabilitation setting. This occurs because, ideally, the evaluation centers on the individual within his/her environment and responds to the diagnostic needs of the person within that environment.

The psychological evaluation in special education and in rehabilitation is unique in that it is concerned with an individual who has a disability (or disabilities) and is goal directed toward identifying the strengths, limitations, and needs of the individual to the extent that these are important for education and rehabilitation. Eisenberg and

Jansen (1983, p. 5) capture the essence of this unique focus in the following statement:

> ... rehabilitation psychologists approach their practice with a significant emphasis on the positive aspects of growth and adjustment and with very much of a developmental orientation. A prime function of the rehabilitation psychologist is to provide psychological services that facilitate healthy growth and development of an impaired individual throughout the life span. Arising from the fact that individuals react differently to impairment, disability, and handicapping conditions, service needs require a unique configuration of treatment modalities. These services are provided from a psychological model wherein key elements in the environment interact with each other to impact upon the lifestyle of the impaired, disabled, or handicapped individual and his/her significant others. The rehabilitation psychologist facilitates the modification of these elements to create an optimal environment.

Jacobs and Wiggins (1976) describe the rehabilitation psychologist as one who attempts to identify and to improve those aspects of a disabled person's physical and social environment that contribute to the disabled state and that present barriers to the disabled person's effective daily living. Grzesiak (1981) adds a somewhat different dimension, stating that rehabilitation psychology "applies psychological knowledge and behavioral science to any and all aspects of physical disability at the individual, group, and systems level" (p. 413).

From these perspectives we see the unique focus of the psychological evaluation within the rehabilitation process as being one which attempts to *identify strengths and limitations of the disabled individual as well as the strengths and limitations of the disabled person's environment and to assist the individual to realize his or her potentials through an enhancement of the environment or ecological circumstances.* This requires of the rehabilitation psychologist not only knowledge and skills in the realm of psychology but also in the areas of disabilities, treatment modalities, and available resources and opportunities for disabled individuals. Without the latter type of specialized knowledge the examiner will encounter major difficulties in relating psychometric and clinical findings to the realities of the disabled person in the world of school, work, and independent living.

Contents of the Psychological Evaluation. The contents of the typical rehabilitation-oriented psychological evaluation consist of the following areas:

1. *Referral Information*. This part of the evaluation consists of a review of the information provided to the examiner by the referring counselor. This includes copies of relevant prior testing results and/or related information on file with the services coordinator. Most coordinators send examiners a completed Referral Form, such as the one on the next page, along with the official agency authorization for services. Such a form contains information to assist the examiner in focusing the evaluation on areas of special concern to the counselor and client. It should be noted that the review of referral information by the examiner takes place prior to the actual clinical interview and testing session.

Some referring coordinators prefer that the examiner conduct the evaluation without first viewing prior testing results. The purpose for this is to obtain an evaluation which depends solely upon the current functioning of the client. These independent evaluations are warranted under special circumstances, and some examiners routinely follow the practice of evaluating a client first before reviewing any prior results. This writer prefers to review records of previous testing and interviewing reports before the evaluation, however, because background information is almost always helpful in more sharply focusing a current evaluation. In regard to furnishing prior evaluation and related reports to examiners, it is important that the coordinator first obtain the client's informed consent for release of this information. Most schools and agencies have specific policies and procedures that govern protection of client privacy, and referral information on a client should conform to these policies.

2. *Clinical Interview*. The clinical interview is one of the distinguishing components of the psychological evaluation. It consists of direct one-to-one communication between the disabled person and the examiner. Through interviewing, the examiner is enabled to learn about the person's communication competencies and style, relevant behavioral characteristics, and personal characteristics that are not readily observable through testing performance. The interview provides an opportunity for the client to furnish information concerning current circumstances and developmental history, self-perceptions, attitudes concerning self and others, self-esteem, self-perceived problem and need areas, motivation, educational and vocational experiences, hopes and aspirations, coping mechanisms for disability-related limitations, and other significant information.

The mental status examination, which is traditionally a major focus of psychological evaluations in clinical settings, may or may not appear in a rehabilitation-oriented evaluation. Often a determinant in the matter is whether the client appears to have significant emotional, mental, or behav-

DEPARTMENT OF REHABILITATION   **Counselor** _____

                                      Date _____

Referral for Psychological Testing

Psychologist _____   Client _____

                                                     (last)   (first)

Tests scheduled for: Group ___ Ind. ___* Address _____

                                              (street)

   Date _____ Time _____   _____

                                       (city)   (zip code)

   Date _____ Time _____

   Date _____ Time _____ Phone No. _____

Marital Status _____ Age _____ Sex _____ Birthplace _____

Major Occupations _____

Last grade completed in school _____ Principal locale of education _____

Disability _____

_____

Other limitations which may affect testing: _____

What RC wants to know from tests _____

_____

_____

Occupational areas being considered _____

_____

Previous test scores and/or reports attached   VP consultation requested

Tests suggested:

Counselor comments _____

_____

*Basis for suggesting individual testing _____

_____

ioral difficulties. The mental status examination is usually either de-emphasized or omitted when there is no history of adjustment difficulties, the referral was made basically for education placement purposes, and the major concern is identification of the client's intellectual and academic skills. However, when it is conducted, the mental health status examination consists of the following areas:

Sensory Abilities and Deficits (Hearing, vision, touch, smell, taste, balance). Assessment of these areas is primarily on a client self-report basis, with appropriate screening tests used when this is needed. Such assessment proceeds from a psychological framework rather than a medical one. At times, however, the findings may lead to a referral for medical or other specialized assessment. The purpose of this screening is to determine whether the examinee manifests abnormalities of a psychological nature in the sensory areas, or has actual impaired sensory abilities. The examiner adapts procedures appropriately when needed to assure a valid evaluation.

Motoric Behavior (Physical coordination, gait and balance, posture, physical activity level). The nature, duration, and consistency of motoric behavior is observed, both for strengths and for symptoms of potential problem areas. Motoric behavior can reflect underlying emotional, mental, and organic difficulties ranging from mild conditions (such as unusual apprehension concerning test performance) to serious ones (such as ataxia, hemiplegia, symbolic compulsivity, and depression). Information is gained through observing the client's manner of walking, sitting, gesturing, and facial expressions as well as directed test performance.

Perceptual Experiences. This part of the mental status examination is directed toward determining if the examinee has normal or unusual perceptions. For example, the client may have false perceptions through hearing, taste, smell, vision, or touch. Such hallucinations can be clinically significant; the full examination will determine whether any reported perceptual experiences have significance.

Affective Display. This area focuses on the client's emotions, feelings, and moods. Their nature, stability, and congruence with external reality considerations are observed. Symptoms such as depression, anxiety, fearfulness, flatness, withdrawal, hostility, anger, suspiciousness, and sadness are noted and considered.

Orientation. Orientation in four areas is tested: person (What is your name?); place (Where are you now?); time (What is today's date?); and circumstances (Why are you here?). Confusion and/or uncertainty in responding to orientation questions may have clinical significance.

Memory. Three components of memory are tested immediate recall, short-term memory, and long-term memory. Deficiencies in any of these components are considered as a part of the total evaluation.

Ideation. The thought processes are observed through statements made by the client to determine whether mental overactivity or underactivity is present, whether the activity level is confusing, and how this affects the person.

Delusions. False beliefs held by the individual, if any exist, are observed and noted. Common beliefs and/or biases that are not necessarily true on a factual basis are distinguished from beliefs generated as psychological defense mechanisms. Examples of the latter might include "People are after me", "Someone is trying to poison me", "The government is out to get me", and "I am God". The nature, intensity, variety, and duration of any delusions present are noted.

Judgment. This aspect focuses upon the client's reasoning abilities and the use of good judgment in coping with circumstances. Examples of questions asked include "What are your plans for the future?" and "How do you spend most of your time?"

Insight. This is concerned with an awareness of one's self and one's circumstances, and the ability to respond to situations in a realistic manner

with reasonable awareness of one's motivations and needs.

Intelligence. This is measured through formal testing, although the interview usually provides the clinician with a broad indication of the individual's general level of functioning.

The clinical interview emphasizes identification of the handicapped person's developmental history and pre- as well as post-disability experiences, with the goal of identifying attitudes, beliefs, abilities, and personal assets that can be helpful in rehabilitation planning. Areas of weakness or deficiencies are also noted in order that remediation may be undertaken where appropriate. The assessment also covers the disabled person's current life circumstances, including the availability of an appropriate support system, training and other treatment resources, independent living opportunities, transportation and public access considerations, communication barriers and resources, financial resources, employment prospects, and similar factors.

3. *Testing*. Following the clinical interview, standardized and clinical tests and inventories are administered. The specific battery used with a given client will depend on the purpose of the referral, the functional limitations of the client, the practices of the examiner, and the nature of the client's circumstances. To illustrate, the VR counselor may have requested an evaluation to assist in determining the client's potentials for college. The client, who happens to be deaf, will need to avoid the tests that require hearing ability (such as the Stanford Binet IQ Test). The examiner may use a trait-factor approach, which involves emphasizing objective, normed tests rather than clinical, projective tests. During testing, the examiner may find that the client displays symptoms of visual motor disturbance and language disturbance, and may add more specialized tests in order to diagnose the nature of these disturbances. Most evaluations follow this type of approach, which responds to the requests of the referral source, the individuality of the client, and the expertise of the examiner. Generally, however, most evaluations include the following:

Intelligence Assessment. Sometimes group paper-and-pencil type tests are used to assess intelligence, but more often individualized testing is the preferred approach. This individual approach permits clinical observation of performance and also is usually more reliable and valid.

Visual Motor Coordination Skills. This involves assessment of ability to integrate and synthesize visual and motor stimuli, and to respond to them in an effective manner. This is a fundamental ability which is instrumental in a broad range of basic learning and performance tasks, including writing, drawing, reading, and language processing. Impairment in this area of abilities may have a profound impact upon communication skills, school performance, and vocational performance. Significantly impaired visual motor coordination skills frequently reflect neurological impairment.

Academic Skills. Academic skills may be assessed through short screening type tests or by indepth achievement testing covering several hours. The former is usually used, although some examiners dispense with achievement tests and instead depend upon the results of a verbal IQ test (such as the Wechsler Adult Intelligence Scale, Revised, Verbal Scale). The two areas most frequently assessed are *reading* and *arithmetic*, since these two skill areas have broad implications for learning.

Vocational Interests. Vocational interests are important in guiding individuals who are undecided regarding their career or occupational goals, and hence vocational interests assessment is important for many clients.

Personality. A major emphasis in the psychological evaluation is personality assessment, which is intended to identify the more enduring aspects of the client's personal makeup as well as transient reactions to situational variables. Personality traits, dynamics, and disorders are identified through testing, interview and test behavior, and self-report inventories.

Other Areas. In some cases the assessment may entail additional testing. Examples would include testing for language disturbances and screening for neuropsychological difficulties. Such cases could, through this type of screening, lead to referral for more specialized examinations. However, basic screening through general psychological evaluation is often important in determining whether referral is needed.

The Report of the Evaluation. The written report of the psychological evaluation presents the findings that the examiner judges to be relevant to the individual case. However, each examiner tends to use the same format for reports even as formats vary from examiner to examiner. The sample reports that conclude several chapters in this book illustrate some of these formats. A common format includes the following headings:

1. Referral information
2. Clinical interview results

3. Tests administered and results (including behavioral observations)
   A. Intelligence
   B. Visual motor coordination skills
   C. Academic skills
   D. Personality
   E. Other
4. Summary of findings
5. Diagnostic statements
6. Recommendations

It is important to emphasize that not all psychological evaluation reports follow this type of structure. Some, in fact, consist of a one page summary written in letter form. Many agencies request that reports follow a recommended format, while others leave this decision to the examiner.

Evaluating the Deaf Person: Special Considerations

The goal of the rehabilitation-oriented psychological evaluation remains the same for all types of disabilities. This goal is to identify client strengths, limitations, and needs, and to recommend appropriate rehabilitation services that will enhance the individual's opportunities for attaining the fullest functioning of which he or she is capable. This goal obviously applies to deaf persons as well. However, because of the unique nature of the communication problems associated with deafness, there are special considerations facing the examiner. These considerations include: (1) the communication skills of the examiner and of the client, (2) the nature of the client's hearing loss and developmental experiences, (3) special areas to explore during the clinical interview, (4) testing problems, (5) interpretation of test results, (6) diagnostic issues, and (7) use of evaluation findings in making recommendations. These are discussed briefly below.

Communication Skills. Deaf persons who seek rehabilitation assistance are a heterogeneous group. Aside from the common characteristic of hearing loss, they represent a cross-section of the general population. Serious hearing loss can occur at any age, and among handicapped persons who come to various rehabilitation programs will be some who have been deaf from birth, others since childhood, and some who have become deaf in adulthood. Communication skills of deaf persons vary from individual to individual. The following communication modalities and skill levels can be expected to be found in various combinations with individual clients:

1. Excellent, good, fair, poor or no speech ability;

2. Excellent, good, fair, poor or no English language skills (for speaking, reading, and writing purposes);
3. Excellent, good, fair, poor or no Manual Alphabet (fingerspelling) skills;
4. Excellent, good, fair, poor or no knowledge of one or more of the several sign language systems used in the U.S.;
5. Good, fair, poor or no skills in using common gestural signs.
6. Good, fair, poor or no residual hearing ability with amplification.

The communication skills of the individual will reflect the influence of many developmental and experiential factors as well as the nature, degree, and age at onset of hearing loss. The psychological examiner with the deaf person, then, in order to effectively evaluate the client, must be familiar with the communication modalities used by deaf persons and must have an understanding of the developmental and experiential influences that lead to their use and/or their absence. Without this knowledge, the examiner will encounter imposing obstacles to conducting a successful evaluation, particularly so when a differential diagnosis (i.e., arriving at a correct diagnosis when several different categories of classification are possible) is needed. Many deaf individuals have additional disabilities and handicaps; deaf people are represented among persons with cerebral palsy, mental retardation, learning disabilities, epilepsy, cardiovascular disorders, emotional disturbance, mental illness, and many other disability categories. There are many instances when a particular problem is attributed to deafness when the cause is actually due to another disability. A case in point is when some of the so-called "language problems of the deaf" are actually created not by deafness but by central nervous system impairment that affects the learning of verbal language. Considerable expertise is required of the examiner in differential diagnosis in such cases.

The use of an interpreter by the psychological examiner who does not use sign language is a common practice with deaf clients. Advocates of this practice argue that a skilled interpreter makes it possible for the deaf person to be examined when otherwise an evaluation would not be possible since there are so few psychologists who use sign language. This argument is certainly valid. However, a legitimate question that should always be considered whenever an interpreter is used during an evaluation is this: Are the evaluation findings valid? This question should be asked of *any* evaluation report, whether an interpreter is used or not, but it should certainly be an even more important question any time the psychological examiner is unable to communicate directly with the examinee. Much of the data emerging from an evaluation is obtained during the clinical interview, and whenever there are communication problems that necessitate the presence of an interpreter, then always in question is the adequacy of the resulting communication. Clearly, when the interpreter is more skilled, the examiner is more experienced in working through an interpreter, and the client has used interpreting services before, then an evaluation can be more valid.

Nature of Hearing Loss and Developmental Experiences. There are many causes and kinds of hearing loss that can occur at different age levels. The examiner needs to be aware of their implications—medical, physiological, educational, social, vocational, and emotional. In illustration, John B. became deaf at the age of 18 from a head wound suffered while fighting in Vietnam. There was no residual hearing. Speech was essentially normal but with indications of grossly inappropriate language usage. Speechreading skills were poor. He had no sign language skills, not having been exposed to sign language up to the time of testing. Directions were provided through demonstration and gestures for testing purposes Now 20 years old, John B. obtained a Performance IQ of 110 on the Wechsler Adult Intelligence Scale, with no unusual strengths or weaknesses on subscales. However, he exhibited severe reading and writing deficiencies, both expressively and receptively. Records from his high school reported pre-trauma academic achievement at grade level (12th grade). An aphasic disturbance was identified, with probable etiology being central nervous system impairment due to cerebral trauma, and John B. was referred for a neuropsychological evaluation for differential diagnostic purposes.

Contrast John B.'s case with that of Robert A. Born deaf, with deaf parents, etiology of hearing loss was reported as heredity. Robert grew up using American Sign Language and lived in a neighborhood where there were several families with deaf children. Robert attended preschool programs for deaf children, and later attended a state residential school for deaf children. Now 20 years old, he obtained a WAIS Performance Scale IQ of 110. Subscale scores were evenly distributed with no unusual highs or lows. He communicated very well using ASL, but he does not use speech and has minimal speechreading skills. He scored at the 6th grade achievement level in reading and at the 11th grade level in math. Overall, Robert A.'s achievements are considered to be consistent with his circumstances. Referral for further assessment was unnecessary.

We see in these two cases the wide variation that may be found to exist between two deaf young adults in the areas of communication skills, etiological factors, developmental and experiential factors, and test performance. In these cases and others, however, the psychological examiner will be better able to understand the individual examinee through good communication and a knowledge of deafness and its impact.

Special Areas to Explore During the Clinical Interview. As explained earlier in this chapter, the clinical interview allows the examiner to obtain historical and current data from the client, and to gather clinically useful self reports in relevant areas of adjustment. Just as the physician attempts to obtain a view of one's physical health, the examining psychologist attempts to obtain a picture of the individual's mental and emotional health. The rehabilitation psychologist's focus in turn is upon evaluating the disabled individual's mental and emotional health, and then relating these to rehabilitation needs. This particular orientation guides the psychologist during the clinical interview. A principle in rehabilitation assessment which may appear simplistic but nevertheless bears stating is that disabled people are first of all people; all that applies to assessment of the non-disabled applies to evaluating the disabled. General disability-related issues applicable to all disabilities are next considered and, finally, concerns that center on the particular disability or disabilities of the examinee are considered.

We may demonstrate this philosophy through a brief discussion. When any individual is evaluated, the basic psychometric and clinical methods and techniques of psychology are used by the examiner. Secondly, as a disabled individual, the examinee is considered in terms of such factors as (a) medical, physical, and other limitations created by the disability status; (b) the impact of disability on the family and the family's impact on the disabled person; (c) the impact on the examinee of being a disabled individual in America, including attitudes, self-esteem, social self confidence, and self expectations; and (d) environmental opportunities and limitations where the examinee lives (since these vary along several dimensions, including religious attitudes toward the disabled, ethnical attitudes toward the disabled, and urban vs. rural social and employment opportunities for the disabled). Thirdly, the examiner must consider the disability-specific variables that are important in the examinee's life. For the deaf person, for example, we must ask specific questions. When did the loss of hearing occur? What was the cause? What is the nature and degree of hearing loss? Has the hearing loss affected language, educational, social, communication, and employment skills development? What was the parental response to their child's hearing loss? Was the child a participating member of the family unit or isolated? Did the child have opportunities to develop normal playmate relationships, peer relationships during school years, and self-esteem enhancing experiences during the developmental years? Was the child overprotected and did dependency traits develop? Did the child go to a residential school for the deaf, to classes for the deaf in public school, or to regular public school with minimal assistance? Does the examinee now know sign language? At what age were signs first learned? Do the parents use sign language, and if so at what skill level and when did this begin? Was the examinee raised through the oral method both at home and at school? What have been the examinee's experiences with hearing people—largely positive, mostly positive, slightly negative, or very negative? Has the examinee demonstrated the ability to cope well with hearing loss in social, educational, and work settings? What aids has the examinee used—TTY (TDD) for telephone communication, closed captioning decoder for television, interpreters, notetakers, flashing alarm clock and/or doorbell signal, etc.? Has the examinee participated as a member of the deaf community and if so in what roles and for how long? Are there other disabilities present, and if so what is the nature of the limitations of these other disabilities and how do they interact with the limitations caused by hearing loss? Are the career aspirations of the examinee limited to those that graduates of his/her school typically enter? Is the examinee realistically aware of the implications of hearing loss in certain occupations, while at the same time not imposing unnecessary limitations on one's self? Is the examinee reasonable in terms of assuming responsibility for success and failure, or does the examinee place responsibility on others to make him or her successful? Is the examinee's educational and/or employment goal based upon a well thought out plan, and does the plan make provisions for adequate compensation for handicaps created by hearing loss? Has the examinee developed inadequate behavioral or emotional responses through frustrations associated with deafness, and if so what are they?

The foregoing are only a few of the special areas to be covered by the examiner. It is hoped that they do illustrate the importance of including such information in the overall evaluation.

Testing Problems. The specific testing problems encountered when testing *some* deaf persons are also encountered in testing *some* individuals who have normal hearing. Further, many deaf persons can be tested without encountering any of these problems. For these reasons, it is misleading to refer to them as "special testing problems with deaf persons". What follows, then, should be considered only as a brief and incomplete listing of some of the problems that are frequently encountered in testing a good proportion of deaf clients typically served by various rehabilitation and education programs.

1. *Limited Test Options.* A large number of prelingually deaf persons have relatively restricted English language skills. The majority of standardized tests used today have a high level of English vocabulary and language structure which, unfortunately, makes them inappropriate for use with deaf individuals (or any other group of persons) who have limited English skills. Additionally, many tests are standardized for administration through spoken means, and these usually cannot be understood by the deaf person unless sign language is used by the examiner or an interpreter is used. The result is that the examiner who evaluates deaf clients having restricted English language skills will find that choices of examining instruments are very limited. This is particularly true in assessing personality and vocational interests.

2. *Test Validity Questions.* Another problem is that only a few tests were developed with deaf subjects included in the standardization sample, and this fact raises questions concerning the validity of test results generally. The Hiskey Nebraska Test of Learning Aptitude and the Stanford Achievement Tests—Hearing-Impaired are two major exceptions. However, skilled examiners have for decades used many kinds of tests effectively with deaf subjects, and most of these examiners, if asked, would most likely offer the professional judgment that they are usually able to perform satisfactory evaluations using available tests even though the standardization samples did not include deaf persons. The argument can also be set forth that it is extremely difficult to identify a *representative deaf population* for test standardization purposes. The deaf population is a highly heterogeneous group; within this larger group are subgroups whose circumstances have introduced significant variables that have profound impacts on development and adjustment. Controlling these factors in the sampling process is extremely difficult. This writer suggests that even if it were possible to actually achieve a stratified random sample of deaf persons representative of the nation's present deaf population, the sample would be representative only for a brief period of time since uncontrolled variables such as the incidence of rubella and other etiological agents, changes in the incidence of multiply handicapping

conditions, and variations in the effectiveness of early identification and early childhood education, for instance, would result in the introduction of changes in the population that would make it different from the original standardization population. However, the fact remains that at this time there are almost no tests having norms for deaf persons. As a consequence, questions concerning the validity of test results are continuing concerns.

Interpretation of Test Results. Owing to the lack of test norms for deaf individuals, the *meaning* of test results is more difficult for the examiner to determine. Unusual factors that are present in the lives of many deaf persons—verbal language deficiencies, developmental gaps stemming from inadequate communication, multiple disabilities, and others—introduce confounding variables that cloud test findings. For example, when a deaf person takes the Minnesota Multiphasic Personality Inventory (MMPI), the results cannot be assumed to mean what they might mean with a hearing individual. We could ask, "Did the deaf person understand the questions at all? Mostly? Almost all?" and "Can these results be accepted, when this deaf individual grew up in a family where no sign language was used and he (or she) could not communicate with other family members, spent twelve years living in a residential setting for nine months of the year, and also grew up further handicapped socially by poor communication skills?" When a 35-year old deaf male takes the Wide Range Achievement Test (WRAT) and obtains a reading achievement grade level score of 2.3, can we conclude that this individual's reading ability is truly comparable to that of a child in the third month of the second grade? What of the 16-year old deaf youth who has just moved to the U.S. from Latin America after years of no education, who does not know sign language and has no speech, and who has just started experimenting with street drugs provided by peers? When he is brought into the detoxification unit of a substance abuse treatment hospital, hallucinating (because of having taken PCP the day before) and making meaningless signed gestures (remember, he does not know sign language, but, recently, had been around teenagers who use sign language), what are we to think when the attending psychiatrist, working through an interpreter, makes the diagnosis of paranoid schizophrenia and, because of this and hyperactivity, places him on Haldol? These are only a few examples of the complexities involved in interpreting the results of standardized and clinical tests with persons who are deaf.

It is beyond the scope of this chapter to list the standardized and clinical tests that are useful with deaf persons. The interested reader should consult

Chapter I and the excellent books by Levine (1960;1981) for this purpose.

Diagnostic Issues. Through the years there have been many systems for classifying mental, emotional, and behavioral disorders. The most widely used nosology (the classification of diseases) in psychology today, although by no means the only one, is that provided in the *Diagnostic and Statistical Manual of Mental Disorders, Third Edition* (1980). Abbreviated DSM III, this classification system uses a multiaxial plan, whereby diagnostic information is reported for five categories. The first category, which is labeled Axis I, calls for a listing of clinical syndromes, conditions not attributable to a mental disorder that are a focus of treatment, and/or additional codes. A code number accompanies the identified diagnosis. Axis II provides for listing the type(s) and code number(s) for personality disorders and/or specific developmental disorders. Axis III provides for listing any physical disorders and conditions. Axis IV calls for a statement on specific stressors precipitating a condition along with a judgment of degree of severity of the stressor(s) (ranging from Code 1 <none> to 7 <catastrophic>). Axis V calls for judgment on the highest level of adaptive functioning of the examinee during the past year, including a code level (ranging from 1 <superior> to 5 <poor>). Taken together, these components of the multiaxial reporting system allow a more qualitative approach to reporting results of psychological and psychiatric evaluation.

There are potential complexities with the DSM III system where deaf examinees are concerned. These flow from two sources; the problems that have been cited above for interpreting clinical interview and testing results, and the difficulties inherent in making clinical judgments within the framework of a structured diagnostic system. It is easy to see that there is room for a great deal of error in making diagnostic judgments when, in the beginning, the reliability and validity of test results are questionable and this error range is extended and magnified when the clinician is forced to make choices from among several possible diagnostic categories that are described according to conceptually-defined symptoms and course of development. For example, DSM III lists five diagnostic criteria for Adjustment Disorder. Three of these are listed as follows:

A. A maladaptive reaction to an identifiable psychosocial stressor, that occurs within three months of the onset of the stressor.

B. The maladaptive nature of the reaction is indicated by either of the following:
   (1) impairment in social or occupational functioning;

(2) symptoms that are in excess of a normal and expectable reaction to the stressor.

C. The disturbance is not merely one instance in a pattern of overreaction to stress or an exacerbation of one of the mental disorders previously described . . .

DSM III, 1980 (p. 300).

The reader can readily see that these criteria require considerable interpretive judgments on the part of the examiner; such judgments can only be as valid as the examiner's data from the actual evaluation. When the examiner has considerable experience with deaf persons, evaluation data will be more reliable and subsequent diagnostic judgments will improve in quality.

DSM III is most useful with clients who have problems that lend themselves to this system. However, it is limited in dealing with many of the concerns of educators, clinicians, and other specialists with clients who do not have the disorders listed in the DSM III system. *For this reason many psychological evaluation reports do not include the DSM III terminology and coding. Many psychologists, in fact, do not use the DSM III system at all.*

Differential diagnosis requires that the examiner make a choice among several possible diagnostic categories when the evaluation findings could place the individual in any one of them, but one is more appropriate than the others. For example, the examiner may be faced with a decision on whether an examinee has an Adjustment Disorder with Anxious Mood or an Adjustment Disorder with Mixed Emotional Features; Alcohol Abuse or Alcohol Dependence; Disorganized Schizophrenia or Undifferentiated Schizophrenia; and Developmental Language Disorder or Developmental Reading Disorder. Many times examiners will disagree among themselves in arriving at differential diagnostic findings, so counselors should not be surprised when they read of differing diagnostic findings on one client. This type of situation is not unusual, but with deaf clients the evaluation challenges that have been cited in this chapter further complicate the diagnostic decision-making process. Again, the expertise of the examiner will be a major factor in limiting the degree of error that can creep into the diagnostic phase of an evaluation.

Using Evaluation Findings in Making Recommendations. One of the major complaints program specialists express concerning psychological evaluation reports is the lack of attention given to the *recommendations* section. At times even when recommendations are made they are often worded in general statements that are difficult to interpret and implement. The examiner indeed is in a good position to make specific, useful recommendations to assist the specialist worker and the client in planning services, but if the recommendations are not presented in an understandable fashion they will not be used.

Examiners are usually happy to have feedback concerning their recommendations. When the counselor or teacher finds that more specific and detailed recommendations are needed then a discussion with the examiner should prove to be helpful in meeting this need.

Evaluation reports which prove to be the most reliable with predictions concerning client success in selected areas, through specific training and/or treatment, are those which closely relate interviewing and testing results to recommendations. For example, one examiner may use measures of IQ, reading and arithmetic achievement, interests, personal adjustment, high school grade point average, and motivation to predict probabilities for success in college training. This examiner takes care to ensure that the measure for each of these variables is within the range of characteristics of entering freshmen who have in the past succeeded in college. Another examiner may be less dependent upon test measures, and instead may use clinical judgment concerning the individual's intelligence, expressed interests, and so forth, as judged from a one-hour clinical interview. Over time, the first examiner will be more successful at predicting who can and who cannot succeed at college.

Questions Commonly Asked by Counselors and Program Workers

This section poses questions most often asked by workers who *use* psychological assessments. Answers are suggested for each question.

1. When should a psychological evaluation be obtained on a deaf client?

There are several main criteria for making a referral. These are (a) when a medical assessment (general medical or specialist medical evaluation) recommends a psychological evaluation; (b) when background records or current client behaviors indicate the need; and (c) when the client is participating in a training or other rehabilitation services program that ordinarily includes a psychological evaluation as a part of the services process. There are other special circumstances that may come up from time to time that indicate the appropriateness of a referral; the service worker will become aware of these through experience in the agency.

Each school, clinic, and agency has policies and procedures for the provision of its services, including evaluation services of many kinds. These policies and procedures include specific criteria for determining when a given evaluation is justified, the fees to be paid, and the qualifications required of the examiner. Many schools and agencies that do not employ psychologists maintain a list of approved outside vendors or providers of services.

Some schools and agencies employ staff psychologists for assessment purposes. When this is the case, most psychological evaluations are performed by these staff psychologists. Other agencies purchase psychological evaluations from psychologists in independent private practice or employed by other organizations.

Most agencies require that the counselor consult with the agency's medical, psychological, or psychiatric consultant to obtain formal approval for ordering a psychological evaluation. Special units within some agencies, however, have designated the psychological evaluation as a routine assessment for all clients, and when this is the case then medical consultation for approval purposes is not required.

A question frequently asked by program workers is, "How can I tell when I should refer a client for a psychological evaluation when no one else has recommended one?" This important question has broad philosophical implications. Some rehabilitation workers believe that a psychological evaluation provides important information for all clients who are seeking any substantial education, independent living, and/or long-term training assistance. These counselors feel that they and their clients can do a more realistic job of decision making and services planning with the help of information from the psychological assessment. From this philosophical standpoint, the psychological evaluation is "problem-oriented" only in the sense that decision making and services planning are difficult without sufficient information on the client. When this philosophy is operational within an agency, a psychological evaluation is ordered whenever long-term rehabilitation services are being considered.

The main practice insofar as psychological evaluations are concerned within rehabilitation programs, however, is that the evaluation is seen as a specialist evaluation to be ordered when the client has significant psychological problems. The challenge for the counselor, then, becomes one of making decisions about whether a client has "significant psychological problems". There are no "cookbook recipes" to guide the counselor in making such judgments, but there are several principles that can be helpful. While these principles are not all-inclusive, they are offered here to assist the counselor in beginning to develop a working view regarding referrals for psychological evaluations. Generally, a psychological evaluation should be considered when:

A. . . . the client is clearly experiencing ongoing inner distress of an emotional nature. Such inner distress may consist of undue anxieties, excess worrying, fears of a specific or more general nature out of proportion to real circumstances, feelings of worthlessness or depression, difficulty in controlling feelings, and other feelings that disturb the individual.

B. . . . the client is experiencing recurring thoughts and/or perceptual experiences that are disturbing or upsetting. These might include thoughts of suicide, harming others, committing bizarre acts, and/or other uncontrollable thoughts, for example. Troublesome perceptual experiences might include hallucinations or recurring sensory experiences that are not consistent with conditions (for example, smelling odors when there are none, feeling unexplainable kinesthetic sensations).

C. . . . the client's behavior is, as a pattern, a problem for the individual and/or others. Examples include obvious long-standing physical tension or nervousness, overly aggressive behavior, unstable behavior, substance abuse, compulsive or phobic behavior of a disruptive nature, unusual mood swings, hyperactivity, depressed or withdrawing behavior, and pronounced difficulties in relating to others.

It is important to re-emphasize that these guiding principles do not represent a complete listing. From a rehabilitation standpoint, particularly, the counselor will want to consider requesting a psychological evaluation whenever the disabled person evidences a significant discrepancy between achievement and potential.

2. What does the counselor or program coordinator tell the client about the evaluation?

Many disabled individuals are well-adjusted. For many other individuals, however, their disability may be a source of great sensitivity or vulnerability. For the latter, any evaluation may be viewed uneasily if not with resistance. The psychological evaluation is highly threatening to many people. For this reason it is especially important that the counselor assist the client in understanding the purposes of the evaluation and its function as a means for helping the person to identify and realize individual potentials. It is helpful to the client to be given a brief explanation of the areas to be assessed (for example, intelligence, academic skills, vocational interests, personal strengths, and aspirations), and how long, approximately, the evaluation will last.

The client should be informed of the confidential nature of the evaluation as well as the fact that he or she has the right to not answer any questions asked during the assessment. Finally, the client should be encouraged to express any questions, anxieties or concerns he or she may have concerning the evaluation. This will enable the person to come prepared for the evaluation in a more positive frame of mind and, consequently, perform at an optimal level during the evaluation.

If the evaluation is being done by an examiner who does not use the client's customary mode of communication, it is important for the client to be involved in the selection of the interpreter.

3. Who discusses the psychological report with the client?

As a rule, the evaluation report should be reviewed with the client by the counselor or case services coordinator. However, with a client who has serious emotional and/or mental conditions it is advisable for the examiner to meet with the client for one or more individual sessions to discuss the evaluation before the counselor reviews the report with the client. There are several reasons for this, all of a therapeutic nature, but the primary reason is that the client may have very strong reactions to some parts of the evaluation which could be potentially harmful.

4. Should the client be allowed to read the psychological report?

In many cases it is desirable for the client to read the report, but in some cases doing so would be harmful. The school or agency will have policies governing the use of client case materials, and, additionally, expert guidance from consultants within the agency is available to the counselor who is unsure whether the client will be harmed by reading any particular report. In the past clients were seldom allowed access to such reports, but with recent legislation protecting the rights of individuals much more information became accessible to them. This is a positive development. However, there are reports which may not help the client, but, rather, may be upsetting and possibly harmful if read. Thus, the counselor will need to make a point of studying agency policies and procedures regarding client access to case information. The psychological examiner can be of significant assistance by preparing reports that in themselves would be helpful if read by the client. Unfortunately, this is not always possible, just as some medical reports by their very nature cannot be anything but upsetting to a client.

A Sample Psychological Report

Below is an illustrative psychological evaluation report which is intended to serve as an example for the discussion presented in this chapter. The report will provide the counselor with a frame of reference for evaluating the quality of rehabilitation-oriented psychological reports which are written for deaf clients. The reader will want to study the sample report carefully.

Confidential: For Professional Use Only
Report of Psychological Evaluation

Name of Examinee: Sample, John Q.

Address: 12345 E. West, Anytown, Anystate 98765

Birthdate: 01/02/58   Current Age: 26 years

Date of Evaluation: April 20, 1984

Referred by: Anystate Division of Vocational Rehabilitation

Examiner: XXXXXXXXXXXXX

****

I. *Referral Information*. JOHN Q. SAMPLE is a 26-year old single Caucasian male who has the disabilities of deafness and cerebral palsy. A client of the Anystate Division of Vocational Rehabilitation, he aspires to attend _____ Community College in his home district. The referring counselor questions the feasibility of this plan since Mr. Sample appears to need comprehensive support services for the deaf and his home district community college does not offer such services. Thus, the referring counselor requests a comprehensive psychological assessment to identify Mr. Sample's rehabilitation assets, liabilities, and needs, with specific attention focused upon his potentials for community college attendance.

Referral information includes academic records from the Anystate School for the Deaf and a psychological report from this school dated 4/25/78. The latter reports a WAIS Performance IQ of 118 along with visual motor coordination impairment.

II. *Clinical Interview Results*. Mr. Sample arrived on time for his scheduled evaluation appointment after having called the previous week on TTY to make his own appointment. On today's date—April 20, 1984— he drove his own car to this office from his home, which is approximately 30 miles away. He was cleanly and neatly dressed, demonstrating good personal grooming and hygiene. He gave the appearance of a friendly, open young man, alert and aware of his surroundings. He was of average height and weight, with clear medium complexion, brown hair neatly combed, and clear hazel eyes. He was polite and well-mannered, and had a likeable, cleancut appearance. He wore no eyeglasses. His teeth were noted to be even, clean, and well cared for. Mr. Sample wore a behind-the-ear hearing aid in his left ear, and explained that he was unable to understand speech but the aid helped him to be aware of sounds around him. He appeared to be relaxed throughout the interview and subsequent testing session,and gave every indication of having a high level of self-confidence.

Mr. Sample communicated very well through a combination of fingerspelling, Signed English, and American Sign Language. He also used his speech and appeared to be able to read lips. Communication for the session was through Mr. Sample's preferred mode of communication as described immediately above. In this mode he was able to understand questions and directions readily and to express himself appropriately and well. When asked about his understanding of the purposes of the evaluation, he demonstrated a good level of understanding and added that his VR counselor had gone over the purposes with him to his satisfaction. He also indicated that he had signed a release of information form allowing the counselor to send me past test scores and for me to provide the counselor with a copy of the evaluation report.

Throughout the session, Mr. Sample was friendly, cooperative, and unguarded in providing information and performing test tasks. The mental status examination did not suggest any unusual problems; he was oriented in all spheres, evidenced no delusions or hallucinations—now or in the past—and gave no indications of mental, emotional, or behavioral disturbance. He indicated that he had never experienced any unusual perceptions or events, had never been involved in any difficulties while attending school, and had never used alcoholic beverages, street drugs, or any substances not prescribed by a physician. He has never used tobacco. He reports no prior psychiatric or psychological difficulties, and has only seen school counselors in the past for academic guidance purposes. He has had a driver's license since age 16, and regularly goes about the community independently. He has a TTY at home and uses it regularly to communicate with deaf friends. He states that he has many hearing and deaf friends, and has gone with a 20-year old deaf woman for two years on a steady basis. He has lived with his parents all his life, but plans to live on his own in an apartment when he begins college.

Mr. Sample reported that he was born deaf, and also with cerebral palsy. He was unable to state the cause of these disabilities, but referral information lists the etiology as Rh factor incompatibility. His early growth and development were normal, he feels. He remembers his home as a happy place, and he was close to his brother (now 22) and sister (now 23), who themselves have no disabilities. The brother is an accountant, and the sister is married and has a one year old son. The father is an engineer, and the mother is a homemaker. Mr. Sample stated that both parents and his siblings use sign language well, and he had always felt a member of his family in all ways. Mr. Sample stated that he attended a program for children with cerebral palsy when he was very young; then he attended preschool for deaf children from age three years until six years, at which time he enrolled in the Anystate School for the Deaf as a residential student. He remembered his school years as a happy time in his life and felt that he did well in school, getting mostly C's and B's, with a few A's and no D's or F's (this was confirmed by his school records). He was unable to participate in school athletics due to his cerebral palsy, but he did play games with the other children and regularly participated in swimming and recreational activities. During his high school years he participated in Jr. NAD activities and Student Body Government activities as a member. He made many friendships during his school years and maintains some of these at present. He had prevocational training at the School for the Deaf in the areas of art, drafting, and typing. He graduated in 1980 at the age of 22, but he elected to work instead of attend postsecondary training since he wanted to gain work experience. His first job after graduation was as a stockroom clerk; he held this job for two years, then transferred to another company as a yard maintenance worker at higher pay. He has had this job since 1982, currently earning $4.50 per hour. He likes the work but aspires to become a commercial artist since he enjoys art work. He has taken evening courses in art at his local community college on a one course per semester basis over the last couple of years, but these were non-credit, non-competitive (i.e., non-graded) courses.

Mr. Sample reported enjoying swimming, driving around and visiting with friends, traveling, art work, attending social events for deaf people, being with his girlfriend, and doing projects at home involving crafts. He felt that he had no problems for which he needs help and reported being in good health with only the usual sicknesses (colds, sore throats, etc.).

Observing Mr. Sample during the interview, the following important aspects were noted: his left arm is seriously restricted in usefulness, with difficulty in using his fingers, hand, wrist, arm, and shoulder. He was noted to use his right hand to assist the left in making movements. When he walked, he favored his left leg. Athetoid rather than spastic cerebral palsy was noted in facial, head, and left arm and hand movements, with degree of involvement accelerated under effort of directed movement. However, Mr. Sample seemed to have developed good control of the rest of his body and consequently has reached a remarkable degree of functional effectiveness even with the condition. Again, however, motoric disturbance becomes pronounced when he exerts himself.

Upon closer questioning concerning his career aspirations, Mr. Sample stated that he really wasn't sure what he wanted for himself and was not confident he could get a competitive position in art due to his cerebral palsy. He is open to suggestions for possible careers. In discussing training options he did express a preference for attending his home district community college, but also expressed an openness to other options.

In summary, this clinical interview revealed no emotional, mental, or behavioral evidences of mental disturbance. Mr. Sample is a pleasant, polite, well-mannered young man who has demonstrated many abilities through successful academic, vocational, social, and personal achievements. He is well-motivated to improve his circumstances, and aspires to obtain additional postsecondary education in order to achieve at a higher vocational level. He is handicapped by deafness and cerebral palsy, but has overcome many of the more limiting aspects of these disabilities and shows much promise for further achievement. He would like for Vocational Rehabilitation to help him toward the achievement of his vocational goals.

III. **Testing Results**. Mr. Sample was administered a battery consisting of the Wechsler Adult Intelligence Scale (Performance Scale only), Wide Range Achievement Test (Arithmetic only), the Gates-MacGinitie Reading Tests (Survey F, Form 1), the Bender Gestalt Test, and the House-Tree-Person Personality Test. Mr. Sample understood test directions readily, evidenced good motivation to do well, and applied himself to each task as presented. No undue test anxiety was in evidence, and in fact he appeared to be generally relaxed and confident except as otherwise noted. Test conditions were favorable, hence the results are considered reliable and valid.

Mr. Sample obtained a WAIS Performance IQ of 118, which is consistent with results reported previously. Subscale scores were Digit Symbol 8, Picture Completion 14, Block Design 14, Picture Arrangement 11, and Object Assembly 17. These results indicated a significant weakness in perceptual motor speed tasks and an unusual strength in working with parts to achieve a whole. He also demonstrated strong abilities in attention to detail as well as abstract thinking and concept formation. However, in manipulating the test materials, Mr. Sample was noted to use his right hand almost exclusively, and small and fine hand movements were noted to require great effort on his part. At times he broke out in fine sweat about his forehead from these efforts. Yet, the outcomes were uniformly impressive, suggesting an unusual degree of tenacity. An analysis of the WAIS-P scores suggested the appropriateness of prorating the scores by eliminating the one significant deficiency—Digit Symbol—and averaging other scores. This procedure resulted in a Performance IQ of 125, which places Mr. Sample in the Superior classification. The standardization sample for the WAIS included 6.7 percent in this classification, with only 2.2 percent scoring higher (Very Superior—IQ of 130 and above). Even without prorating, Mr. Sample scored in the Bright Normal Range (IQ 110-119). Giving consideration to Mr. Sample's motoric handicaps, this examiner is of the opinion that even the prorated IQ of 125 represents an underestimation of Mr. Samples' actual intelligence.

In the visual motor coordination skills area, Mr. Sample's performance on the Bender Visual Motor Gestalt Test was within the normal range. He functioned quite well drawing the designs, but depended almost exclusively on his right hand. His left hand, again, was seldom used even to control placement of the drawing paper. Beads of sweat were again noted on Mr. Sample's forehead as he focused strenuous efforts on producing exact copies of the design cards. His performance suggests that his visual motor coordination skills are normal, but the cerebral palsy effects require him to strain himself in actual motor performance involving small and fine hand movements.

On the WRAT Arithmetic Test, Mr. Sample's performance resulted in a grade level placement of 3.9, with a percentile rating of 5 in his age group. His working speed was noted to be quite slow due to his cerebral palsy, yet his limits were reached within the time limits of the test so that it is not felt that his motoric handicaps penalized him on this task. The results, overall, suggest that Mr. Sample's arithmetic skills are an area of relative weakness for him.

On the Gates-MacGinitie Reading Tests (Survey F, Form 1), Mr. Sample obtained a standard score of 30 (the mean is 100) and a percentile rating of 2 for Speed & Accuracy, Number Attempted; standard score of 30, percentile rating of 2 for Speed & Accuracy, Number Right; standard score of 30, percentile rating of 2 for Vocabulary, Number Right; and, standard score of 29, percentile rating of 2 for Comprehension, Number Right. These results indicate a severe deficiency in Mr. Sample's English vocabulary and reading skills. These results are not entirely explained, in this examiner's judgment, by congenital deafness alone. The combination of his unusually high IQ, favorable family circumstances, early childhood education, extensive specialized education (a total of 20 years), and effective signing skills would suggest a higher level of verbal acquisition and performance. Consequently, the results suggest rather strongly the presence of central nervous system impairment impacting on verbal language processing functions.

In the *personality* area, Mr. Sample's drawings for the House-Tree-Person Test are consistent with background information and interview observations. He is revealed as a well-integrated young man with healthy self-perceptions and good ability to relate to his environment. His ability to relate to objects and people in his world appears in a positive light. He is open to others and observant as well. No evidence of unusual emotional needs or symbolism is present. Small indicators of dependency are noted but these are explained and understood in terms of his circumstances as a multiply handicapped individual who has received extensive assistance over the years. No evidence of anger or hostility complicate these dependency features, however. The results suggest that Mr. Sample has attained a healthy level of personality development and may be expected to relate well to others in his social environment.

IV. **Summary of Findings**. In summary, John Q. Sample is a 26 year old single Caucasian male who has been deaf all his life and additionally handicapped by athetoid cerebral palsy which significantly affects the left side of his body and general upper body movements. However, no spasmodic movements are present. He has had extensive specialized education and a supportive family background, and these have enhanced his overall development. A high school graduate who has been employed competitively for four years now, he currently aspires to attend a community college and enhance his vocational potentials. However, despite interest in art, he is aware of the limitations his motor handicaps impose on his performance and is open to other vocational possibilities although he does not know at present just what these might be. Testing reveals an exceptionally high level of intelligence, with strong abilities in concept formation, abstract thinking, ability to work with parts to achieve a whole, and attention to small details. His determination is very impressive, indicating a high level of motivation and goal-directedness. Visual motor coordination skills are normal but slowed by his cerebral palsy disability. Arithmetic skills are marginally developed, and English vocabulary and reading skills are extremely limited, so much so that the evidence would indicate central nervous system impairment in language processing areas. However, his signing skills are very effective, and except for English language limitations he is a good communicator. He has a pleasant way about him, is likeable, and has a healthy, well-integrated personality. His ability to get along with others should be considered one of his major vocational strengths. Physical strength considerations are important in vocational planning for this young man since evaluation observations indicate highly significant weaknesses on his left side which would appear to be associated with his cerebral palsy condition. He has many interests and social involvements, and has demonstrated ability to get around in the community. These, too, are assets in rehabilitation planning. His family should be considered another strong support system in his rehabilitation. Learning to live independently is a desirable goal and a definite prospect for him. While he is interested in attending college in his home district, his academic limitations indicate that he needs a program having very strong support services to help him with his academic deficiencies.

V. **Diagnostic Findings**. Based upon this current evaluation of John Q. Sample, which included a review of background information, clinical interview, and standardized and clinical assessment, this examiner offers the following diagnostic findings (using DSM III classifications):

AXIS I: Clinical Syndromes and Conditions
V62.30 Academic problem

AXIS II: Specific Personality and Development Disorders
315.50 Mixed specific developmental disorder (Provisional)

AXIS III: Physical Disorders and Conditions
1. Profound bilateral sensorineural hearing loss (by report, due to Rh factor incompatibility)
2. Cerebral palsy, athetoid, with mild generalized motoric effects and specific serious left side body effects (by report and by clinical observation, reportedly due to congenital Rh factor incompatibility)

AXIS IV: Severity of Psychosocial Stressors
Not applicable

AXIS V: Highest Level of Adaptive Functioning Past Year
Not Applicable

VI. **Recommendations**. Based upon the findings of this present evaluation of Mr. Sample, the following recommendations are made:

1. It is recommended that Mr. Sample meet with this examiner to review these evaluation findings and their implications for academic studies;
2. It is recommended that Mr. Sample attend the XYZ Community College in XXXXXXXXX, which has a very strong program of support services for deaf students generally and deaf students with learning difficulties specifically;
3. It is recommended that Mr. Sample's first semester at XYZ Community College include (a) vocational program sampling, which would acquaint him with a broader range of occupations and help him identify those that he would be able to pursue in line with his interests and abilities, (b) an indepth assessment of his specific learning difficulties by the deaf services diagnostic staff so that appropriate learning and study methods can be assured for him during his education. He will not be able to learn effectively through study of materials and books emphasizing English, so appropriate means will need to be provided to enhance his learning;

4. It is recommended that Mr. Sample receive assistance from the Anystate Vocational Rehabilitation agency's Independent Living Training staff for deaf adults and that he be assisted in learning to live independently in the community as a part of his first year of college;

5. It is recommended that Mr. Sample's VR counselor obtain his approval for a meeting with his parents and that in this meeting the family be informed of these recommendations, and their support be enlisted in implementing the rehabilitation plan;

6. It is recommended that Mr. Sample be provided with a physical assessment by a physician specializing in physical medicine and rehabilitation, with the possibility in mind of designing an appropriate plan for strengthening Mr. Sample's left leg, arm, hand, and finger functions.

Thank you for the opportunity of conducting this evaluation for Mr. Sample and your agency. It has been a privilege to be of assistance with this fine young man, who is most deserving of assistance.

Respectfully submitted:
XXXXXXXXXXXXXXXXXXXXXXXXX
Psychologist
Anystate License No. XXXXX

References

American Psychiatric Association. (1980). *Diagnostic and statistical manual of mental disorders. (Third edition)*. Washington, D.C.: Author.

Eisenberg, M., & Jansen, M. (1983). Rehabilitation psychology: State of the art. In E. Pan, T. Backer, & C. Vash (Eds.), *Annual review of rehabilitation, Volume 3*, (pp. 1–31). New York: Springer Publishing Company.

Grzesiak, R. (1981). Rehabilitation psychology, medical psychology, health psychology, and behavioral medicine. *Professional Psychology*, *12*(14), pp. 411–413.

Jacobs, D., & Wiggins, J. (1976). Psychologists in health and rehabilitation. Unpublished book proposal.

Levine, E. (1960). *Psychology of deafness*. New York: Columbia University Press.

Levine, E. (1981). *Ecology of early deafness*. New York: Columbia University Press.

McGowan, J. (1969). Referral, evaluation, treatment. In D. Malikin & H. Rusalem (Eds.), *Vocational rehabilitation of the disabled: An overview*, (pp. 111-127). New York: New York University Press.

Woody, R. (l980). Introduction: A conceptual framework for clinical assessment. In R. Woody (Ed.), *Encyclopedia of clinical assessment, Volume l*, (pp. xxx-xl). San Francisco: Jossey-Bass.

CHAPTER III

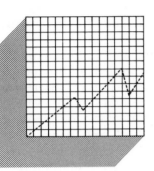

Psychological Assessment: Another Perspective

David P. Yandell

Introduction

Psychological assessments are frequently obtained for deaf individuals as a part of services in educational, rehabilitation, and mental health programs. When a mental disorder constitutes an additional disability, or such a determination needs to be made, the psychological evaluation becomes a more focused clinical procedure within a program's context. In view of relatively widespread and well-documented incidents of insensitivity to the unique characteristics of deaf persons by psychologists and other members of the mental health community, specialists who are skilled in serving this population are understandably concerned about the quality of psychological reports and the extent to which they can rely on the findings and recommendations. This chapter summarizes some of the basic issues and considerations in evaluating deaf persons. Rather than attempting to go into detail regarding the special qualifications psychologists need to serve this population, the focus is on assisting non-psychologists to better understand the role of the psychological interview, testing, and diagnosis in the development of a psychological report useful in serving deaf individuals who also have a mental disorder.

Foundations

The skill of the psychologist remains the single most important factor in producing a useful psychological report. "The most serious obstacle," Smith (1984) contends, "is the examiner (who) is not only

the collector but the perceiver and interpreter. In subtle ways the process can go awry" (p. 189). While the ways in which the process can go awry may well be subtle, the consequences may be substantial. When amplified by a lack of sensitivity to the complex issues of deafness, the results can be disastrous. Moores (1978) implicates "well-meaning but misinformed hearing individuals" (p. 151) and concludes that, "For the most part, inappropriate tests have been administered under unsatisfactory conditions and results have been compared with unrealistic norms" (p. 146). The psychologist who has had little opportunity to work with deaf persons is at a marked disadvantage and prone to questionable judgments. Even when the conclusions are appropriate, they may remain under a cloud of doubt in the minds of both the psychologist and the recipient of the report and have a less than optimal impact on the client's program.

The psychological assessment of a deaf client should be conducted in the language or language modality preferred by the client by a psychologist having such communication skills or, as a second choice, with the assistance of a certified interpreter acceptable to the client. The psychologist also needs to have background and experience with deaf culture as well as the psychological, social, educational, and vocational consequences of the various severities and times of onsets of hearing impairment. Without these minimal qualifications, the psychologist runs a risk of doing a disservice to the client. Another highly desirable characteristic is for the psychologist to have experience as a psychotherapist. The psychologist who is not also a therapist will be limited in making treatment recommendations, which are often needed for individuals with a mental disorder. Skill and experience in implementing therapeutic recommendations contribute to the quality and practicality of recommendations contained in the psychological report.

Underlying the questions from referral sources are more basic issues which the psychologist must address on the way to answering specific referral questions and to arriving at useful predictive statements. One helpful working concept in this regard is the "projective hypothesis" which, as Rapaport, Gill, & Shafer (1968) explained, "implies that every action and reaction of a human being bears the characteristic features of his individual make-up" (p. 52). It is, of course, these "characteristic features" of the client that the psychological report attempts to summarize, since they illuminate the meanings of the client's 'action and reaction'. By conducting a series of systematic observations (in this case, a psychological assessment), these characteristic features that typify an individual, make up one's identity, and allow for reasonable predictions consistent with that individual, may be understood. Shapiro (1965) has termed these characteristic features "style," that is, "constancies of individual functioning . . . giving shape alike to symptom and nonsymptom, to defense against impulse and adaptive expression of impulse" (p. 4). The assessment process identifies an individual's style or characteristic features regarding coping strategies, belief systems, intellectual efficiency, social behavior, motivation, and more. It then becomes possible to differentiate adaptive from nonadaptive features, and to identify, for example, anxiety that serves as an effective motivation for achievement as opposed to anxiety that produces inefficient behavior, or confidence that is reality-based and constructive as opposed to confidence that is defensive and fails to take into account real limitations.

The Clinical Interview

The initial part of the psychological assessment is the clinical interview which allows for the development of the case history and provides opportunities for behavioral observation. The organization of the interview will be more or less shaped by the information elicited and will follow selected paths of inquiry related to the individual client. The interview is substantially tailored to each individual client in accordance with communication skills and willingness to cooperate, and provides a context for descriptions, explanations, diagnoses, and recommendations. Such biographical information has,

of course, serious limitations. There will inevitably be omissions and distortions, intended or not, which may mislead the psychologist. It is, for example, of importance to know that a client was in fact expelled from school for repeated assaultive behavior as opposed to quitting because, "I didn't like school, they didn't teach me anything." The client's statement may be true, but it is misleading without the perspective provided by the other information. From the vantage of the client, however, it is not the objective events which account for behavior, but the beliefs that he or she holds concerning the events. It is through understanding an individual's perceptions and interpretations of events that characteristic behaviors, both adaptive and nonadaptive, can be comprehended. Additional understanding can be obtained from discrepancies between the client's interpretation of events and those of others, including hypotheses about judgment, insight, reality testing, and the nature of the client's social milieu. Though not always possible, it is helpful to have the insight and interpretation of others concerning crucial events. Eliciting memories of specific events, or "behavioral incidents" as Pascal (1983) terms them, provides insight into how the event was perceived and its possible role in present behavior. For example, a prelingually deaf man recalled childhood incidents of traumatic separations from his parents in order to attend a residential school. These memories were described with intense emotion as proof that his parents did not love him and had rejected him despite the fact that his parents loved him dearly and also found the separations painful. This client's thoughts, feelings, and behavior were not in accordance with the objective events but were, instead, consistent with inaccurate interpretations established in childhood, referred to and modified over a period of years, and integrated into his personality. Such discrepancies suggest areas for focused therapeutic activity provided the client has the potential for productively reconsidering such emotion-laden beliefs.

Testing Considerations

Psychological testing is itself a kind of extended interview which allows for more systematic behavioral observations in a wider range of situations. Testing differs from and compliments clinical interviewing by adhering to standardized procedures which provide a common situational background against which individual attributes can be clarified. One approach to understanding the characteristic features of an individual through testing is by comparing the quantifiable aspects of test responses with those of a normative group. Such an approach has proven highly productive especially in the areas of intelligence and achievement. This normative approach however, poses special problems for the assessment of deaf persons since scores often reflect the influence of uncontrolled variables related to language, communication, and culture. Even when the test scores and their normative interpretation are acceptably valid and reliable, we need to look beyond the scores to the test responses themselves. The quantification of responses focuses attention on one aspect, but every test response communicates more than can be scored. Several persons may have identical test scores and yet they remain unique individuals. The psychologist's task at this level, while not discarding the scores, is to exercise judgment in identifying the meanings of the responses, how they relate to the client's characteristic style, and their diagnostic, treatment, educational, and rehabilitation implications. In discussing his approach to psychological testing, Hirsch (1970) notes that even when using intelligence tests he looks beyond the scores and is, at this level:

> . . . less concerned with the degree to which 'the IQ' score is accurate, and more concerned to find out, for example, what personal characteristics the individual uses to deal with tasks, what kinds of blockages and emotional detours occur while he works them, what are the significances to the individual of dealing with the test problems, what sorts of interactions go on between the person taking and the one giving the test . . . Validity, in the usual sense, therefore, has only the smallest role in the way that psychological examinations are used here.

(p. 15)

Normative test scores and statistical analysis are obviously useful, even with deaf clients. Nonetheless, even when the psychometric aspects are crucial, such as in neuropsychological assessment or the documentation of mental deficiency, it is still important to understand the person behind the scores and describe who that individual is with words rather than numbers.

Levine (1980) has pointed out that a common complaint about psychological reports on deaf persons has been the overemphasis on scores: ". . . almost as if psychologists are so preoccupied with testing that they cannot see the individuals for the test scores" (p. 340). This preoccupation is especially significant in view of the frequently criticized normative data available on deaf populations. While not underestimating the value of quantifiable patterns, we need to keep before us that test scores are, as Holt (1968) contends, "a set of abstracted dimensions from a much richer reality" (p. 23). Perhaps it is because of communication

limitations and cultural unfamiliarity that psychologists assessing deaf persons at times seem to be less aware of the "richer reality" that is the deaf person and take refuge in statistical considerations.

Psychological testing, in addition to standardized procedures, allows for increased comprehensiveness of behavioral observations with respect to content, functions, and structure (Allen, 1984). Tests can systematically elicit content on many themes which may not have been approached in the interview, including dependency, autonomy, sexuality, aggressiveness, achievement, etc. A variety of functions can also be readily investigated such as perceiving, remembering, sequencing, abstracting, calculating, psychomotor coordination, and judging. Structure is another test variable which can range from tasks with clear guidelines and right and wrong answers to relatively unstructured tasks allowing for a broad range of responses. A determination of the extent to which externally imposed organization and structure facilitates or impedes optimal functioning can be among the most useful information presented in the psychological report since it has obvious educational, rehabilitation and therapeutic implications.

The following paragraphs present examples of behavioral observations that can produce viable hypotheses. These examples are by no means comprehensive and are offered only as illustrations. It should also be kept in mind that psychologists seldom make conclusive interpretations based on a single observation. While there are, of course, exceptions, it is typically the characteristics that emerge as patterns that are of importance rather than isolated instances. The test examples are illustrative of a range of structure, from highly structured intelligence testing to projective techniques which are much less clearly defined. These latter considerations are largely independent from the scoring aspects though they need to be taken into account along with the objective psychometric findings.

The Wechsler Adult Intelligence Scale-Revised can provide a wealth of information about the characteristic features or style of an individual, quite apart from the IQ score. On the Block Design subtest, for example, the client is to reproduce designs with colored blocks. One source of information is, of course, the score on the individual tasks and on the entire subtest. Another source is observing the client's responses to the tasks: Are the instructions readily understood? Does the client seem eager to do well or seem intimidated? Does the client laugh and claim to be too old to "play with blocks?" Are the blocks assembled carefully or haphazardly? Are they assembled with one or both hands? At what point do the designs become difficult for the client and how is the difficulty confronted or avoided? What problem-solving strategies are employed, and do mistakes follow a pattern? Does the client become frustrated, give up, become angry, throw the blocks on the floor, or persevere calmly even though unrewarded by success? How does the client respond to encouragement? Does the client assert that the designs cannot be made or accuse the psychologist of trickery? Is the client aware of incorrect responses and how is this information used? Does the client recover after incorrect responses and provide correct responses? Is the quality of performance inconsistent, with easy items performed less adequately than difficult ones?

The Bender Gestalt is another useful test for many deaf persons. Even clients with little or no language are usually able to complete it. This test consists of nine designs which are copied onto a sheet of paper. The drawings can then be interpreted by an experienced psychologist in terms of what they suggest regarding the individual. Most of the issues raised regarding the Block Design subtest of the WAIS-R are relevant here as well. Additional considerations include: Are the designs reproduced accurately, expansively, constrictedly, overly controlled, sequentially organized, distorted, incomplete, or rotated? Are mistakes neatly erased or impulsively crossed out? Are second attempts improvements or are errors perseverated? Is the pencil line excessively heavy or light? Are tremors present? Did the client count the number of dots or estimate the number; was the number of dots drawn correct? Was the time required excessive or brief? An important part of the Bender Gestalt is the recall phase. After completing the initial copying of the designs, all materials are placed out of sight and the client is instructed to draw them from memory. The results can be compared to the initially copied designs to obtain an estimate of the efficiency of the client in functioning on the basis of recent memory in the absence of the stimulus cards. The manner in which an individual organizes and presents the designs provides insights into the characteristic ways of organizing and presenting him or herself.

The Diagnosis

The role of diagnosis in terms of a standard nosology is as relevant to the assessment of deaf persons as other populations despite its history of inconsistent application. A systematic utilization of a common language of mental disorders by the professional and scientific communities is a prerequisite for the provision of quality services and the development of improved techniques through research. Just as communication difficulties have posed conceptual problems between hearing and deaf individuals, conceptual inconsistencies in the absence of a commonly accepted language of diagnosis also leads to misunderstanding. As Chapter II notes, the *Diagnostic and Statistical Manual of Mental Disorders*, Third Edition (1980) (DSM-III) is the most widely-accepted standard in the United States at this time. It is an attempt to classify concepts of psychopathology descriptively rather than on the basis of various theoretical or etiological considerations. The generic concept of 'mental disorder' set forth in DSM-III is:

> . . . a clinically significant behavioral or psychological syndrome or pattern that occurs in an individual and that is typically associated with either a painful symptom (distress) or impairment in one or more areas of functioning (disability).

(p. 6)

The DSM-III task force has emphasized that what is classified are disorders and not persons, attributes of individuals and not the individuals themselves. We avoid, therefore, referring to a person as, for example, 'a schizophrenic' or 'an alcoholic' and refer instead to 'an individual with Schizophrenia' and 'an individual with Alcohol Dependence' (p. 6). Thus, it is no more accurate to reduce a person to a mental disorder than to any other attribute, including, of course, deafness.

The multiaxial format of DSM III provides several advantages over the previous approaches to diagnosis: it acknowledges explicitly that different types of disorders may coexist simultaneously; it acknowledges the importance of identifying physical disorders and conditions; and it provides a broader basis for making prognostic estimates.

The role of Personality Disorders in the DSM III system merits special attention. Personality Disorders are diagnosed when long-standing personality traits, recognizable by adolescence or earlier, become "inflexible and maladaptive and cause either significant impairment in social or occupational functioning or subjective distress . . . [The diagnosis should be made only when] . . . the characteristic features are typical of the individual's long-term functioning and are not limited to discrete episodes of illness" (p. 305). By encouraging the diagnosis of both Clinical Syndromes (Axis I) and Personality Disorders (Axis II) when both exist, DSM-III acknowledges that Personality Disorders can not only exist along with Clinical Syndromes, but may predispose the development and course of a Clinical Syndrome and have implications for treatment and outcome. It should be noted that Personality Disorders are diagnosed less reliably due to the difficulty in separating these long-standing traits from other symptoms and the conceptualization of Personality Disorders as extentions of normal traits often without clearly defined boundaries (Frances, 1980).

The inclusion of Physical Disorders and Conditions (Axis III) allows for the identification of non-mental variables that are relevant to diagnostic understanding and treatment planning. While a psychologist does not make medical diagnoses, Axis III provides a method for summarizing physical disorders and conditions and the source of the information including client self-report. In this way, DSM-III increases the likelihood of a more comprehensive diagnosis, ensuring the important information will not be ignored. Axis III is also utilized when Axis I diagnosis of Psychological Factors Affecting Physical Condition is made; Axis III then identifies the relevant physical condition.

The last two axes provide information especially useful in planning treatment and predicting ability to benefit from educational and rehabilitation programs. Axis IV provides for a systematic rating of precipitating stressors and Axis V a rating of the highest level of adaptive functioning during the preceding year. These ratings contribute to establishing prognosis for recovery. For example, a person with Major Depression would have a more favorable prognosis if the depression were precipitated by a specific, identifiable psychosocial stressor. The prognosis would still be more favorable if the individual had been functioning at an acceptable level of adaptive behavior prior to the precipitating stressor since the client will often return to the previous level of functioning. Similarly, an individual with a long history of impaired adaptive behavior will be less likely to recover as satisfactorily.

An example of how a DSM-III diagnosis can summarize the findings of a psychological assessment is as follows. The client was a congenitally deaf man who became severely depressed following the sudden death of his older, hearing brother with whom he had lived many years and upon whom he was excessively dependent. He had a history of periodic alcohol abuse and an inconsistent employment history. He had lost two jobs the previous year though he was working at the time of his brother's death. He was frightened of the prospect of living on his own. He has no other familial resources. Testing revealed an IQ of 78.

Axis I	296.22	Major Depression, Single Episode
	305.02	Alcohol Abuse, Episodic
	V62.89	Borderline Intellectual Functioning

Axis II	301.60	Dependent Personality Disorder
Axis III		Congenital deafness by self-report
Axis IV		Psychosocial Stressors: Death of older brother with subsequent anticipation of independent living for first time in life. Severity: 6—Extreme
Axis V		Highest level of adaptive functioning past year: Excessive dependence on deceased brother, periodic alcohol intoxication, inconsistent employment: 4—Fair

While the above diagnosis summarizes an extensive amount of information and professional judgment about the client, it also leaves out a good deal more that is necessary. The psychological reports should provide the additional information that is relevant. Holt (1968) advised that "A diagnosis is not a sufficient classification but a necessary constituent of a personality description" (p. 14). The diagnosis is an important part of the personality description, that is, the psychological report, but it remains only one part. The diagnosis is a tool which exists to facilitate this understanding of the client as well as to meet various programmatic needs: eligibility, funding, demographics, research, program development, and others. Beyond this, the report exists to assist in formulating short and long-term goals and the methods for their achievement.

The Report

As Chapter II has explained, the organization of the psychological report will vary greatly among psychologists. There are numerous formats which can be entirely appropriate. All reports, however, need to address the issues sufficiently to allow the user of the report to proceed confidently. Levine (1981) has assembled a thorough list of topics that are relevant to the psychological report for hearing-impaired persons (pp. 382–384). The only recommended addition to this format is, of course, a DSM-III diagnosis which is of importance in assessing deaf individuals for documenting or ruling out the presence of a mental disorder. The psychologist should also list the client's assets and strengths. An important eligibility requirement for some programs is that the client must have demonstrated sufficient potential to benefit from the services, that he or she not be so severely disabled as to preclude participating in the education or rehabilitation program. This is especially important when considering individuals with multiple disabilities such as deafness with a mental disorder. The psychological report should, therefore, include a summary of the strengths and resources of the client. A report limited to a recital of deficiences, defects, and disorders is incomplete and misleading. Even if a client's strengths are severely limited, a forthright discussion of them will present a more complete picture and convey that the psychologist's efforts to find assets has been as thorough as the efforts to find problems.

A psychological report contains a broad range of personal and technical information and should not be made available to the client without careful consideration. The *Ethical Principles of Psychologists* (American Psychological Association, 1981) requires psychologists to "respect the client's right to know the results, the interpretations made, and the bases for their conclusions" (p. 637). However, providing such information must be done within the broader context of the ethical obligation to "make every effort to promote the welfare and best interests of the client" (p. 637). Allowing the client to actually read the report may or may not be in his or her best interest. Learning one's IQ score or formal diagnosis does not necessarily result in constructive insight. It may instead be upsetting and jeopardize future therapeutic efforts. Such destructive consequences may result regardless of whether the report is correctly or incorrectly understood. While legal procedures may, at times, remove such considerations from the purview of psychologists and other professionals, it is preferable that the client be provided with oral, signed, or written summaries of the report explained and interpreted in a manner consistent with the client's ability to comprehend and constructively utilize the information. For deaf clients with a mental disorder, considerable skill and sophistication in communication and psychology are prerequisites to reviewing a report with the client. The client's motivation for wanting the information is also important and such requests should not be taken simply at face value. The psychologist, educational, and rehabilitation specialists should be sensitive to issues underlying the request and be responsive to them.

Sample Report

Referral Information

Mr. J was referred by a psychological evaluation by his Vocational Rehabilitation counselor. Mr. J is applying for VR services at this time and his counselor is seeking documentation of a possible mental disorder and recommendation for rehabilitation planning. Records of previous psychiatric hospitalizations are not yet available.

Background Information

Mr. J is a 27 year old congenitally deaf, Caucasian male who has been in the _____ area for the past six weeks. He is residing with his father and stepmother. He is an only child. His father accompanied him to the evaluation and participated in a portion of the interviews. His father and stepmother are both hearing and communicate only marginally in sign language. Mr. J's father does not believe that communication is a major problem. The client, however, is frustrated when trying to communicate and at one point angrily walked out of the interview.

Mr. J resided in the state of _____ with his mother since his parents were divorced when he was 12 years old. However, much of his time was actually spent in a residential school for the deaf about 100 miles from his home with infrequent visits during the school year. Summer vacations were divided between his mother and his father. He graduated from high school in 1977, apparently with poor grades. He was previously a VR client in the state of _____ and he reports participating in training in a print shop though the details of this are not clear. His VR program was disrupted when he was psychiatrically hospitalized for 3 months in 1978. While Mr. J relates that he was hospitalized "for a rest" his father explained that he had become unmanageable by his mother who had contacted him requesting that the client move in with him. He reportedly would be up all night and was taken to a hospital emergency room by the police who found him at 3 a.m. stopping cars at an intersection looking for "the devil" which he believed was in one of the cars. Mr. J's father believes he has had two subsequent psychiatric hospitalizations of three to four weeks each. He is presently taking Mellaril 150 mg hs and 75 mg PRN for agitation. These were prescribed by Dr. _____ of the County Hospital in the state of _____. Mr. J has only another three weeks supply.

Mr. J has no work history since his initial hospitalization in 1978 and had been content to stay at home and help his mother around the house. His previous work history was limited to part-time janitorial work for less than one week.

Clinical Interview

Mr. J made only a marginal appearance. He was clean though unshaven and at times became exasperated and even angry. He became more cooperative as the evaluation progressed. He communicates adequately in American Sign Language and the evaluation was conducted in ASL. When he became angry his signing became grossly exaggerated and, in view of his tall stature, could easily be seen as threatening. He has little insight into his previous psychiatric condition. He states that he takes his current medicine to help him "sleep better." He denies hallucinations though admits to communicating to God, though not for several years. He used to be awakened by these "communications." He cannot recall the content of these. He explains that he moved to his father's home because he didn't get along with his mother though he can offer no further insight into this.

Mr. J reports learning to sign at the age of six when he was placed in a day school for the deaf. He expressed resentment towards his parents for not attending sign language classes and became angry in discussing this. When his parents divorced (when he was 12) he and his mother moved to _____ to be closer to her family though this necessitated his entry into a residential school which had the consequence of separating him from both of his parents. Mr. J minimized any difficulties in school and was not very communicative. He denies getting into trouble, though his father later explained that he had been suspended briefly on two occasions for drinking and fighting and had been retained an additional year because of academic difficulties. Mr. J's father believes his son is capable of above average work and attributes his lack of achievement to "stubbornness". Mr. J was nonresponsive when asked how he had felt about his parents divorce and placement in the residential school except to say "OK". He was willing to express anger toward his parents on other issues, however. For example, he accused his mother of stealing his SSI check when he lived with her, and blamed his father for not taking his side in this. Mr. J had written letters to various officials about his complaint in addition to his father. In discussing this, Mr. J was unable to seriously consider possible alternative explanations for his mother's management of his check and insisted that she had no right to steal his money. He was momentarily quite angry discussing this though quickly calmed down when the subject was changed.

Mr. J has never dated and denies any interest in women. He was unable to explain this beyond stating that "they are no good for you." He claims no interest in making friends or socializing and spends his time watching television. He helps do some work around the house but refuses to mow the lawn or do other outside work because "it's too hot!" His refusal to help routinely has been a source of con-

flict which is placing additional stress on the relationship between his father and stepmother.

Mr. J says he would like to work though has little insight into the implications of employment. In discussing his vocational interests he said emphatically that he did not want to work in a print shop. His first choice would be to "work with computers." He could not explain what he would do with computers except to "work" with them. He seems willing to consider other occupations.

Tests Administered and Results

WAIS-R, Bender Gestalt, Projective Drawings

The WAIS-R places Mr. J in the normal range of intelligence based on the performance subtests. The specific scores are:

Picture Completion	10
Picture Arrangement	7
Block Design	11
Object Assembly	8
Digit Symbol	8
Performance IQ	92

Mr. J is able to visually discriminate relevant from irrelevant details within normal limits though his performance on the Picture Completion subtest was somewhat inconsistent. He was typically slow to respond not wanting to commit himself to a response until he had considered several possibilities. His score was lowered somewhat because he couldn't arrive at a decision within the time limit. The Picture Arrangement subtest revealed considerable underlying confusion demonstrating Mr. J's inability to consistently understand social situations and exercise good judgment. While his score remains at the low-normal level, his social judgment is rather tenuous and represents a significant obstacle for a successful vocational adjustment. His highest score was on the Block Design subtest which is well within normal limits. Mr. J was much more comfortable on this task and worked consistently. He suggested that the most difficult design was "impossible" though this was offered with a smile. His Object Assembly score is at the low end of the normal range, and would have been higher except for his conceptual difficulty in understanding what the last puzzle was as he was working on it. He stayed with the task and completed it correctly after the time limit. The Digit Symbol subtest was within normal limits.

The Bender Gestalt designs were reproduced accurately with no major distortions. However, he required 19 minutes for the initial copying phase which is excessive. He erased and reworked several of the designs which improved their quality. The recall phase was completed in 4 minutes and Mr. J reproduced 5 of the 9 designs from memory. The quality of the designs was less adequate though still without gross distortions. It is significant, however, that he could not recall more of the designs in view of his having worked with them initially for an extensive amount of time.

The projective drawings (House, Tree, Person) also required extensive time and effort with inappropriate attention to irrelevant details. For example, on the house, he began drawing every shingle on the roof, tired of this after several minutes, and left out the remainder of the shingles. His drawings reflect the inconsistencies observed during the interview and testing. He was largely unwilling to discuss the drawings and when asked about then said only that it was "silly" to talk about them.

The Information and Comprehension subtests of the WAIS-R were also administered. Mr. J received scaled scores of 7 and 5 respectively. Though not indicative of his intelligence his responses contribute to understanding him further. Considerable time and effort was required to get his responses though on the Information subtest he was often, though inconsistently, able to provide a correct answer. By contrast, his poor judgment was a major factor on the Comprehension subtest. He became frustrated when the questions were repeated and clarification requested. In response to the question "Why do people who are deaf have trouble learning to talk?" he initially said he didn't know and he specified that he could sign. When questioned further he gestured resignedly, "God."

Diagnostics

Axis I:	295.32	Schizophrenia, paranoid, chronic
Axis II:	V71.09	No diagnosis
Axis III:		Congenital deafness
Axis IV:		Severity of psychosocial stressors: conflict with mother precipitating move to _____; conflicts and adjustment problems with father and stepmother; entry into VR program. Severity 4—moderate.
Axis V:		Highest level of adaptive functioning past year: unemployed; helping with household tasks; very limited socializations. Severity 5—Poor.

Mr. J appears to be manifesting schizophrenia, paranoid type, chronic. This is partially controlled by his medication. He is of basically normal intelligence though he has moderately impaired judg-

ment and lacks insight into his condition. His expressed vocational goals are inappropriate. He can be expected to continue to be a source of conflicts at his father's home.

I recommend that he be referred for psychiatric supervision and continued medication. He and his family could benefit from psychotherapy to provide emotional support and exploration of problem-solving alternatives. Without access to therapy he is at risk for being asked to leave his father's home and for further acute psychotic episodes. His father and stepmother should explore their own values and make some decisions concerning what they want their future role to be with respect to Mr. J. Developing greater skill in manual communication should be a high priority. His condition is chronic and not likely to improve substantially in the foreseeable future. He may be capable of semi-independent living in a group home specifically designed to serve deaf individuals though without such structure he would not function well outside of his family. Vocational assessment is needed. In view of his poor judgment and inconsistent social skills, work tasks should be routine to minimize his becoming confused.

I believe Mr. J can productively participate in a vocational rehabilitation program. He will probably be a good candidate for work adjustment training. Please contact me if I can provide any further information.

Sincerely,

_____

Psychologist

References

Allen, J. (1984). The clinical psychologist as a diagnostic consultant. In F. Shectman, & W. H. Smith (Eds.), *Diagnostic understanding and treatment planning* (pp. 220–229). New York: John Wiley & Sons.

American Psychological Association (1981). Ethical principles of psychologists. *American Psychologist*, Vol. 36, No. 6 (pp. 633–638).

American Psychiatric Association (1980). *Diagnostic and statistical manual of mental disorders* (Third Edition). Washington, D.C.: Author.

Frances, A. (1980). The DSM-III personality disorder section: A commentary. *American Journal of Psychiatry* (pp. 1050–1054).

Hirsch, E. (1970). *The troubled adolescent as he emerges on psychological tests*. New York: International Universities Press.

Holt, M. (1968). Foreword. In D. Rapaport, M. Gill, & R. Schafer (Eds.), *Diagnostic psychological tests*. New York: International Universities Press.

Levine, E. (1981). *The ecology of early deafness*. New York: Columbia University Press.

Moores, D. (1978). *Educating the deaf*. Boston: Houghton Mifflin Co.

Pascal, G. (1983). *The practical art of diagnostic interviewing.* Homewood, IL: Dow Jones Irwin.

Rapaport, D., Gill, M., & Schafer, R. (1968). *Diagnostic psychological testing.* New York: International Universities Press.

Shapiro, D. (1965). *Neurotic styles.* New York: Basic Books.

Smith, S. (1984). Psychological testing and the mind of the tester. In F. Shectman, & W. H. Smith (Eds.), *Diagnostic understanding and treatment planning* (pp. 185–190). New York: John Wiley & Sons.

CHAPTER IV

Characteristics and Assessment of Students in Transition

Patricia M. Sullivan

Introduction

This chapter addresses the psychological characteristics and assessment of deaf students in transition from school to the world of work. This categorization of disabled individuals represents a national priority towards improvement of the transition from school to working life. Between 50 and 80 percent of working age adults with disabilities are jobless (U.S. Commission on Civil Rights, 1983; U.S. Bureau of the Census, 1982). In the mid-1970's, every handicapped child was guaranteed a free and public education, and millions of dollars have been invested in this endeavor. However, employment statistics of disabled individuals suggest that attention needs to be given to the transition from public education to gainful employment to insure that public investment in special education leads to full, or some form of, community participation in adult life. This chapter defines transition and its component processes and services. Applications to deaf clients for each component process are presented. Some of the psychological characteristics of the client population are discussed. Finally, the ideal components of a psychological assessment for deaf clients in transition are presented and described, with particular emphasis on interpretation of the resulting psychological report by the rehabilitation counselor.

Transition Defined

Transition, or change, plays an integral role in normal life. How one is able to adapt to change is key to an individual's survival and indicative of one's psychological adjustment. Individuals develop and change throughout their lifespans. Life entails a series of transitions that require adaptation of the individual.

The transition from school to working life is only one such transition. It demands a series of choices about career options, living arrangements, social life, and economic goals. This transition is difficult for everyone. However, it is particularly difficult for some deaf individuals for obvious reasons. Deaf students typically leave an organized provider system with a complex network of support services that is readily available to them. They enter a more complex and confusing world of work where few, if any, support services are available. These services include peers and supervisors with sign language skills, interpreters, easy access to TDDs, counseling, and social work services, to name a few. Students from residential schools often have become accustomed to these readily available support services and experience a kind of culture shock when they are not available to them on-the-job. Students from mainstreamed settings may not suffer as much culture shock because they have become accus-

37

tomed to the absence of these support services or may be able to function somewhat independently without them. Other mainstreamed students have been insulated and overprotected during their school years and have difficulties coping without the special treatment provided them in high school. Unfortunately, both residential and mainstreamed programs generally foster too much dependency in high school students.

The successful transition from school to working life is an outcome-oriented process that encompasses a broad array of services and experiences that lead to employment (Will, 1983). This transition is a developmental process that includes the high school years, graduation, additional postsecondary education, and the beginning years of employment. A hallmark of this transition is the successful resolution of the adolescent dependence-independence conflict. This encompasses the ability to leave the security and structure afforded by the school environment for the opportunities and risks of adult life.

A successful transition also requires that the major developmental tasks of adolescence (Erickson, 1951) are addressed and resolved, to whatever extent possible, at the secondary level. However, this may not be a realistic expectation for some multihandicapped deaf adolescents (Brier and Demb, 1981). These developmental tasks include:

1. Attainment of emotional independence from parents and the residential school;
2. Establishment of a meaningful and stable identity;
3. Development of a commitment to work;
4. Development of a personal value system;
5. Development of a capacity for lasting relationships and both tender and genital love;
6. Development of an ability to return to parents or the residential school in a new relationship of relative equality.

The final components of a successful transition from school to the working world are adequate support services at the point of school leaving and opportunities and services, if needed, in adult situations (Will, 1983). Thus, transition success is a shared responsibility of deaf educators at the secondary level, Vocational Rehabilitation counselors at both the secondary level and postsecondary levels, and the networking between professionals and employers at all levels. Networking, as described by Naisbitt in *Megatrends* (1984), is a communication process that creates linkages between people and clusters of people through the sharing of ideas, information, and resources. It is a powerful tool to bring about social action and is a direction that will most probably define service delivery models of the future.

Components of Transition Services

Transition services are grouped into three classes that reflect the nature of services required to provide support as the passage from school to work is completed (Will, 1983). These include no special services, time-limited services, and ongoing services.

No Special Services

The first mode of bridging the developmental change from school to work is employed by most individuals without disabilities. It entails reliance on individual resources or those generic resources that are generally available to all citizens. The individual is able to locate and take advantage of work opportunities without the assistance of special disability services. Examples include students who obtain employment at the end of high school programs as a direct result of contacts made during secondary level work experience programs; others are able to locate employment through family or community contacts; some volunteer jobs may result in permanent employment; and other individuals are able to gain entrance to postsecondary institutions on the merits of their own endeavors without the assistance of specialized disability services.

Statistics on the number of deaf individuals who use this pathway are currently unavailable. However, it is assumed that they encompass a minority percentage of the deaf post-school-age population. This is because clinical experience of both psychologists and VR counselors serving older deaf adolescents suggests that most require some type of assistance in either obtaining employment or enrolling in a postsecondary educational institution. Until data become available on percentages of this service population, this chapter will assume that it comprises, at most, 10 percent. This figure allows for the best and brightest students who consistently function at the upper end of the normal distribution and for the few who benefit from fortuitous life experiences.

Time-Limited Services

This bridge from school to work consists of temporary services that are designed to result in employment. Examples typically include the gamut of vocational or academic oriented education, and/or other specialized job training programs. The presence of a significant hearing impairment qualifies an individual for this cascade of services and often provides special support benefits for participation. Some deaf individuals are able to find employment after receiving minimal services in rehabilitation facilities. Others require a specific job training course of study before employment is secured. Time-limited services are usually accessed only by those deaf individuals who are deemed good risks for securing gainful employment upon their successful completion. This type of service is the crux of traditional Vocational Rehabilitation services.

Again, statistics are unavailable on the percentage of deaf students in transition within this service category. In this chapter, it is assumed that these students constitute a majority, or some 60 percent, of the deaf population served by Vocational Rehabilitation.

Ongoing Services

The third bridge from school to the working world consists of ongoing services in whatever form necessary to secure and obtain some type of employment. Most deaf individuals within this service category require the provision of structured living and work-support services throughout adulthood. Some individuals within this service category live at home and attend day activity programs which provide a regimen of instruction in daily living skills, social activities, and part-time semi-skilled employment. Others live in group homes or semi-independent living facilities and participate in some type of sheltered workshop vocational setting during the day. Some require institutionalization and participate in minimal pre-vocational or vocational activities throughout the day.

Multihandicapped deaf individuals clearly comprise the majority of this transition population. Current demographic estimates suggest that this group encompasses 30 percent of the deaf school age population (Jensema & Mullins, 1974).

Conclusions

Successful bridging, irrespective of the type of transition service, ultimately requires employment opportunities (Will, 1983). These opportunities are dependent upon factors both within and without the educational and Vocational Rehabilitation service domains. Factors within these domains include quality education programs that precede arrival at the transition plateau, availability of adequate and viable transition services to meet individual needs, and available employment. This availability is most often dependent upon factors outside of education and Vocational Rehabilitation. Such factors include the overall status of the economy, unemployment levels, structural unemployment affecting both skilled and unskilled workers, the extent of job dis-

crimination, and job availability in a given individual's chosen field of endeavor and training. Unfortunately, Vocational Rehabilitation counselors are often faced with seemingly insurmountable barriers in placing deaf clients in employment positions, largely because of economic conditions beyond their control. Hopefully, supported employment alternatives and government incentives provided to employers will somewhat alleviate these difficulties.

Applications to Deaf Clients

The successful transition of a deaf individual from school to work has been described in this chapter as an outcome oriented process that is dependent upon networking and the sharing of responsibility between secondary programs, Vocational Rehabilitation counselors, postsecondary programs, and employers. This concept of successful transition represents the ideal situation wherein the necessary training programs and jobs are readily available. Vocational Rehabilitation counselors serving at the "front" of the transition battle, however, are too often confronted with conditions relating to availability of services and jobs that are far from ideal. Any consideration of the deaf student in transition must address key factors that are indigenous to the population served and the zeitgeist with which the Vocational Rehabilitation counselor must cope. It is impossible to use all types of clients encountered by VR counselors as examples. Therefore, the author has selected typical cases to illustrate general points covered.

Heterogeneity of Deaf Population

The deaf population does not comprise a homogeneous group (Moores, 1978). Many variables may impinge on the deaf individual's physical and environmental life space which contributes to his/her basic human uniqueness and may necessitate specialized services. These include: etiology of the deafness (Vernon, 1969), presence of additional handicapping conditions, parental acceptance of deafness, self-acceptance of deafness, oral vs. total communication early intervention techniques, residential vs. mainstreamed educational placements, placement transitions and subsequent adjustment, parental and educational expectations (or lack thereof), deaf culture issues, degree of hearing loss, age at onset, and general hard-of-hearing vs. deaf issues. Professionals serving the deaf population are well advised to conceptualize this client population as individuals with hearing impairments rather than as hearing-impaired individuals. The heterogeneous nature of the population necessitates a thorough understanding of the psychological aspects of deafness and idiosyncratic interaction of numerous deafness specific variables as a prerequisite for appropriate referral and transition placement services. The reader is referred to Moores (1978), Vernon (1969), and Gannon (1981) for a discussion of these issues.

Attainment of Adolescent Developmental Tasks

Unfortunately, it cannot be safely assumed that deaf students in transition who apply for Vocational Rehabilitation services and are subsequently referred for psychological evaluation to assist in appropriate transition referral have successfully mastered Eriksen's (1951) developmental tasks of adolescence. Clinical experience supports this general statement. Like most generalizations, it applies to some but not all deaf students in transition. Several hypotheses are presented to explain this phenomenon. Deaf students with hearing parents who attend residential schools from an early age are often more emotionally bonded or attached to the residential school than to their natural parents. Long periods spent away from the family, ease of communication and acceptance within the residential school, and identification with the deaf community probably account for this factor. Many deaf students consider the residential school to be their family and experience depression and withdrawal symptoms as graduation approaches. Suicidal gestures or attempts may be made. These are most probably cries for help in coping with the transition process. These difficulties are exacerbated if the relationship between the student and the residential school is a particularly dependent one. Students from mainstreamed settings may experience similar difficulties. The thought of coping without the resource teacher and/or school provided interpreter who have kept them "afloat" throughout their school career is frightening for some students. These fears are exacerbated when some postsecondary or job facilities to which they apply do not provide these support services.

Parents often contribute to the emotional dependence of deaf youth by not allowing them to attain pre-adult rites of passage at the normal ages allowed hearing siblings and peers. Examples include obtaining a driver's license, dating, and part-time teenage employment. Some parents either require their young adults to live with them during the transition period and after or do not want them to leave home or the community to obtain work. This factor most probably reflects over-protective tendencies and decreased expectations of deaf offspring on the part of some hearing parents.

Some deaf students have difficulties establishing a meaningful and stable identity because they have not accepted their deafness and have pronounced self-concept difficulties. Both parental and school factors may contribute to these problems. Examples include parents with chronic acceptance problems of their child's deafness and mainstreamed settings that do not foster interaction with hearing-impaired peers.

The development of a commitment to work is hard to engender in deaf youth when some are encouraged to expect Social Security disability benefits only because they possess the required degree of hearing impairment to qualify. Further, some deaf youth are given pseudo-jobs in their respective schools and are paid, as it were, for showing up to work rather than as remuneration for services rendered. Proper work ethics and attitudes are learned and should be emphasized in all secondary level programs for deaf youth. Competition in today's job market is keen and our deaf youth must be prepared for it.

Many deaf youth are unable to handle the new social freedoms afforded them in postsecondary educational facilities. This is probably due, in part, to lack of or inappropriate sex education programs within the secondary schools, both in residential and mainstreamed settings. Parents assume the school is handling the topic adequately, schools assume parents are addressing some aspects of sex in the home, and the deaf youth is often adrift in a sea of misinformation. An increasing number of deaf students appear to be the victims of sexual abuse (Sullivan, Scanlon and LeBarre, in preparation). This state of affairs makes it difficult for students to develop a capacity for lasting relationships and to engage in a transition social activity of seeking and choosing a life mate.

The successful attainment of these developmental tasks is a necessary component of a successful transition from school to work. Students usually become eligible for Vocational Rehabilitation services at 16 years of age. At this time an assessment of a student's progress towards these developmental milestones should be obtained by means of a clinical interview with the student, his/her parents, and appropriate school personnel. Cooperative efforts between secondary level school personnel, the Vocational Rehabilitation counselor, psychologist, and the student's parents should then ensue to assist the student in realizing his/her potential in attaining these milestones. If needed, specific behavioral objectives should be included in the student's Individualized Educational Program (IEP). This will ensure that the deaf youth comes equipped to make the transition passage several years later.

40

VR Counselors as Gypsies

Folklore provides us with one of the safety valves or defense mechanisms when things do not turn out as hoped or expected. This convenient means of projecting blame and guilt on an innocent uninvolved party is expressed by the English idiom: "blame it on the gypsies". It is often the lot of the VR counselor who is faced with providing transition services to a deaf youth who is ill-prepared for the crossing or who lacks the prerequisite skills for entrance into the career program of his/her family's choice and probably will never be able to realistically acquire them. This situation creates great consternation in the youth and his/her family and vitriolic feelings, remarks, and blame are often leveled at the VR counselor for "failing" to provide desired services. Many parents are unaware that an approximate eighth grade reading level is required for entrance into the most prestigious colleges for the deaf. Such parents are shocked to learn that their child did not pass the Gallaudet or NTID entrance examinations and, at nineteen years of age, with a high school diploma, is reading at an approximate fourth grade level. These parents were either uninformed by school personnel about their child's reading progress or did not "hear", in the client-centered sense, what was explained to them. Many parents misinterpret the "A" and "B" grades earned in school as automatic passports to college. The VR counselor inherits the task of giving the parents and deaf youth the bad news of reality and earns the accolades that follow all harbingers of despair.

This is only one example of the VR counselor's sometimes experienced fate as gypsy. No wonder this profession has a high burn out rate (Meadow, 1981). Antidotes include early involvement with the deaf youth, his/her parents, and school personnel at the pre-transition service level. A complete psychological evaluation at this juncture followed by an open and honest parent conference with the VR counselor present should abate the formation of castles-in-the-air with this particular type of client. This example keenly illustrates the need for cooperative networking and shared responsibility between deaf educators, VR counselors, psychologists, and postsecondary school personnel.

Clients Between the Cracks

Tantamount to the nature of psychological and Vocational Rehabilitation services is the categorization of individual characteristics as a nexus to services. Specialized services require certain characteristics for entrance. These categories of characteristics, most often subsumed under the label of diagnoses, are often inflexible, ostensibly in the name of pure scientific nosology. Blue birds should not compete with yellow birds, to borrow an analogy from most of our first grade reading groups.

Problems arise when an individual does not seem to "fit" into any one category but may exhibit the characteristics and service needs of several categories. Given this state of affairs, the client has the dubious distinction of "falling between the cracks" of the service cascade. A classic example is the client with borderline intelligence and marginal adaptive behavioral proficiencies who needs services available for the mentally retarded but misses qualification for such services by three IQ points. An equally classic example is the multihandicapped deaf youth with mental retardation, primitive personality, and socially inappropriate behavioral manifestations. The individual is refused services for the mentally retarded because of his/her deafness, programs appropriate for the other multiple handicaps reject the person because staff members do not know sign language, and available programs for the deaf do not accept the multihandicapped! The trolls guarding the bridges to such programs frequently argue over which is the primary handicapping condition and, in effect, accept the individual on the basis of one handicap and simultaneously reject him/her on the basis of another.

Such dilemmas are not easily resolved. The crux of the problem appears to rest in failure to respond to the individual's total service needs, rather than responding to each as a separate entity. These are the clients that try VR counselors' souls. The ultimate solution lies in less rigid entrance criteria and a service rather than category oriented philosophy. However, until this shift in philosophy becomes commonplace, the VR counselor is left to his/her own creative devices to gain entrance for clients into appropriate transition programs. The exception, of course, is when a complete service cascade of appropriate programs is available for all possible classification permutations of deaf clients. However, this is the luxury of only a few geographic areas.

A strategy that has been effective, in the author's clinical experience, in gaining program entrance for client's who typify the examples given in this section involves creative networking between the VR counselor and the psychologist. Sometimes all that is needed is a conference between the two professionals wherein the VR counselor requests that the psychological report emphasize a particular handicapping condition over another. Examples include reporting the standard error of measurement for the IQ score in the borderline client's report and emphasizing the appropriateness of MR programming in the recommendations section. With multihandicapped clients, it is sometimes possible to gain program entrance on a trial or probationary basis. This strategy may be used with clients who possess several handicapping conditions. The service site is selected by the VR counselor and psychologist on the basis of client primary need. This is often a program that serves hearing mentally retarded individuals which typically has excellent vocational, social, behavioral and living skill behavior modification-based programs. Also, the hearing clients of such programs often have some form of communication disorder. The key is to convince admissions personnel to accept the client with the hope that the service site learns that it is quite capable of serving deaf multihandicapped clients appropriately. However, this type of networking requires a great deal of ongoing consultation and follow-up with the placement site by both the VR counselor and psychologist. This strategy is particularly effective with clients who have been rejected or failed in several community programs and have reputations, both real and imagined, that precede and follow them along the service site circuit.

Conclusions

This section has described some of the psychological characteristics and issues that confront educators and VR counselors in providing services to deaf youth in transition. The heterogeneous nature of the population served and variable availability of appropriate transition services necessitates the implementation of networking (Naisbitt, 1984) among professionals along the transition continuum. Transition itself is a developmental process that roughly corresponds from the middle adolescent years, when a youth becomes eligible for VR services, to the late adolescent or young adulthood years, when the client is able to secure and maintain some type of employment. A given individual may require intervention and services at several points along this continuum. This is particularly true with the multihandicapped, with the teenagers who are not making adequate progress toward successful completion of the developmental tasks ordinarily achieved in adolescence, and with the clients who do not conform to the traditional hierarchies of service delivery models. Difficulties encountered by deaf students in transition are not the exclusive property of VR counselors. Transition success results from the sharing of responsibility and networking between the secondary school, VR counselor, psychologist, postsecondary facility, and prospective employer.

Psychological Evaluation for Transition Clients

A VR counselor who refers a deaf student in transition for a psychological evaluation should expect a report that provides useful information in determining the kind of transition service(s) appropriate to the client's abilities and needs. The nature and scope of the psychological evaluation in rehabilitation are described and discussed in Chapters II and III. They, therefore, will only be discussed here as they relate to transition clients. Emphasis will be placed in this section on the kinds of assessment and diagnostic information the rehabilitation counselor should be able to garner from psychological evaluations of these clients. The kinds of information the counselor needs to provide the psychologist are delineated and described. Finally, a sample psychological report of a transition client will be presented.

Components of a Transition Psychological Evaluation

A psychological evaluation of a deaf student in transition should include the standard components dictated by state-of-the-art clinical practice. These include the following.

Reason for Referral: This section should delineate the reasons which prompted referral and specific referral questions to be answered in the psychological report. Examples include the determination of the appropriateness of college entry and eligibility for mental retardation services, and an assessment of the behavioral and emotional status of the client as they relate to adjustment in a particular service facility. This section informs the counselor that the report addresses aspects of the client's psychological status that will be of assistance to him/her.

Test Administered: This section lists all tests administered and their results which were employed to answer the referral question(s). These should be reviewed by the counselor to determine their appropriateness for use with deaf clients. The reader is referred to Zieziula (1982) and Sullivan and Vernon (1979) for a discussion of appropriate tests. This review is unnecessary, if the counselor has access to a psychologist with experience in working with deaf persons and fluent communication skills with deaf clients for referral purposes.

Behavioral Observations: The client's behavioral characteristics during the psychological evaluation offer important diagnostic information. For example, clients with consistent impulsive response patterns may have difficulties with impulse control which can interfere with learning in a transition program and contribute to behavior problems within that program and the ultimate place of employment. This section should alert the counselor to these possible client behavioral characteristics. It should also provide a statement of the psychologist's opinion of the reliability of test results. If these are judged to be only a fair or minimal estimate of the client's functioning level, then the counselor should consider referral for another psychological evaluation at a later date. A client's behavior during testing and rapport with the examiner have a significant effect on the reliability of testing results.

Case History and Background Information: A psychological assessment and the interpretation of results are not performed within a vacuum. This section briefly surveys the client's developmental status and includes major aspects of his/her medical, cognitive, educational, motor, communication, audiological, family, and social history. A counselor should glean this section of the report for information on etiology of the hearing loss, results of previous psychological evaluations, medical and medication status, school and communication mode histories, and pertinent family and social variables. These factors are germane to placement decisions and should be synthesized in the report as they relate to the client's individualized psychological response to deafness.

Diagnostic Impressions: This section of the psychological report discusses the results of each instrument administered and information from the clinical interview. It usually includes the following.

1. **A Measure of Intelligence:** This typically includes the results and interpretation of the client's performance on a nonverbal or performance measure of intelligence. The counselor needs this information to determine if the client meets intellectual functioning criteria for admission to certain programs and to determine the client's potential to benefit from particular placements. If the client plans to attend college, then a measure of his/her verbal intellectual abilities is appropriate. Although not a valid measure of intelligence with deaf clients, results of verbal intelligence tests correlate with achievement in language related academic subjects at the same level of magnitude ($r = .50$) in hearing and deaf adolescents (Sullivan & Weiss, in preparation). Results of verbal intelligence tests provide an indication of the client's potential to succeed in college level academic pursuits. Clients with scores in the Average range of verbal abilities are often able to do this. There is invariably a discrepancy between the client's verbal and nonverbal intellectual abilities, with the nonverbal being greater in magnitude.

2. **An Evaluation of Personality Structure and Behavioral Status:** This section should report the results of a personality and a behavioral assessment. Results typically include both projective and objective measures. This section often includes the results of the clinical interview and mental status examination. Behavioral checklists should be completed by individuals most familiar with the client's behavior. Parents, dormitory counselors, school counselors, and teachers provide pertinent information in this area. The counselor is able to garner from this section of the report information about the client's personality dynamics, the presence or absence of a mental disorder, adaptive behavioral assets and deficits, and behavior management difficulties that may affect placement decisions or indicate a need for psychotherapy, counseling, and/or behavior modification interventions within a given placement.

3. **A Measure of Educational Achievement:** This section should provide an estimate of the client's skills in the core academic areas of reading, mathematics, and spelling. Depending upon the extent of assessment, it may include vocabulary, science, and social studies scores as well. This information is invaluable in determining a client's potential to complete college work, benefit from a vocational-technical program, or handle the reading requirements of a specific job-training course. It is also beneficial in determining if the client possesses basic academic survival skills in reading and math to function independently in society. Survival academic objectives may be garnered from this section of the report for multihandicapped clients.

4. **Neuropsychological Screening/Assessment:** All psychological reports do not typically include this kind of assessment. If given, this section reports information about a client's preferred cognitive style, learning strengths and weaknesses, memory, and processing skills. This is useful in determining if the client will require instructional modifications within a transition program to insure optimal learning.

5. **Summary and Recommendations:** This section provides a succinct summary of the client's cognitive, affective, behavioral, academic, and neuropsychological functioning. Test results are integrated across these domains and a diagnostic classification is given. Strengths and weaknesses may be delineated. Special problems and suggestions for remediation are provided and based upon these findings. Specific services, remediation procedures, viable resources, and programming options should be recommended to ensure that the psychological evaluation has a proactive effect on the client's life.

What the Counselor Should Provide the Psychologist

The referring counselor or referral source can generate a positive effect on the quality assurance of psychological evaluations of deaf youth in transition. This is accomplished by networking with the psychologist regarding the client at counselor-determined necessary points along the transition continuum. Networking is a service oriented communication process that has been emphasized throughout this chapter. Suggested continuum junctures for this communication are as follows:

1. At 16 years of age, when the client becomes eligible for VR services and the initial VR referral for a psychological evaluation is often generated;
2. After high school graduation, when the client may need evaluation to determine eligibility for transition services;
3. Six months after entrance into a transition training program to determine its appropriateness and the effectiveness of the psychological recommendations made to assist the client in completing the program successfully; and,
4. At any time the counselor or other case service worker deems necessary to improve the psychological well-being of the client.

A complete psychological evaluation need not be undertaken at each of these junctures.

The counselor also needs to provide the psychologist with certain kinds of information to foster quality assurance in psychological evaluations. This includes the following.

1. *A specific referral question(s).* This provision is most helpful to the psychologist because it pin-points the purpose of the evaluation and enables him/her to focus on those psychological characteristics of the client that will be most useful to the counselor and beneficial to the client.
2. *Relevant case history and background information.* The referring counselor often has access to extensive files on clients that psychologists do not. This is often the case when referral is made to a psychologist who functions independently from school and rehabilitation services. This information must be accessible to the psychologist to ensure that an adequate evaluation is completed.
3. *Assistance in completion of behavioral checklist data.* An accurate behavioral assessment depends upon information obtained from persons with direct knowledge about the client's behavior. The referring counselor should identify those individuals for the psychologist and, if necessary, assist them in completing the forms.
4. *Liaison contacts between client, family and referral options.* The psychologist often needs assistance in making these contacts. The referring counselor is the logical person to assume this role.
5. *Information regarding viable programs and options.* The referring counselor is most often more knowledgeable in this area than the psychologist. Consultation with the psychologist about viable options can prevent unrealistic programming recommendations for which rehabilitation services are unable to provide assistance. This consultation should also abate angry interactions between counselors and parents who cannot understand why an agency will not pay for a specific program recommended in their child's psychological evaluation.
6. *Implementation of recommendations.* The agency counselor should attempt to implement all viable recommendations made in the psychological evaluation.
7. *Follow-up and feedback regarding the effectiveness of recommendations.* This is an imperative role of the referring counselor if he/she realistically expects to receive viable suggestions and recommendations from psychological reports of clients in transition.

In conclusion, rehabilitation and education professionals need to be cognizant of the fallibilities of psychologists and psychological evaluations and not expect from them magical cures or services for clients which they cannot realistically provide. Reality dictates that some clients will not receive ideal services or even those that offer special support services for deaf clients. In such cases, the psychologist and counselor must work together to create a patchwork of services that will meet some of the client's needs. Finally, some clients may be beyond help. An example is a mentally retarded individual with a primitive personality and aggressive tendencies multiplied by poor impulse control. These cases are a sad fact of a clinician's life and are particularly resistant to intervention techniques (Rodda, 1974). This is not to imply that attempts to serve such clients are futile. Rather, service sites which accept them are scarce. The poorly served and the unserved were a target population of federal legislation in the last decade to provide disabled students the right to an education. An unprecedented number of disabled students are nearing school leaving age. They represent a challenge to rehabilitation personnel to assist them in the transition to higher education, competitive work, or supported employment.

Sample Psychological Report

It is difficult to select a psychological report of a student in transition that illustrates the points made throughout this chapter. This is because the deaf student in transition is not a homogeneous client categorization. The variability of client characteristics has been stressed in this chapter. For these reasons, the reader is cautioned that this report does not represent a typical case, but one case, of a deaf youth in transition.

CLIENT: T   DATE SEEN: 10-10 and
                                           11-4-83
D.O.B.:   11-29-63
CA: 19 years, 10 months

Psychological Evaluation

Reason for Referral

T was referred for psychological evaluations by his Vocational Rehabilitation Counselor for intellectual, behavioral and academic assessment to ascertain his potential for college work.

Tests Administered

Wechsler Adult Intelligence Scale - Revised (WAIS-R):
(Scaled scores between 7 and 13 are broadly considered to be within the Low Average to High Average range. The Average score is 10 with a standard deviation of 3.)

Verbal Tests	Scaled Score
Information	13
Digit Span	10
Vocabulary	11
Arithmetic	8
Comprehension	10
Similarities	13

Performance Tests	
Picture Completion	11
Picture Arrangement	11
Block Design	10
Object Assembly	10

Verbal Score: Average Range
Performance Score: Average Range (Prorated)
Full Scale Score: Average Range

AAMD Adaptive Behavior Scale

Factor	Scaled Score
Personal Self-Sufficiency	1
Community Self-Sufficiency	1
Personal-Social Responsibility	7
Social Adjustment	11
Personal Adjustment	7

Stanford Achievement Test

Subtest	Grade Equivalent	Hearing-Impaired %ile Rank
Vocabulary	12.6	99
Reading Comprehension	10.0	98
Math Concepts	7.8	80
Math Computation	8.3	70

Child Behavior Checklist

Meadow-Kendall Social-Emotional Assessment Inventory for Hearing-Impaired Students

Thematic Apperception Test (TAT)

Clinical Interview

Relevant Case History and Background Information

T is a 19 year, 10 month old young man with a severe-to-profound, bilateral sensorineural hearing loss attributed to maternal rubella which was contacted in the first trimester of pregnancy. Additionally, T presents with mixed quadriplegic cerebral palsy with spastic features and diabetes mellitus. He is confined to a wheelchair, has received special education services throughout his educational career in the public school system, and is currently a senior in high school. According to his father's report, T earns average to above average grades in his academic program. T is interested in attending college and the current psychological assessment was requested by personnel from Vocational Rehabilitation to ascertain his potential to do college work.

Behavioral Observations

T was accompanied for psychological evaluation by his father who was present through the first testing session on October 10, 1983. A second session was undertaken on November 4, 1983 because it was not possible to finish all testing with T in the given time limit. His cerebral palsy makes it difficult to test T within given time limits because his motor difficulties make it quite difficult for him to complete items rapidly. T was very cooperative throughout testing and rapport was easily established. He is generally a delightful and pleasant young man with whom to work and displayed a good sense of humor throughout testing. All testing was undertaken in Total Communication, i.e., the simultaneous use of speech, sign language and/or fingerspelling. T's expressive sign language and fingerspelling is somewhat difficult to read because of his motor spasticity. However, T will repeat fingerspelling or sign language for the reader as needed.

It is emphasized that T's cerebral palsy makes it extremely difficult to find appropriate assessment instruments to measure his intellectual potential. Verbal intelligence tests require a language response on T's part and more validly measure the language difficulties caused by the hearing impairment rather than intellectual potential. Nonverbal intelligence tests, although appropriate for use with the hearing impaired, require fine-motor responses and award bonus points for rapid performance and penalize T unfairly because of his cerebral palsy and resulting motor difficulties. However, current testing results are felt to be a reliable estimate of his current functioning level as best as they can be measured. Further, they suggest that his intellectual abilities are at least what is measured and quite possibly may be somewhat higher.

Diagnostic Impressions

T was given both the Verbal and Performance Scales of the *Wechsler Adult Intelligence Scale-Revised (WAIS-R)*. The Verbal Scale was administered to T in Total Communication, i.e, the simultaneous use of speech and sign language. T responded through speech, sign language and/or fingerspelling. T was also given some of the subtest questions to read and this appeared to enhance his comprehension of the question posed. T earned a score which places him within the Average range of intellectual functioning in comparison to normally hearing peers. It is emphasized that results of the Verbal Scale are not really a valid estimate of his intellectual abilities in this area because they also measure the language difficulties caused by the hearing impairment. The fact that T was able to score within the Average range on a verbal intelligence test suggests that he has exceptional abilities in this area for a hearing-impaired individual. Most hearing-impaired individuals score significantly below the Average range on verbal intelligence tests. However, T was able to earn scores on the six individual subtests of the Verbal Scale which ranged from the Average to Superior range. Again, it is emphasized that this is an exceptional performance level for a hearing-impaired individual. At an average rate, he was able to repeat digits presented in sign language both forward and backward, define vocabulary words, solve arithmetic word problems and answer verbal comprehension type questions about common sense things in his envi-

ronment. He was able to score within the Superior range on tasks which required him to answer questions requiring factual information and to abstract commonalities between words. Results of verbal intelligence tests are fairly good predictors of academic achievement in both the hearing and hearing-impaired population. T's test scores would suggest that he may be realistically expected to be able to achieve at an average rate or above in academic subjects which would require verbal/language-related reasoning abilities. It is felt that this level of verbal intellectual functioning suggests that he is capable of doing college level work. On the Non-verbal or Performance section of the *WAIS-R*, T earned a score within the Average range. He was not administered the Digit Symbol subtest because this is a fine-motor task that requires speed of motor coordination and it was felt that his cerebral palsy would unduly penalize him on this test. The other three of the four subtests that were given are timed and, again, T's cerebral palsy significantly interfered with his performance on the Picture Arrangement, Block Design and Object Assembly subtests. He was, however, able to complete these items at an average level in comparison to hearing peers and his performance would, therefore, suggest that his abilities in these areas are at least average and might possibly be somewhat higher if he were able to perform them rapidly and earn bonus points for this rapid performance. T's Full Scale Score, which is based on verbal and nonverbal abilities, is also within the Average range.

In summary, intellectual assessment would suggest that T has the intellectual potential to do some college work. He has exceptional intellectual abilities in verbal areas for a hearing-impaired individual. Generally, given the fact that it is difficult to measure intellectual potential in an individual with cerebral palsy, current testing results should be interpreted as indicative of the lowest level of work that T is able to complete.

The *AAMD Adaptive Behavior Scale* was administered to garner an estimate of T's adaptive behavioral proficiencies and independent functioning abilities. His overall performance level is compared to youngsters within regular grade placements. Some 46% of peers within the regular classroom placement receive scores lower than T's comparison score. This would suggest that T's comparison score most closely resembles those obtained by the regular classroom reference group. However, T's scaled scores across the five factor domains suggest that he is exhibiting some adaptive behavioral deficiencies in the areas of personal self-sufficiency and community self-sufficiency. All of these difficulties, however, may be directly attributed to his cerebral palsy and the fact that he is confined to a wheel-chair. For example, T is not able to bathe himself completely without help, is unable to perform many of the motor actions necessary to take care of his clothing or dress himself, has poor body balance, and is unable to walk or run alone. In the Community Self-Sufficiency domain, T is exhibiting some difficulties in that he is unable to independently take public transportation, cannot use the telephone because of his hearing impairment, and is not able to complete complex jobs or chores which require motor actions. All of these areas of deficits are felt to be directly related to his cerebral palsy and should not be considered actual weaknesses.

Further behavioral assessment was undertaken by having T's father complete the *Child Behavior Checklist* and the *Meadow-Kendall Social-Emotional Assessment Inventory for Hearing-Impaired Students*. The *Child Behavior Checklist* measures social competence and behavior problems and compares T to hearing peers of the same chronological age group. As rated by his father, T scored within normal limits on the social competence scale. He does engage in several hobbies, attempts to perform some jobs around the house and is fairly responsible in job completion if he is capable of performing the motor actions required, belongs to one organization, and generally gets along well with other people. He also is performing quite well in school, is not in a special class, has never repeated a grade and is not exhibiting any school problems. However, Mr. T indicated that T did not have any close friends and did not have many social or recreational activities with peers. T also scored within normal limits on the behavioral problem scale suggesting that, currently, he does not present with any significant behavior management difficulties. The *Meadow-Kendall* assesses social and emotional adjustment and self-image and compares T to hearing-impaired peers. Again, as rated by his father, T scored within normal limits across all scales assessed. This would suggest that he is exhibiting adequate social and emotional adjustment for a hearing-impaired individual and has a good self-image regarding his hearing impairment and additional handicaps.

During the interview, T was relaxed and cooperative. He stated that he enjoyed school and would like to attend college. His career goal at the present time is to become a computer programmer.

On the TAT, T evidenced some impressive psychological strengths. He appears to have a strong desire to develop interpersonal relationship skills. He described others as helpful, giving and supportive. Described relationships were long-term and tolerance for mixed feelings was evident. However,

isolation was a common theme in stories involving interpersonal relationships. T's coping abilities, as measured by the TAT, were impressive. He appears to have considerable insight into the feelings and motivations of others as well as his own feelings. Ego functions appear to be adequate and stories are logical and plausible. His stories reflect age appropriate concerns about career goals and age appropriate conflicts around independence from his parents. There is some suggestion of possible self-esteem problems related to being accepted by others. He appears to satisfy a need for acceptance by pleasing others rather than himself. In summary, the TAT indicates that T has good emotional stability, excellent coping abilities, good ego functions, and adequate reality testing with logical thought content. Some possible problems appear to be in the areas of self-esteem and social isolation. However, these may be a direct result of his multiple handicaps.

As a measure of academic achievement, T was given the advanced battery of the *Stanford Achievement Test*. The Vocabulary, Reading Comprehension, Math Concepts and Math Computation subtests were administered. T's scores would suggest that, currently, he has a vocabulary that approximates a late 12th grade level, he is able to comprehend what he reads at a 10th grade level, and has math concept and computation skills at an approximate 8th grade level. These grade equivalents are all adequate to complete college work. Additionally, when T's performance on the *Stanford* is compared to that of other hearing-impaired youngsters who took the same level of the *Stanford*, he is functioning anywhere from the 70th to the 99th percentile. This is an exceptional academic achievement profile for a hearing-impaired individual.

Summary and Recommendations

In summary, T is a 19 year old young man with a severe-to-profound, bilateral sensorineural hearing loss. He is confined to a wheelchair because of cerebral palsy with spastic features. Additionally, T has diabetes which is adequately controlled by insulin. T's multiple handicaps render intellectual assessment quite difficult because of the lack of appropriate tests to tap accurately the intellectual potential of an individual who is hearing-impaired and has cerebral palsy. Current intellectual assessment would suggest that T is functioning within the Average range of verbal intellectual abilities, Average range of nonverbal intellectual abilities and has overall intellectual abilities within the Average range. However, these testing results are felt to be a minimal estimate of his true intellectual potential and are felt to indicate the lowest level of abilities at which he is able to function. That is, his intellectual abilities are at least as measured and might possibly be somewhat higher. Intellectual assessment would suggest that this young man has the potential to do college work and he should be encouraged to do so. He is exhibiting some adaptive behavioral difficulties in the areas of community and personal self-sufficiency. However, these are felt to be directly related to the fact that he is confined to a wheelchair because of his cerebral palsy. Social competence and behavior are generally within normal limits. Personality assessment suggests good emotional stability, adequate reality testing, and possible problems in self-esteem and social isolation. Academic assessment would suggest that this young man has exceptional academic skills for a hearing-impaired individual. This includes the areas of vocabulary, reading comprehension and math concepts and computation. Specific recommendations follow:

1. Results of the current psychoeducational evaluation suggest that T has the potential to do college work. He, therefore, should be encouraged to apply to some type of postsecondary institution. However, it is emphasized that the college T attends be selected carefully. Specifically, he will require some support services designed specifically for hearing-impaired students. These will include interpreter services, note-taking assistance, and some individual tutoring because of the fact that T's hearing loss may cause him to miss some concepts presented in classroom lectures. T's cerebral palsy and the fact that he is confined to a wheelchair will also necessitate that the college he attends be totally accessible and perhaps have some type of a domestic aide to assist him in personal self-sufficiency areas that he is unable to complete himself.

2. On behavioral checklist data, Mr. T indicated that T did not have any close friends. Personality assessment suggested self-esteem and social isolation difficulties. It is suggested that steps be undertaken to secure some individuals for T to socialize with in the hopes that he would acquire a friend. There may be other youngsters with cerebral palsy within the public school system who are also mainstreamed who are unaware of the existence of each other. T should be encouraged to attend socialization activities within his school.

If there are any questions regarding this report, please contact me.

References

Brier, N., & Demb, H. (1981). Adolescence in the developmentally disabled. *Psychiatric Annals, 11*(3), 57–65.

Erickson, E. H. (1959). *Identity and the life cycle.* New York: International Universities Press.

Gannon, J. R. (1981). *Deaf heritage: A native history of deaf America.* Silver Spring, MD: National Association of the Deaf.

Jensema, C., & Mullins, J. (1974). Onset, cause and additional handicaps in hearing-impaired children. *American Annals of the Deaf, 119,* 701–705.

Meadow, K. (1981). Burnout in professionals working with deaf children. *American Annals of the Deaf, 126,* 13–22.

Moores, D. F. (1978). *Educating the deaf: Psychology, principles and practices.* Boston: Houghton-Mifflin.

Naisbitt, J. (1984). *Megatrends.* New York: Warner Books.

Rodda, M. (1974). Behavioral disorders in deaf clients. *Journal of Rehabilitation of the Deaf, 7,* 1–13.

Sullivan, P., Scanlon, J., & LeBarre, A. (in preparation). Assessment and intervention techniques with sexually abused deaf children.

Sullivan, P., & Vernon, M. (1979). Psychological assessment of hearing-impaired children. *School Psychology Review, 8*(3), 271–290.

Sullivan, P., & Weiss, S. (in preparation). The relationship between IQ and academic achievement in a residential deaf school population.

U.S. Bureau of the Census (1982). Labor force status and other characteristics of persons with a work disability. Washington, D.C.: Author.

U.S. Commission on Civil Rights (1983). Accommodating the spectrum of disabilities. Washington, D.C.: Author.

Vernon, M. (1969). *Multiply handicapped deaf children: Medical, educational, and psychological considerations.* Washington, D.C.: Council for Exceptional Children.

Will, M. (1983). Programming for the transition of youth with disabilities: Bridges from school to working life. Washington, D.C.: Office of Special Education and Rehabilitation Services.

Zieziula, F. (Ed.). (1982). *Assessment of hearing-impaired people: A guide for selecting psychological, educational and vocational tests.* Washington, D.C.: Gallaudet College Press.

CHAPTER V

Neuropsychological Assessment

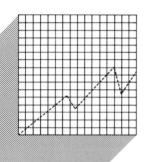

Amy M. Wisniewski
Asa J. DeMatteo
S. Margaret Lee
Forrest C. Orr

Introduction

Impairment of the functioning of the human brain is typically associated with disturbance in the behavior of the individual. Neuropsychological evaluation involves formal assessment of behavioral expressions and manifestations of impaired brain functioning. Formal neuropsychological evaluation includes the systematic examination of cognitive functions, of sensory-perceptual and motoric abilities, and of the emotional and motivational aspects of personality. Neuropsychological examination of these areas of functioning is accomplished by utilizing standardized tests, clinical procedures, and observational data that have been demonstrated as clinically useful and psychometrically valid in discriminating individuals with impaired brain function from those without such impairment.

In clinical and rehabilitation settings, neuropsychological evaluations are most often performed for one or both of the following important reasons: first, to aid in determining if an individual has an *organic brain disorder* that might be responsible for disturbances in behavior and functioning—literally to diagnose brain dysfunction; second, to facilitate the planning and implementation of appropriate treatment, rehabilitation, disposition, and management efforts with a particular client (Lezak, 1983). In addition, neuropsychological evaluation can be useful in assessing the effectiveness of specific interventions with a client, in evaluating the effectiveness of a treatment or rehabilitation program, in monitoring the course of a neurological illness, in providing information relevant to legal/forensic decision-making, and in the research investigation of brain-behavior relationships (Strub & Black, 1981).

In this chapter an overview of neuropsychological evaluation is presented; the special issues and problems of performing neuropsychological assessment with deaf clients and the relevance of such assessment for this population are examined.

Use of Neuropsychological Evaluation in the Identification and Diagnosis of Brain Disorders

General Considerations. Perhaps the most crucial use of neuropsychological evaluation is to determine the presence or absence of a brain disorder in the individual client who complains of or manifests disturbance in some area(s) of behavioral functioning, and for whom the possibility of brain dysfunction constitutes a diagnostic issue. Specifically, the results of a neuropsychological evaluation are used to determine if the diagnosis of a neurologic or neuropsychiatric syndrome is warranted or whether the behaviors of concern have an environmental or psychosocial basis. In performing a neuropsychological examination, the neuropsychologist makes use of multiple sources of information regarding the client's cognitive, perceptual-motor, and emotional-motivational behavior. After gathering these data, the neuropsychologist interprets the results by using a variety of inferential methods to draw conclusions about the probability of a brain disorder being present. The methods of inference used to draw conclusions are based upon: (a) The level of a client's performance on quantified tests and measures as compared to normative data for expected performance (e.g., number of errors on a sequencing task, or score on a measure of memory function). This method defines as deficits, or "negative" symptoms of brain dysfunction, those scores that fall beyond a cut-off point on the distribution of normative scores; (b) The presence of specific pathognomonic signs of brain disorder. Pathognomonic signs are "positive" symptoms of a brain disorder, that is, specific abnormalities in behavior that are not present in the neurologically normal but are typically present in specific neurological syndromes (e.g., perseveration—the inappropriate persistence of a motor response which was appropriate to a previous stimulus but is not appropriate to the current stimulus); (c) The presence of identifiable constellations of spared and impaired abilities, of efficient and deficient performances, and of specific pathognomonic signs that are recognized as characteristic of specific neurologic and neuropsychiatric disorders. For example, poor performance on recent memory tasks, and good performance on immediate and remote memory tasks with no deficit in any other areas of cognitive, perceptual-motor, and emotional-motivational functions implies a neurological amnestic syndrome. Such amnestic syndromes are associated with damage or dysfunction in specific areas of the brain-the midline diencephalon and hippocampal areas of the mesial-temporal lobe; (d) Comparison of the sensory-perceptual and motor functions of one side of the body with the same functions on the other side (e.g., testing ability to distinguish geometric shapes by touch alone using the right hand vs. using the left hand). In essence, one side of the body serves as a control or monitor against which to evaluate the performance of the other side of the body.

By using the methods of inference outlined above and the behavioral data gathered in the neuropsychological examination, the neuropsychologist can draw conclusions regarding the probable *presence or absence* of a brain disorder. The terms "brain disorder" or "brain dysfunction" are regarded as general labels indicating impaired brain functioning which may be due either to structural anatomic alterations in the brain tissue itself, or to abnormalities in the physiological or metabolic

functioning of the brain without identifiable alterations in brain anatomy. The labels "brain damage" or "brain lesion" are restricted to those types of brain dysfunction in which anatomic alterations of brain tissue have clearly occurred (i.e., tumors, hemorrhages, etc.). In general, brain damage represents a permanent injury. Once injured, brain tissues do not regenerate. Moreover, damage at one site can lead to cell degeneration and loss in surrounding tissues. Furthermore, neuropsychologists can frequently do more than simply detect the presence of brain dysfunction. They may be able to make more specific inferences regarding the *location* of the dysfunction within the brain. Dysfunction may involve the whole brain (i.e., diffuse or generalized dysfunction), only one of the cerebral hemispheres (i.e., dysfunction lateralized to the right or left hemisphere), or only a specific area within a hemisphere (i.e., focal or localized dysfunction).

In addition, the neuropsychologist may be able to offer inferences regarding the probable *onset* of the disorder (i.e., sudden or gradual; recent, remote, or congenital), the likely *course* of the disorder (i.e., rapidly progressive, slowly progressive, static, episodic, or recovering), and the *severity* of the disorder (i.e., mild, moderate, or severe). Typically, there is an acute phase just after the onset of structural brain damage when the individual suffers more severe and generalized deficits in functioning. As recovery proceeds, a great deal of functioning may return. Usually, however, certain deficits of a chronic or slowly progressive nature remain.

In cases of dysfunction not associated with injury or other structural changes in the brain (i.e., dysfunction associated with metabolic disorder, blood flow restriction, toxic conditions, etc.), the prognostic implications of the dysfunction are not so clear. In some cases, the deficits seen initially will clear completely with proper medical treatment. In other cases, chronic deficits remain.

In some instances, the neuropsychologist may be able to offer an opinion about the probable *etiology* or cause of the brain dysfunction. Possible etiologies include the following: (a) *Cerebral tumors* (or neoplasms) can destroy or displace brain tissues causing neuropsychological deficits ranging from mild and subtle to severe and obvious. (b) *Cerebrovascular disorders* (or defects in the blood vessels which supply the brain) can result in reduced or absent blood supply to certain parts of the brain, or can lead to hemorrhages (i.e., bleeding) which destroy brain tissues. (c) *Head trauma* is a very common cause of brain injury in individuals under the age of 40. It can cause tearing, bleeding, and compression of tissues initially, and later compression effects caused by swelling, bleeding, or obstruction of the flow of cerebrospinal fluid. (d) Certain *intracranial infections* such as neurosyphilis, encephalitis, meningitis, Creutzfeld-Jakob disease, and others can cause permanent brain dysfunction, although many infections result in only transient symptoms. (e) *Seizure disorders* are often symptomatic of or secondary to some other illness, but may also represent a primary disorder of the brain (i.e., idiopathic epilepsy). The brain dysfunction associated with seizures can be related to cognitive deficits, personality disorders, and psychoses. (f) *Dementing illnesses* (e.g., Alzheimer's disease) can produce brain injury at the neuronal level leading to cell loss and subsequent neuropsychological deficits. (g) Certain *degenerative disorders* such as Parkinson's disease, multiple sclerosis, and Huntington's chorea, or other disorders such as lupus erythematosus can cause various damage to brain structures resulting in neuropsychological deficits. (h) *Metabolic disorders* and *vitamin deficiencies* associated with severe, chronic malnutrition or alcohol abuse can lead to brain dysfunction, both transient and permanent. (i) *Endocrine* and *toxic disorders* such as hyperparathyroidism or hypothyroidism and mercury or lead poisoning can have profound effects on both cognitive and emotional-motivational aspects of functioning. (j) *Anoxic events*, in which the oxygen supply to the brain is interrupted, may produce neuropsychological deficits. Finally, (k) *Congenital* or *genetic disorders* may result in abnormal brain physiology and/or anatomy and significant disturbance of neuropsychological functions.

The neuropsychological evaluation has a number of advantages not shared by most other standard neurodiagnostic techniques: (a) It is noninvasive and carries no risk of mortality or morbidity. (b) It can provide important descriptive and prognostic information that other diagnostic procedures cannot (Strub & Black, 1981). Despite the tremendous advances in medical diagnostic procedures (i.e., computerized axial tomography, positron emission tomography, nuclear magnetic resonance), there are many conditions in which scans and other laboratory data are not diagnostically helpful and in which neuropsychological findings can be crucial (Lezak, 1983). For example, neuropsychological assessment has proven especially useful in discriminating between psychiatric and neurological symptoms and in identifying brain dysfunction not associated with structural abnormality.

Issues of Relevance to the Deaf Population. The deaf population is no less vulnerable to the most common causes of brain dysfunction than is the hearing population. Head trauma, cerebral tumors, toxic disorders, alcoholism, and most other causes of brain pathology are as probable occurrences in deaf as in hearing persons. Moreover, when deafness is caused by maternal rubella, Rh incompatibility, prematurity, anoxia, or meningitis, there is an increased risk of brain dysfunction (Isselbacher, Adams, Braunwald, Petersdorf, & Wilson, 1980; Vernon, 1968) as these conditions result in an assault on the fetus' or child's developing central nervous system (CNS). The risk of neurologically-based impairments in addition to hearing loss has increased as the causes of deafness have changed. The shift from childhood meningitis to maternal rubella as a major cause of deafness illustrates the potential for damage or dysfunction to occur earlier in fetal development. Also, the percentage of people with hereditary deafness as opposed to disease-caused deafness must necessarily decrease as disease-based mortality rates decrease (DeJong & Lifchez, 1983). It seems likely that in the years to come, the medical technology that decreases mortality rates will also result in an increase in the percentage of multiply handicapped deaf individuals.

It has been shown (Schlesinger & Meadow, 1972; Wilson, Rapin, Wilson, & Van Denburg, 1975) that deafness caused by an insult to the CNS rather than an hereditary etiology results in a larger proportion of individuals labeled as "severely disturbed" and/or showing evidence of brain dysfunction. The problem of diagnosing and delineating neurological dysfunction in the deaf population is complicated by the fact that some of the behavioral deficits most commonly seen in a clinical deaf population (i.e., impulsivity, low frustration tolerance, difficulties with cause/effect relationships, etc.) may be signs of neurologically-based learning disabilities, attention deficit disorders, or other neurologic disorders, or may be related to functional disturbances. In general, the types of neurological dysfunction seen in the deaf population tend to be subtle and easily confused with developmental psychosocial problems or functional linguistic deficits.

It is extremely important for the human service professional to have an accurate evaluation of the client in order to provide relevant and appropriate services. The deaf client who has poor language skills and difficulty maintaining attention, and who tends to behave aggressively at the job site because of neurological dysfunction may present the same symptoms and problems as the emotionally disturbed deaf individual who grew up in a family without communication, who is without sufficient socialization, and whose functional developmental deficits make it difficult for him or her to monitor feelings or to develop good relationships. Although these two individuals may present a very similar picture in terms of their patterns of behavior, their service needs and potential for benefitting from services are quite different.

Additionally, deafness can mask brain pathology. The possibility of failure to detect signs and symptoms of brain dysfunction is more likely when the "low verbal" deaf individual presents with poor language skills and lack of a well-organized lifestyle which may be assumed to be a result of deafness, linguistic deprivation, and lack of socialization. Undiagnosed and, by implication, untreated brain pathology could have life threatening consequences. Even in cases in which the undiagnosed and untreated brain disorder poses no threat to life, it can severely impair the individual's ability to function and can limit quality of, and satisfaction with, life. Referral for appropriate medical care, rehabilitation services, educational and psychosocial interventions depends upon initial identification of those clients having brain disorders.

In general, neuropsychological evaluation of deaf clients is likely to present complex differential diagnostic problems. In some cases, the use of quantified tests (whose norms and cut-off points were developed with a normal hearing sample) in evaluating deaf clients may confound rather than clarify assessment issues. Also, the patterns or constellations of abilities and disabilities that neuropsychologists use to identify specific neurologic syndromes may not be completely applicable when evaluating deaf clients. For example, comparisons between linguistic abilities and nonverbal skills are used to define and localize neurological dysfunction. Poor language abilities in a deaf client, including specific organic appearing deficits, may be associated with early linguistic deprivation rather than neurological dysfunction. Furthermore, many neuropsychological procedures that do not specifically assess language skills are, nonetheless, language dependent (and, in particular, English-based) in terms of directions and instructions. Poor performance by a deaf client on such a task may indicate a brain dysfunction, but could also indicate an inability to understand the task requirements. Deafness puts an individual at risk for communication and language deficits, emotional problems, and depending on the etiology, brain pathology. Deafness, and assumptions about it, can result in the masking of neurological problems. Similarities in symptomatology between the potential impact of deafness on psychosocial development and learning, and certain neurological syndromes can result in misdiagnosis and inappropriate treatment.

Use of Neuropsychological Evaluation in Planning Interventions

In many cases neuropsychological assessment is not needed for diagnostic purposes (i.e., in cases where the client is obviously brain damaged on cursory examination or already has a definitive neurologic diagnosis). Neuropsychological assessment can, nonetheless, provide useful, and even crucial, information for planning appropriate client management, rehabilitation, disposition, and treatment. Such assessment ideally provides a detailed description of the client's cognitive and intellectual status, language skills and capabilities, sensory-perceptual and motoric functioning, and personality characteristics as well as gives information about the specific behavioral changes associated with his or her neurological condition. Clearly, appropriate planning depends on an understanding of client's capabilities, limitations, and changes in behavior related to their brain dysfunction. For example, service providers may need to know a client's capacity for self-care, for adhering to a program, for making appropriate judgments, and so forth. Given all the information gathered during the neuropsychological evaluation, examiners can recommend how clients might best compensate for their deficits and, more importantly, whether and how retraining could be profitably undertaken (Heaton & Pendleton, 1981). Further, neuropsychological assessment measures, taken repeatedly over time, can provide appropriate and reliable information on the progress of retraining.

There is currently a group of individuals whose deafness includes an etiology of maternal rubella stemming from the epidemics of the early 1960's. As these adolescents and young adults reach vocational age, the pressure of their disabilities moves from the educational system to the vocational rehabilitation system. The largest proportion of referrals to the University of California, San Francisco, Center on Deafness for evaluation services involve deaf individuals with a history of maternal rubella. Many of these individuals have experienced behavioral and educational difficulties during their school years and may have continuing difficulties in vocational planning, training, and job performance. Assessment of strengths and specific neuropsychological deficits allows the vocational rehabilitation specialist to provide a better assessment of what services a deaf individual needs and to analyze more effectively the type of job situations that individual is capable of handling. Vocational rehabilitation specialists may find themselves in a central, coordinating role with deaf clients, needing to interpret test results, skills, and weaknesses to various professionals who may be involved with a client but who have no knowledge of deafness or ability to communicate directly and adequately with the deaf individual.

The fact that many neuropsychological deficits are relatively permanent losses in functioning that may prove resistant to attempts at remediation is of great importance in understanding how rehabilitation efforts might be most successfully directed. A neuropsychological deficit does not represent a lack of learning or otherwise remediable gap in the individual's functioning. Rather, it is a hole in the fabric of the individual's abilities. Such deficits must be worked around, generally by the development of compensatory or alternative mechanisms which substitute for the missing function. Thus, if the rehabilitation client has memory retrieval problems with a neurological basis, it may be of little use for the rehabilitation specialist to train and rehearse the client in memory tasks. Instead, the specialist might assist the client by counseling the use of a compensatory mechanism such as keeping lists and a daily calendar or appointment book.

Neuropsychological Evaluation: Who Provides the Service?

Most neuropsychological evaluations are performed by *clinical* (rather than research or experimental) neuropsychologists or by clinical or counseling psychologists who have had specialized training and experience in neuropsychology. Most psychologists providing neuropsychological services have completed a doctorate in psychology (i.e., the Ph.D. or Psy.D.) and have had pre- and post-doctoral training plus supervised clinical experiences providing neuropsychological assessment and consultation services. Most are licensed in the states in which they practice. Providers of these services all have extensive training in brain-behavior relationships in normal and pathological populations plus experience in evaluating the status of brain functioning based on behavioral indicators.

Although some rehabilitation facilities have a neuropsychologist among their permanent staff members, frequently clients must be referred to private practitioners in the community. Unfortunately, there are few neuropsychologists who also have an understanding of deafness or experience working with deaf individuals. At this time, there are only a handful of agencies and clinics in the United States that are seriously investigating the special issues of neuropsychological assessment with deaf individuals.

In addition to neuropsychologists, various other professionals perform assessments with deaf individuals focusing on differential diagnosis and identification of areas of neurological dysfunction. Among this group are more generally trained clinical and counseling psychologists, school psychologists, and learning disability specialists. These professionals may be excellent in delineating capabilities and differentiating emotionally- from neurologically- based problems. The school psychologist and the learning disability specialist may be particularly skilled in developing educational plans for both children and adults. Such professionals are less likely to be able to pinpoint site of dysfunction in the brain or to identify known neurological syndromes. However, those professionals who are associated with schools for the deaf may have a deep understanding of the impact of deafness on behavior and of the need to adapt available assessment tools as well as fluency in one or more sign language systems.

When looking for a possible referral, the rehabilitation specialist is likely to be unable to find an experienced neuropsychologist who is familiar with deafness and fluent in sign language. In order to get an accurate assessment, the neuropsychologist may need consultation regarding the need for and use of an interpreter as well as to obtain consultation services by telephone with one of the mental health programs that serve the deaf population.

Nature and Scope of the Neuropsychological Evaluation

Psychologists providing neuropsychological evaluation services come from widely divergent training backgrounds, have a variety of models for conceptualizing brain-behavior relationships, and serve clients with a broad spectrum of medical and psychosocial disorders. For these and other reasons, a number of different approaches to neuropsychological assessment have evolved. Whether the approach used by a particular neuropsychologist meets the needs of a rehabilitation specialist serving a client is an issue the specialist must decide for him- or herself based on the usefulness of the report. In working over a period of time with a neuropsychologist, the rehabilitation specialist will find the neuropsychologist becoming increasingly familiar with the special issues of deafness and of the need to adapt particular tests and procedures. A long-term goal would be to develop a network of professionals throughout the country with skills and experience to provide high quality neuropsychological services to the deaf community.

For most neuropsychologists, the initial components of the evaluation roughly parallel the initial aspects of a general psychological evaluation. Moreover, the structure of the evaluation report typically corresponds to the assessment procedure itself and to the inferential processes used by the neuropsychologist to draw conclusions regarding the presence, location, onset, cause, severity, probable etiology, and behavioral correlates of a suspected brain disorder.

Referral Questions and Issues. In order to perform a neuropsychological evaluation that is tailored to the needs of the referring professional, the neuropsychologist must have an understanding of the purpose of the assessment and how the information is to be used. "Tell me everything you know about Mr. X" leads to frustration for psychologists or neuropsychologists. They are unable to focus the examination and may provide information that is useless to a vocational rehabilitation specialist while omitting data that are relevant to specific issues for a client. It is important to consider carefully the questions one would like answered before making the referral. Possible questions are these: "Is this person's poor language due to a neurological dysfunction like aphasia or to language deprivation?" "This person appears to have memory deficits. What is the etiology, and will they interfere with work such as a clerical/filing job? Can this person learn compensatory mechanisms?" "Is this person capable of structuring her own life and living independently?" "This client is alcoholic. Has there been any permanent neurological damage related to alcohol abuse?"

At the point of referral, it may also be helpful for the referring professional to provide any understanding that he or she has of the client, particularly as it relates to deafness. An example might be the following: "This elderly deaf client uses many signs that are not common; however, my experience indicates that they are the standard signs that were used long ago." It is also often useful to assess the neuropsychologist's awareness of the need to use a certified sign interpreter (not a family member) and of how to locate an interpreter familiar with testing situations.

Background, History, and Symptoms. Acquisition and organization of information regarding a client's past history may involve interviewing the client, interviewing informants from among the client's family and friends, and gathering information from medical records and reports of psychosocial, educational, and other human service providers. Types of background and historical data gathered include information about family of origin, childhood and adolescent development, educational and vocational experiences, relationships and marital status, legal and criminal justice problems, use and abuse of alcohol and other sub-

stances, medical history (especially accidents, injuries, illnesses, and their treatment), and history of psychosocial difficulties including psychiatric disorders and mental health intervention. With a deaf client, it is also important to obtain information regarding the hearing status of the parents, the client's language environment and modality, past educational setting, and etiology of deafness (if known).

Following history taking, the psychologist often reviews current symptoms and complaints and may systematically inquire about areas of functioning in order to assess whether any symptoms or signs are present that the client may not have noticed or regarded as significant. Typically, signs and symptoms are reviewed regarding each of the sensory-perceptual modalities (i.e., sight, hearing, smell, taste, touch and kinesthetics, etc.), language, thinking and memory, movement, dizziness, loss or disturbance of consciousness, seizures, pain, sleep, appetite, sexual function, and changes in mood or personality. The assessment of language provides a particularly difficult area for the professional who is unfamiliar with a deaf population. American Sign Language (ASL) structure can sometimes appear to the unsophisticated observer like the disorganized thinking of a schizophrenic or the language of a fluent aphasic. The wide variety of language systems and proficiencies makes the assessment of language very difficult even for the experienced psychologist.

While most neuropsychologists collect information on history and symptoms and integrate these data into the evaluation, some do not. By virtue of their training and model for practice, some neuropsychologists gather only the barest of demographic data (i.e., age, education, socioeconomic status, and gender—factors that influence interpretation of test findings) and base their evaluations solely upon test findings and observations. Some few neuropsychologists never even see the client, but have all test data gathered by trained technicians. Following data gathering, they make inferences solely on the basis of test results and minimal demographic information; essentially, they make blind interpretations and inferences.

Observations. During the background interview and administration of standardized neuropsychological tests and procedures, the psychologist usually observes the following aspects of the client's behavior: appearance, level of alertness, psychomotor behavior (i.e., posture, gait, facial expressions, gestures, etc.), attitude toward the examiner, cooperativeness, motivation, and concern about performance. In addition, the psychologist takes note of any other influences that may affect the reliability and validity of test data. Such influences may include patient factors (i.e., fatigue, pain, loss of eye glasses, sedative medication, intentional malingering, resistance, confusion regarding the purpose of evaluation, etc.) or environmental factors (e.g., poorly ventilated room, insufficient lighting, unexpected interruption, etc.). Another important influence on test performance is the deaf client's ability to understand the task; understanding must be carefully assessed if valid inferences are to be made regarding the client's neuropsychological status.

Tests and Procedures Administered and Results. A wide variety of standardized tests and clinical procedures are available for assessing neuropsychological functioning. Certain assessment approaches have been developed as comprehensive test batteries (i.e., groups of tests routinely used together). Some of the best known neuropsychological test batteries include the Halstead-Reitan Neuropsychological Test Battery (Reitan & Davison, 1974), the Luria-Nebraska Neuropsychological Battery (Golden, Hammeke, & Purisch, 1980), the Benton-Iowa Battery (Benton, Hamsher, Varney, & Spreen, 1983), the Boston VA Battery (Goodglass & Kaplan, 1979), and the battery proposed by Lezak (1983). However, none of these approaches have been standardized or normed on a deaf population. Also, patterns of neuropsychological results that imply a specific neurologic syndrome or permit localization of brain damage in the hearing may not be applicable to all or part of the deaf population. Research evidence (Manning, Goble, Markham, & LaBreche, 1977; McKeever, Hoemann, Florian, & VanDeventer, 1976; Poizner, Battison, & Lane, 1979; Poizner & Lane, 1979) suggests that language functions in deaf individuals may not be controlled in the same parts of the brain that mediate language in the hearing population. Further, some of the tests in these batteries rely heavily on use of English for communicating test directions and for client responses during testing tasks; therefore, their use in determining intellectual functioning in the verbal area for most deaf clients is inappropriate. They may, however, provide useful information to clinicians who wish to compare a deaf client's performance to that expected for a hearing client. At present, there exist no standardized neuropsychological tests specifically designed for the deaf population. Thus, neuropsychological assessment of deaf individuals presents a unique challenge and an opportunity for development of needed techniques.

Certain portions of standardized psychometric tests and available neuropsychological instruments can be appropriately used with a deaf pop-

ulation. Moreover, there are behavioral techniques, some formal and some informal, which can aid in identifying brain-dysfunctional deaf individuals in much the same way that brain-disordered hearing individuals are detected. It is beyond the scope of this chapter to present all the specific methods a qualified psychologist might employ in a neuropsychological evaluation of a hearing-impaired client. Instead, an outline is offered of the areas of behavioral functioning that are routinely examined during a neuropsychological evaluation. Mention is made of some tests that may be utilized in the assessment of a particular aspect of functioning.

1. *Attention, concentration, orientation, and lateral preference.* Prior to assessment of higher cognitive functions, it is important to determine if the client is able to focus attention and resist distractions. The inability to attend selectively and to maintain attentional focus may be a sign of brain dysfunction, an attention deficit disorder, or a psychiatric disorder. Vigilance and span of attention can be assessed by means of cancellation tasks (e.g., striking through all of the *M*'s in an array of letters) or sequenced block tapping (e.g., Knox Cubes or Corsi Blocks). Concentration can be evaluated by having the client count backwards from twenty or draw lines connecting a series of numbered circles in the correct order (e.g., Trail Making Test, Part A). These are all tasks that, for the most part, can be easily used with a deaf population.

Assessment of orientation requires that the client be able to communicate awareness of events in four spheres: *person* (i.e., the client's own name), *place* (i.e., name of the agency, and the city and state in which the agency is located), *time* (i.e., year, month, date of the month, day of the week, time of day), and *circumstance* (i.e., why the client is at the agency). Assessment of orientation is important as individuals with disorders of recent memory (i.e., *amnestic disorders*) usually fail to maintain correct orientation in changing spheres such as time and place. Orientation can also be disrupted by other major mental disturbances such as schizophrenia.

Lateral dominance, or preference for using one side of the body (i.e., the right or left side) to perform a motor task that can only be performed with one side of the body, is usually assessed early in the examination. Neuropsychologists often evaluate lateral preference in two spheres, namely, manual preference or handedness and eye preference or optic dominance. Most people (approximately 90%) are right-handed; the remainder have mixed (or no) hand preference or are left hand dominant. Many people are right eye dominant, but a substantial proportion are left-eyed, and some have mixed (or no) eye preference. Hand preference is important to assess prior to having the client perform motor speed or coordination tasks since most people who have clear hand preference are expected to perform about 10% better with their dominant hand than with their nondominant hand. Variation from this expected pattern may be a sign of a lateralized brain lesion. Further, individuals who have mixed hand preference and/or mixed eye preference, and individuals who have hand-eye crossover (i.e., clear hand preference for one side of the body with eye preference on the opposite side) are at higher risk than strongly lateralized individuals without crossover for such problems as learning disabilities, mental retardation, and psychiatric disorders. The Lateral Dominance Examination from the Halstead-Reitan Neuropsychological Battery can be adapted for use with hearing-impaired clients.

2. *Level of general intellectual functioning.* Estimates of current level of overall intellectual functioning are presented. These may be based upon test scores, history of educational and vocational performance, impressions gathered during interview, or some combination of these factors. Tests commonly used with deaf clients include the Hiskey-Nebraska Tests of Learning Aptitude, the Performance Subtests of the Wechsler Intelligence Scales, or the Leiter International Performance Scale. A determination is usually made about the probability that the currently obtained IQ score manifests an accurate indication of level of functioning, and whether current functioning represents any change (i.e., improvement or deterioration) in overall functioning.

3. *Sensory and perceptual functions.* Basic sensory and more complex perceptual processes are usually examined in two major modalities with deaf clients, namely, vision and somesthesia (i.e., skin and body senses such as touch, pressure, pain, temperature, body schema, kinesthetics, and proprioception). Visual assessment may include a gross screening of visual acuity and of visual fields (i.e., how far peripheral vision extends up, down, to the right, and to the left when the eye are fixated on a central point). Problems in visual acuity are often the result of eye rather than brain dysfunction (i.e., end organ defects rather than dysfunction of the CNS). Visual field defects (i.e., inability to detect an event in a section of the usual visual field) and visual neglect syndromes (i.e., failure to detect an event in a peripheral section of the visual field *only* when a competing event takes place simultaneously in the opposite right or left peripheral field) may indicate the presence of a brain lesion in the posterior portions of the right or left cerebral hemisphere.

Inability to recognize and discriminate colors, shapes, sizes, objects, designs, and human faces visually when visual acuity is adequate may be a symptom of dysfunction in the occipital, parietal, or posterior temporal regions of the brain. Visual recognition and discrimination are usually tested by having the client pair or match like stimuli or match pictures or drawings of objects to the objects themselves. Further testing of visual organization abilities might require the client to discriminate the essential versus irrelevant features of a visual stimulus (e.g., Wechsler's Picture Completion) or the presence of two or more simultaneously occurring visual stimuli. Assessment of voluntary control of eye movements and ability to track visual stimuli may also be included in the neuropsychological evaluation.

Basic evaluation of cutaneous senses commonly involves testing to determine if the client can detect (without visual input) when a single stimulus has been applied (usually to the hand or the face), and when two stimuli have been applied simultaneously to both upper limbs or both sides of the face. Anesthesia of one side of the body and somesthetic neglect syndromes (in which bilateral simultaneous stimulation is perceived as unilateral single stimulation) are strong indicators of pathology in the cerebral hemisphere opposite the affected body side. Anesthesia of a smaller body area or of only the distal portions of the body (i.e., hands and feet) may indicate dysfunction not of the brain, but of the sensory end-organs (i.e., skin disorder), peripheral nerves, or spinal cord. Ability to localize touch (i.e., to discriminate where one has been touched: elbow, shoulder, wrist, thumb, ring finger, etc.), to discriminate touch involving one versus two (or more) points of contact with the skin, and to differentiate sharp versus dull stimuli, light versus heavy pressure, and hot versus cold temperature may also be assessed. Some neuropsychological examinations include assessment of stereognosis (i.e., the ability to discriminate and identify three-dimensional objects by touch alone). Stereognosis is usually assessed with each hand separately, and consistent inability to discriminate objects on one side of the body is a serious indicator of brain pathology when other tactile sensations are intact. Evaluation of graphesthesia involves discrimination (without visual cues) of numbers, letters, or simple geometric shapes traced on the skin. Kinesthesia and proprioception can be evaluated by placing a client's hand in a certain position, then having the client repeat that position without the aid of visual input. Sensory-perceptual assessment items from the Halstead-Reitan Neuropsychological Test Battery or the Luria-Nebraska Neuropsychological Battery can be easily modified for use with deaf clients.

4. *Motor functions.* Basic motor evaluation includes appraising the client's ability to initiate, repeat, alternate, and stop/inhibit movements of the limbs, fingers, and oral/facial musculature in a voluntary or volitional manner. It also includes ability to assume and to maintain a position. The motor speed, strength, and coordination of each upper limb is assessed separately to evaluate the possibility of lateralized brain lesion. Then, bilateral speed and coordinated activity (involving both hands working together) is assessed. Tasks that require fine and more gross degrees of motor control are used. Praxis, or the ability to perform and pantomime skilled, purposeful movements (e.g., chewing food, using a key to unlock a door, pouring and preparing a cup of coffee) is also evaluated. The Finger Oscillation (or Tapping) Test and dynomometer (to test strength of grip) from the Halstead-Reitan and the Motor subtest from the Luria-Nebraska have been used successfully to assess motor skills with deaf clients.

Unimanual and bimanual visual-motor (i.e., hand-eye) speed and coordination may be evaluated using the Purdue Pegboard, the Grooved Pegboard, Wechsler's Coding or Digit Symbol Subtest, and figure drawing tasks. Complex, tactually guided motor performance may be appraised with the Halstead-Reitan Tactual Performance Test.

5. *Spatial organization and constructional skills.* Examination of spatial orientation determines if the client understands and can manipulate basic spatial relationships (i.e., above, beside, etc.), can reliably use clocks to tell time, can recognize faces, and can navigate successfully through a familiar building or neighborhood. By observing the client assembling simple jigsaw puzzles (e.g., Object Assembly from the Wechsler scales), and copying geometric designs with paper and pencil (e.g., Bender Visual-Motor Gestalt Test and the Rey-Osterreith Complex Figure) or by building with blocks (i.e., with two- and three-dimensional block design tests), and matching photographs of faces (e.g., Facial Recognition Test), or geometric designs in rotated position, the neuropsychologist can determine if the client manifests any disturbances in the organization of spatial relationships typical of various disorders. In general, these tests are easily adapted to the deaf population as instructions can be mimed or tasks demonstrated if necessary.

6. *Language and communicatin skills.* Comprehension and production of signed and gestural communication may be evaluated. Valid assessment requires that the assessor be fluent in the sign language of the client or that a certified sign interpreter familiar with the constraints and demands of testing be employed. Typical aspects of language production that might be assessed include ability to repeat signed words and phrases, ability to produce the correct sign label for common objects or pictures of objects, ability to produce over-learned language sequences (i.e., numbers from one to twenty and months of the year), ability to communicate fluently in signed conversation using vocabulary and formational structure consistent with the signer's language history and without word finding difficulty (i.e., inability to recall the correct sign) or the substitution of inappropriate signs and incorrect formational properties of the signs (i.e., hand shape, movement, place of articulation on the body or in the signing space). These specific aspects of language are evaluated to aid in determining whether communication deficits exist and, if so, whether the deficits are those usually seen in *aphasic* language disorders or are the results of limited education and socialization or other environmental factors limiting sign acquisition. Assessment of language may be especially difficult with the "low verbal" deaf persons, particularly those who have experienced linguistic deprivation and/or have substituted simple gestures or "home" signs for standard signs. More complex linguistic tasks, such as the verbal subtests of the Wechsler scales must be used with extreme caution. These tests are heavily English-based, at times have a difficult language format, or when signed, provide clear cues for correct responses. With these tests, the examiner might be unable to determine if he or she is testing understanding of language or ability to perform various specific, language-based tasks.

If the deaf client can be expected (by educational history and/or prior performance) to have significant facility with written English, reading and writing of English may also be evaluated to discover if the deaf client manifests any of the impairments in written word recognition and discrimination that characterize certain *dyslex disorders.* For example, a client with excellent English training and a history of good functioning with written English may be found to make frequent, and possibly subtle, errors in decoding written words (i.e., producing the sign "brother" in response to the written word "both," fingerspelling "top" in response to "pot," or making errors in copying written English). In such cases, evaluation of reading and writing abilities may prove diagnostically significant. However, in most cases it must be kept in mind that English is most likely a second, rather than a native, language for the prelingually deaf individual, and that in such cases, inappropriate assessment of reading and writing skills may confuse rather than elucidate neuropsychological diagnostic issues.

7. *Calculation skills.* Recognition and discrimination of numbers, comprehension of numerical differences (i.e., bigger than, less than) and understanding of basic arithmetic processes (i.e., addition, subtraction, multiplication, division) are examined. Learning disabilities and aphasic disorders can impair the ability to discriminate numbers and to do even simple calculations. Brain disorders and learning disabilities which disturb spatial relations may impair the ability to place hold in writing numbers and to carry in performing calculations. Again, assessment of disorders in this area assumes that the deaf client can be reasonably expected to have had the basic skills premorbidly (i.e., prior to onset of brain dysfunction); if a client cannot be expected to have had requisite skills, assessment of calculation abilities can cloud diagnostic issues.

8. *Reasoning, abstraction, and cognitive flexibility.* Examination of these "higher cognitive functions" may involve language-mediated and nonlanguage-mediated processes. To assess the ability to form concepts, maintain conceptual set in the face of interference or distraction, and flexibly shift set in response to changing environmental requirements and contingencies, the psychologist might employ such nonlanguage-mediated tasks as the Weigl-Goldstein-Scheerer Color Form Sorting Test, Wisconsin Card Sorting Test, Categories Test, and some language-mediated tasks such as Wechsler's Similarities and the Trail Making Test, Part B. Deficits in forming simple conceptual sets (i.e., concreteness) and in shifting sets appropriately (i.e., perseveration) are among the most common behavioral indicators of impaired brain function. Neuropsychologists usually assess ability to reason logically, to sequence events temporally, to appreciate consequences of actions, and plan ahead (e.g., with Wechsler's Picture Arrangement, Raven Progressive Matrices, Cattell Culture Fair Tests) as deficits in these areas often suggest certain learning disabilities and/or dysfunction of the frontal lobes of the brain. Practical judgment in real-life problem situations and awareness of social conventions may also be assessed to aid in determining if reasoning deficits reflect an organic brain dysfunction, a psychiatric disorder, or lack of appropriate socialization. With some deaf individuals, lack of adequate language can impair scores, particularly on more complex tasks where internal, verbal labeling and processing may be important for problem solving.

9. *Memory functions.* Impairment of memory is the behavioral symptom most commonly seen in brain disorders, regardless of the etiology of the disorder. Because memory is not a simple function, but rather a complex, multidimensional process, careful evaluation is critical in determining if a defect in memory is present and, if so, the type of memory deficit manifested. Memory is examined with reference to its temporal aspects (i.e., *immediate* recall of events in the preceding 10 to 15 seconds; *recent* memory for events that occurred in the past few minutes, hours, and days; *remote* memory for public and personal events from the distant past), the type of information to be stored (i.e., *language* vs. *figural/spatial*), the sensory modality through which the information was received (i.e., *visual, tactual, olfactory*, etc.) and the format for recall (i.e., *free* recall, *cued* recall, or *recognition*/multiple choice).

Immediate recall is usually tested using procedures similar to tests for attention span. Tests commonly used to assess recent memory with deaf clients include immediate and delayed recall for the Visual Reproduction subtest of the Wechsler Memory Scale, the Benton Visual Retention Test, Memory for Designs, immediate and delayed recall of the Rey-Osterreith Complex Figure, and the memory and location portions of the Tactual Perception Test. Tests of language-related recent memory using signed words, phrases, and stories are almost nonexistent and represent an area in which standardized test development for the deaf population is sorely needed. As part of efforts at the University of California Center on Deafness, a language memory task is being utilized that requires recollection of four signed words immediately and after a period of 20 minutes in a free recall, cued recall, and recognition format. Remote memory is usually examined informally by inquiry into memory for life events in the more distant past.

10. *Personality features.* Many, but not all, neuropsychological evaluations include assessment of the client's personality features or psychodynamics. This is important because a variety of neurological disorders first present with disturbances in emotional and motivational functioning. Further, it is common to have as a referral question the differential diagnosis between a psychiatric and a neurologic disorder as the basis for the disturbed behavior.

In conducting personality assessment, the neuropsychologist typically evaluates these basic areas: (a) the presence of distortions in perception and reality testing; (b) evidence of disturbance in thought process, ideational content, and beliefs; (c) type, range, control over, and appropriateness of emotional experience and expression, and predominant mood; (d) identity development and self-perception; (e) interpersonal relationships and social skills; (f) major conflicts or problems and typical coping styles and defense mechanisms. Tests used for personality appraisal include the commonly used projective techniques (e.g., Rorschach Inkblots, Thematic or Children's Apperception Test, House-Tree-Person or Draw-a-Person). Instruments requiring knowledge of English, such as the Minnesota Multiphasic Personality Inventory or the California Personality Inventory, may be employed if the client's reading proficiency is high enough (i.e., at least 6th grade vocabulary and comprehension) to permit reliable and valid comprehension of test items.

11. *Summary conclusions and diagnostic impressions.* This section of the neuropsychological evaluation should be tailored to respond to the referral question(s) or issue(s). Most often, this section of the report can be organized into three broad areas: (a) Behavioral or functional implications includes brief restatement of level of intelligence, specification of type and degree of deficits and strengths in the areas of cognition, perception, motor performance, and personality adjustment, and the implications of the pattern of strengths and deficits for the client's ability to live independently and to participate in educational, vocation, and social opportunities. (b) Neurologic implications involves determining if the results of the evaluation are consistent with the presence of a known brain syndrome. If possible, the neuropsychologist may not only make inferences regarding the presence of a brain disorder, but may also specify the location, severity, onset, course, and probable etiology of the brain disorder. (c) Psychiatric implications involves determining whether a specific psychiatric syndrome is indicated based upon the evaluation results. Usually DSM-III methods and terminology are employed when psychiatric diagnoses are warranted.

12. *Recommendations.* Recommendations are typically related to the three areas delineated above. Again, the orientation and specificity of any recommendations depends upon the referral question(s) and issue(s). Recommendations may include suggestions for further evaluation and diagnostic workup, referral to a particular training, treatment, assistance, or service program, ways to work successfully with the client, techniques to aid the client in maximizing ability to function in certain situations, settings, and so forth.

When to Refer for Neuropsychological Assessment

The rehabilitation specialist is often the first person to become aware of functional deficits or other symptomatology suggesting brain dysfunction. It is important, then, that rehabilitation specialists acquaint themselves with some of the gross indicators of brain dysfunction and with specific symptoms and/or symptom complexes which indicate a need for neuropsychological assessment. In general, specialists will attend to the behaviors exhibited by their clients, for it is in behavior that the dysfunction can be seen. In certain cases, however, behavior reported by others will lead rehabilitation specialists to suspect dysfunction. In this section of the chapter, the following is discussed: (a) gross indicators of neuropsychological dysfunction frequently observable, or reported, in the client interview, and (b) general chronic symptoms of brain dysfunction, including specific deficits suggesting a neurologic substratum.

Gross Indicators of Brain Dysfunction. Many neuropsychological symptoms can be obvious in the client interview, if the observer is aware of what to look for. Is the client alert and oriented? Does he or she seem lethargic or to display a fluctuating level of consciousness? Conversely, does the client appear to be hyperalert, restless, and unable to moderate his or her behavior? Brain-dysfunctional deaf clients may have difficulty finding signs to encode what they wish to say, may use some signs idiosyncratically, or may make various sign formation errors when, by history, they would be expected to have good signing skills. A client may move in specific ways which seem bizarre or otherwise unusual. Recurrent failures of memory, both for remote events and for events within the interview itself, can suggest dysfunction. In some neurologic disorders, there is paradoxical emotion. That is, there may be an outward show of laughter, tears, or rage that does not match the client's inner state or is inappropriate to the content of his or her speech. Conversely, the client may be quite unresponsive, with blunted affect.

It may be noted that the signs and symptoms of brain dysfunction observable at interview match, or mimic, those often seen in functional psychiatric disorders. In general, neuropsychologic disorders can grossly mimic any functional psychiatric disorder. This fact does not mean that on observing the presence of a symptom shared by both psychiatric and neurologic disorders, the rehabilitation specialist must then refer for differential neuropsychological assessment. Rather, it suggests that any psychiatric symptom should be investigated further with an eye toward a possible neuropsychological basis for the behavior. Therefore, any psychiatric symptom is suspect (i.e., mood changes, emotional lability, dissociative state, hallucinations, illusions, feelings of depersonalization, etc.). The reports of others acquainted with the client can also be important and should lead the rehabilitation specialist toward further investigation. For example, family or employers may say that the client is "just not his old self," reporting differences such as absent-mindedness, withdrawal from ordinary activities, bouts of anxiety, sudden rages, changes in eating or sleeping patterns, and so forth.

It is also important to remember that the client, or those in the client's environment, will often have some plausible psychogenic attribution for these changes. In other words, there may be events in clients' histories which appear to "explain" their current behavior in psychological rather than neuropsychological terms. Psychological and neuropsychological difficulties can and do coexist in the same individual, and because organic events must be incorporated into the client's self view, he or she is likely to interpret them in terms of personal history and/or psychopathology.

1. *Chronic Symptoms.* The chronic symptoms of brain dysfunction can be divided into five major areas: (a) loss of cognitive flexibility, (b) memory deficits, (c) loss of specific skills, (d) sensory and motor deficits, and (e) emotional disturbances. Each of these are discussed below.

(a) *Loss of cognitive flexibility.* The first characteristic of loss of cognitive flexibility (or inability to change mental sets) is concrete thinking, exemplified by a certain "stimulus boundedness." In the hearing individual, this quality is often manifested in proverb interpretation. Asked to explain, for example, the proverb "people in glass houses shouldn't throw stones," the concrete thinking hearing individual might say, "Stones break glass, so you shouldn't throw stones or you will break the glass in your house." Concrete proverb interpretation may not have the same implications for the deaf client, however, unless there is independent evidence of very high premorbid functioning in English. Nonetheless, observable and remarkable concrete thinking can be detected in the brain-dysfunctional deaf client, particularly where the site of the dysfunction is in the frontal lobes. A good example can be found in the sample report included in this chapter. When asked to sign a release for the examiner to obtain his school records from a state school for the deaf in a particular town, the client stated that he attended school in another town. Although it was explained to him in great detail that the school had moved to new facilities in another town, the client was unable to escape the "stimulus boundedness" of having attended school in the first town. In his dysfunctional state, his having attended school in that town meant that his record were there. This client's inability to shift the mental set of "where his records were maintained" was not attributable to low intelligence. Indeed, despite his lesion, his general intellectual functioning was measured variously as falling within the low average to average range.

Goldstein and Scheerer (1941) have defined concrete thinking in more general terms. Specifically, they define concrete thinking as having none of the attributes of abstract thinking, and state the attributes of abstract thinking as comprising the following conscious and volitional modes of behavior: (a) to detach oneself from the outer world and from inner experiences, (b) to assume a mental set, (c) to account for one's acts to oneself and to communicate the account, (d) to shift reflectively from one aspect of a situation to another, (e) to hold in mind various aspects of a situation simultaneously, (f) to appreciate the essentials of a given whole while being able to break up the whole into parts, isolate them, and synthesize them, (g) to abstract common properties reflectively and to form hierarchic concepts, (h) to plan ahead mentally, and (i) to think and perform symbolically.

The second characteristic of loss of cognitive flexibility is an inability to learn. The individual may be capable of rote memory, but be unable to use the information for problem solving. For example, a client may be able to repeat and understand instructions, but may be unable to modify his or her behavior in response to those instructions. More generally, the individual may have difficulty in modifying behavior in response to environmental feedback.

The third characteristic of loss of cognitive flexibility is perseveration. In testing, it usually appears as stereotypic repeated solutions or responses. However, perseveration may manifest itself as an inability to shift conversational topic, difficulty in shifting activities, or even difficulty in initiating activity (a perseveration of inactivity). It is as if the individual were engulfed in his or her own self-perception and cannot imagine doing anything except the immediate activity.

The assessment of loss of cognitive flexibility in a prelingually deaf individual presents particular hazards. The types of behavior taken as symptomatic of loss of cognitive flexibility in a hearing individual may not have the same implications for, say, a "low verbal" deaf client. In particular, the low functioning deaf client may operate at a very concrete, rather than abstract, level not because of specific brain dysfunction, but rather because of socialization and, most importantly, language deficits. Language itself serves as a means of forming categories and hierarchies (i.e., dogs vs. cats vs. animals), provides the symbols with which one manipulates one's inner world of thoughts and feelings, and is the epitome of abstraction. If the deaf client's language learning background is deficient, then deficits in abstraction, in ability to follow directions, and in inability to conform one's behavior to the demands of situations may follow—without specific brain dysfunction.

(b) *Loss of memory.* Loss of memory, or amnesia, is one of the more pervasive symptoms of brain dysfunction and can occur with dysfunction in almost any area of the brain. Memory loss, particularly for immediate memory, can appear in any function and may be modality specific. Thus, the client may be able to remember visual-verbal language material (i.e., signs) but be unable to hold purely visual-spatial material (i.e., designs) in memory. Conversely, memory for visual or figural material may be intact but language memory deficient.

(c) *Loss of specific skills.* One way of conceiving of complex and molar general behavior is to characterize it as a summation of smaller, more molecular, specific behaviors. If there is some deficit in a specific molecular behavior, then the larger, more complex behavior will suffer. The general areas of specific skill loss likely to be seen by the rehabilitation specialist are loss of language abilities (i.e., the aphasias), loss of ability to organize sensory stimuli (i.e., the apraxias), and disturbances of sensation (i.e., the sensory disorders).

The asphasias are disturbances of language in its communicative function. In the hearing individual, aphasias are almost always associated with left hemisphere dysfunction; however, the picture is not so clear with prelingually deaf individuals. Chiarello, Knight, and Mandel (1982) presented a very complete description of the neuropsychological functioning of a 65-year-old prelinqually deaf woman who suffered a cerebrovascular accident (i.e., stroke) focused in the left parietal lobe. The woman had been fluent in ASL prior to the CVA and manifested severe language deficits subsequent to the brain injury. Although the woman presented with numerous signs and symptoms classically seen in hearing aphasics, the pattern of deficits was somewhat incongruent with that expected in a hearing individual with a similarly situated lesion. This clinical study suggests that while the left hemisphere appears to be dominant for language in prelingually deaf individuals as well as hearing individuals, the brain organization of

those functions within the left hemisphere may be different. Other research (i.e., Manning, et. al., 1977; McKeever, et. al., 1976; Poizner, et. al., 1979; Poizner & Lane, 1979) has suggested greater right hemisphere involvement in sign language processing by prelingually deaf signers. Despite such possible differences in language organization, the behavioral deficits that the rehabilitation specialist is likely to see at interview or reported in an assessment are apparently similar to those seen in the hearing aphasic.

There are several specific dysphasic/aphasic symptoms that the rehabilitation specialist is likely to encounter. The client may be unable to give the correct language label for an intended referent (i.e., the client may use incorrect signs, such as signing "story" for "sign", or may simply be unable to come up with a sign at all). Signed discourse may be marked by circumlocutions, that is, sentences such as (in translation to English), "I put it on the (pause) you know (pause) the thing in my office where my typewriter is" when what is meant is "I put it on my desk." Often the client is able to use correct signs in conversational signing but is unable to produce the correct sign on confrontation (i.e., in response to a question such as, "What is this?"). The rehabilitation specialist may notice that the formational properties of the client's signing are disturbed. For example, the deaf client may make a sign with an incorrect hand shape, an incorrect place on the body or in the signing space, or with an incorrect movement. Or the client may make semantic errors, using the wrong word or sign for the intended meaning (e.g., the deaf client may sign "car" for "train" or "chair" for "table.").

Agnosia refers to loss of the ability to recognize sensory stimuli in the presence of intact sensory receptors. Usually the impairment is quite specific and is confined to a particular sensory modality. The rehabilitation specialist might note that the client is unable to read, despite a history of appropriate training and prior ability. There may be a failure to recognize objects by sight or touch (e.g., change in one's pocket), or be unable to recognize faces reliably. The client may be noted to drop objects or to miss them in reaching for them. Left/right orientation may be difficult or impossible for the client. The client may even fail to recognize his or her own body parts. Each of these behaviors may be related to specific brain impairment but can be easily mistaken for malingering or for some functional psychiatric disturbance.

Praxis, as noted above, refers to the ability to perform purposeful voluntary motor acts. In particular, praxis involves complex, learned motor sequences such as riding a bike or drying a dish.

Apraxia, then, refers to the loss of ability of perform specific motor sequences voluntarily, although such acts can occur automatically, especially in the appropriate environmental circumstance (such as in the kitchen with clean, wet dishes). There are several symptoms of apraxia the rehabilitation specialist might note. A client may be unable to express a word in written form, although the individual knows the word and has appropriate training in written language. There may be a disturbance in the ability to spell words with the correct letters in the right order, although the person knows how to spell (this condition would have special significance for deaf signers, who use many fingerspelled words in normal sign conversation; however, the present authors have not seen, and know of no reports of, spelling apraxias in deaf individuals in the absence of more global aphasic conditions). Loss of the ability to perform arithmetic functions, to do line drawings, to prepare a meal, or to dress oneself are less likely to be seen at interview, but may well be reported in referral data. Other specific apraxias are possible, but are less likely to be encountered by the rehabilitation specialist.

(d) *Sensory and motor deficits.* Sensory disorders can be peripheral (i.e., based on organ dysfunction outside of the CNS) or central (i.e., based on brain dysfunction). Often it is difficult to distinguish the two. Some of the disorders that might be reported to the rehabilitation specialist are spontaneous sensation (i.e., experiencing sensation without external stimulation in any sensory modality), or complete or partial loss of sensation in one or more modalities. For example, the client may have a visual field cut, or a loss of a portion of the visual field, often without the individual's being aware of the loss. This condition may only be represented by the client's consistently running into or tripping over objects in one side of the visual field.

Movement disorders are marked by difficulty in initiating, terminating, or controlling movements. They are different from the apraxias in that the latter refer to performance of complex, voluntary motor sequences. Often movement disorders are quite apparent and have led to medical diagnosis prior to the client's coming to the attention of the rehabilitation specialist. Some movement disorders are quite subtle, however, and may be overlooked. In general, the rehabilitation specialist should suspect any abnormal slowness of movement in the presence of proper motivation and ability difficulty in continuing purposive acts such as holding a certain position (e.g., the individual may be unable to keep his or her eyes closed), or difficulty in stopping purposive movements, particu-

larly those of a repetitive nature. The more obvious movement disorders (i.e., sudden jerking movements, undulating movements of the arms, neck, and/or trunk, disturbance of gait, or tremors) always indicate neurological or neuropsychological assessment.

(e) *Emotional disturbance.* Emotional disturbance of various sorts (i.e., depression, elation, violent anger, suspiciousness, etc.) can cue the rehabilitation specialist to the possibility of neurological dysfunction. The most telling sign is that the emotional disturbance is "ego alien" (i.e., unacceptable to the client and not a part of the client's usual experience of him or herself). Further, emotional disturbance related to neurologic dysfunction often has a sudden onset which is not related to specific environmental, circumstantial, or social events in the client's life.

Final Considerations

Two final issues warrant discussion at the conclusion of this chapter. The first issue arises *prior* to formal initiation of the neuropsychological evaluation, and involves *preparation* of clients for assessment. Adequate preparation of clients by the vocational rehabilitation specialist is necessary in order to instill motivation to perform as well as possible with reasonable effect and care, and in order to facilitate cooperation with the neuropsychological examiner. Also, appropriate preparation may help reduce clients' anxieties and fears about assessment and lessen the impact of these factors on test performance. Thus, adequate preparation of clients will help ensure that test findings are a valid and reliable reflection of a client's abilities and current status.

Clients need to understand why testing is being done, what the tests will tell the specialist, how the test findings will effect the specialist's decisions and the particular client's opportunities and choices, and approximately how long the testing will take (e.g., approximately how many hours divided into how many sessions over how many days or weeks). Further, prior to testing, clients need to know that they will receive some payoff for all the time and energy put into testing—that once all the testing is completed, they will get feedback about the results of the evaluation, will learn what the test findings are, and what the results mean for everyday life. In addition, preparation needs to take place early in the referral process so that clients have ample opportunity to ask questions regarding the evaluation and to express their concerns and anxieties.

The specificity and degree of detail used in describing the reasons for testing should be tailored to the needs and capabilities of the individual client. Some clients are satisfied with brief, general explanations; others need clearly detailed and concrete examples of what the tests are like and what each test tells the examiner. The explanations offered to clients should clarify their understanding and enhance motivation without increasing anxiety. For example, one client may be given this rationale: "You know the meningitis you had as a baby caused your deafness. This illness may also be responsible for the memory problems you have and the long time it takes you to learn a new skill. I want you to take these tests so that you and I will have a clear idea of what things you are good at, your strengths, and what things are hard for you to do, your weaknesses. Once we know more about your strong abilities and your weaknesses, I can better help you find the right training program for a job." Another type of rationale might be presented: "Your boss says you have been having problems forgetting things at work. He said you forget to lock the cabinet after you put the tools away, you can't remember where you put things, and that you get lost going to the cafeteria. These are all new problems you never had before. I would like you to have some testing done to help find out what is causing you to forget things and how we can help you with this problem."

In some instances, it is useful to have the vocational rehabilitation specialist and the neuropsychologist discuss beforehand the rationale to be presented to a client. In all cases, the neuropsychologist must be aware of the rationale that the vocational rehabilitation specialist has presented. Often, it is advisable for the specialist to accompany the client to the initial meeting with the neuropyschological evaluator.

Testing is a time-consuming, demanding, and often frustrating and anxiety-producing experience. If adequately and appropriately prepared beforehand, clients will be more likely to engage in the testing process actively, to see themselves as partners in a joint effort, and to regard testing as something the psychologist does *with* rather than *to* them.

The second issue that deserves careful consideration at this chapter's conclusion involves the provision of *feedback* to the client *after* the neuropsychological evaluation has been completed. In many cases, clients and/or parents of guardians have a legal right of access to the information that results from the evaluation. In most cases, the client, parent, or guardian needs feedback of the information to better understand the client's problems and to make informed choices regarding treatment, jobs, education, or other services. Moreover, offering the client feedback about the test findings often enhances motivation and cooperation during testing. On occasion, it may even be helpful to share test results (with the client's consent) with others who interact with or provide services to the client— a supervisor at work, spouse or other family members, or other human service providers.

Feedback to clients about test results should always be conducted in the context of face-to-face comunication. Providing the client with a copy of the written test report may be appropriate and a legal right of the client in some cases. However, providing the client with a photocopy of the report is never adequate by itself and should be accompanied by a face-to-face meeting in which the findings are presented and discussed, unfamiliar or technical language is clarified, and an opportunity for questions is available to the client. Individual agencies have policies regarding client access to written information. Awareness of these policies is especially crucial when access to the test information may prove harmful or upsetting to the client.

Discussion of test findings with clients can assume many forms; three of the most frequently used methods are outlined below. All three methods require that the neuropsychologist and the vocational rehabilitation specialist discuss the evaluation results prior to any feedback meeting with the client. During this discussion, alternative methods for informing the client may be explored and an optimum method agreed upon for the individual client. The three most common methods include: (a) the client, vocational rehabilitation specialist, and neuropsychologist all meeting together for a feedback session, (b) the specialist alone presenting the results to the client after discussion with the neuropsychologist, and (c) the neuropsychologist meeting with the client (without the specialist present) to provide feedback. Each method has its advantages (e.g., opportunities for immediate clarification of questions among all three people focusing rather than diffusing efforts with the client) and disadvantages (e.g., cost, scheduling).

In discussing test findings with clients, it is always helpful to present a balanced picture—to emphasize strengths and skills as well as explain deficits and impairments. In general, it is helpful first to present results summarized in terms of specific areas of behavioral functioning (i.e., memory, language, motor coordination, etc.) rather than in a test-by-test fashion, which can be overwhelmingly complex and unnecessarily confusing to clients. Next, implications of the test results—what the test findings mean in terms of the original referral question—are discussed. These implications may be vocational or educational in some cases. In other instances the implications may involve identifying a medical or neurological disorder and preparation of the client for referral to a medical, neurological, or psychiatric specialist for appropriate diagnosis or treatment. For example: "The test results do not show any real problems with your memory or ability to learn new things. What the tests did show was that you probably are feeling very sad, depressed, worried, and upset, and that these feelings are probably the reason why you are having difficulty forgetting things at work. I think you might feel better and do better at work if you had the chance to talk about your feelings with a counselor who understands, and can help with feelings. Would you like to talk with a counselor?" Another example: "The test results show that you are having serious problems using your left hand to do small, careful movements, and that you can't recognize objects by touch alone with your left hand. You also have a lot of trouble finding your way around your old neighborhood and get lost often. These problems are probably due to a medical or neurological illness that needs attention. I want to send you to see a doctor who specializes in these problems so you can get the proper medical care as soon as possible." A last example: "The test results show you do have serious memory problems and that it takes you a lot longer than most people to learn something new. These problems were probably first caused by the same infection that caused you hearing loss years ago. But now your memory seems to be getting a little worse as you get older. This is something that usually happens as people get older. You need to find ways to help your memory along—like keeping a daily calendar with all your appointments and things you have to do written in it. You may also need to put notes or pictures up around your apartment and at work so that you don't forget to do things. Maybe your work supervisor could help you make a list of things you need to do every morning when you first come to work, and you can tape it to a corner of your work table to help remember what needs to be done."

When discussing test results and their implications with clients, it is wise to avoid the use of technical jargon. In some cases it may be appropriate to share the formal diagnosis with the client; in other instances these labels may prove unnecessarily alarming or even devastating. Caution should always be used in sharing psychiatric or neurologic diagnostic labels with a client. Again, awareness of agency policy regarding revelation of diagnoses and use of consultation with colleagues/supervisors to help formulate the best strategy for patient feedback is always recommended.

Sample Report
NEUROPSYCHOLOGICAL EVALUATION
(For professional use only)

NAME : John Q. Sample
DATE OF BIRTH : 6/3/57
AGE : 26
HANDEDNESS : Right
TEST DATES : 1/10/84, 1/25/84, 1/31/84

Identifying Information

John Sample is a 26-year-old single Caucasian male referred by John Doe, a private practice vocational rehabilitation counselor with the firm of Doe and Associates, for neuropsychological assessment. Mr. Doe does not have reliable historical data on his client, but does know that the client is currently living in a "convalescent home". According to Mr. Doe, John Sample was involved in an accident with a printing press at his former place of employment. The result was damage to the tendons of his left (nondominant) hand with loss of fine motor control but retention of some gross mobility. There is currently a Workman's Compensation Insurance disability case in process. Mr. Sample carries a diagnosis of sensorineural hearing loss, profound, and a mixed seizure disorder with both grand mal and focal motor manifestations. Mr. Doe requested assessment to help him understand his client's problems and limitations, and the causes of these problems. Mr. Doe noted two specific aspects of the client's behavior that are of concern; first, Mr. Sample seems unable to learn new skills and is very distractible. The counselor would like information about the client's overall level of intellectual functioning and about his specific cognitive abilities—especially memory and ability to learn. Are the memory problems related to Mr. Sample's long-standing seizure disorder, to some new neurological problem, or is depression playing a role in the client's apparent learning deficits? Second, what has been the impact of Mr. Sample's tendon injury on his psychological state.

Background, History, and Symptoms

Mr. Sample has been seen at this clinic previously. He was referred by his vocational rehabilitation counselor at that time, Mr. John Smith, in September of 1976. Mr. Smith said that Mr. Sample had been "kicked out of his room and board situation for behavior problems" and "needed to talk to someone." First contact with Mr. Sample was not achieved until January of 1976 through the intervention of his parents. As that time, Mr. Sample was described as "multiply handicapped—deaf, seizures, possible MR." His seizure disorder was being followed by a local neurologist, Dr. _____.

According to history gathered from the parents, John Sample began school at five years of age as a residential student at the *Firststate* School for the Deaf. The family moved when the client was eight years old, and from eight to ten years of age, he attended the *Secondstate* School for the Deaf. The family then moved to *Thirdstate* in 1967, and Mr. Sample transferred to the *Thirdstate* School for the Deaf. He graduated in June of 1976. Following his graduation, Mr. Sample entered a work evaluation program on referral from Mr. Smith. Records from or descriptions of that evaluation were not available for the present assessment.

Records from the *Thirdstate* School for the Deaf indicate that Mr. Sample presented many behavioral problems there. He was often reprimanded for fights with other students. He was caught shoplifting. He once stabbed another student just above the eye with a sharp pencil. He did not make friends well with other students. Also reported in the records was an IQ estimate obtained at approximately age 8 of 83 (low average); considered to be of suspect validity owing to Mr. Sample's inattention and hyperactivity. Mr. Sample obtained a Wechsler Intelligence Scale for Children Performance Scale IQ score of 97, and a Draw-a-Person IQ estimate of 98, at age 10 years, 5 months. These scores indicated average intellectual functioning at that time. On the other hand, a Vineland Social Maturity Scale score of 84 indicated slow development of social and self-care skills.

Further testing in 1974 at age 16 indicated higher cognitive functioning at the 32nd percentile (IQ estimate 93), numerical aptitude below the 1st percentile, form recognition at the 70th percentile, motor coordination at the 13th percentile, finger dexterity at the 6th percentile, and manual dexterity at the 48th percentile. In general, these results indicate that Mr. Sample had, at that time, mild to moderate deficits in gross and fine motor coordination.

Academic testing at age 17 in 1975, before his last year of school, indicated the following grade-level equivalents in academic skills: word meaning—2.5; paragraph meaning—2.3; spelling—3.1; English—2.8; arithmetic computation—2.2; arithmetic concepts—4.0; arithmetic applications—2.7; social studies—3.6; science—3.1. These scores indicate that Mr. Sample left school with minimal academic skills and was markedly deficient in academics even taking into account the impact of his deafness.

Mr. Sample had had no psychiatric history prior to his presentation at this clinic. There apparently had been a Bender Visual-Motor Gestalt Test administered at ten years of age, with the examiner suggesting some instability in fine motor coordination and/or personality functioning. A differential diagnosis between emotional disturbance and organic involvement was not made at that time.

Mr. Sample's seizure disorder dates back to the age of four weeks when he had pneumococcal meningitis. From that time until 1971 (age 14), his seizures were generalized in nature and always associated with fevers. He then began to exhibit focal motor seizures involving the buccal musculature and the left arm. A CAT scan in early 1977 (age 19) revealed a prominent right frontal lobe lesion as well as dilatation of the right lateral ventricle and slight rightward displacement of the third ventricle. Mr. Sample's seizures had been controlled with Dilantin, phenobarbital, and Tegretol. His deafness has also been attributed to the meningitis. His parents stated that Mr. Sample was diagnosed as profoundly deaf shortly after the infection resolved and that there has been no change in his hearing status since that time.

Interview and Test Behavior

Mr. Sample was brought to the clinic by Mr. Doe, his current vocational counselor. Mr. Sample is a moderately attractive man of average build and height. He was casually dressed in clothing appropriate to his age and gender, but was rather unkempt and rumpled looking. He was unshaven, his hair was uncombed, and his hands were dirty. His presentation would probably be judged as somewhat inappropriate to the situation. At interview, he was at times pleasant, affable, and cooperative, but several times became angry and upset over trivial matters. For example, he threatened to walk out of the interview when his release was requested for the clinic to obtain his school records from the *Thirdstate* School for the Deaf in *Firsttown*. He stated that he had not attended school in *Firsttown* but rather in *Secondtown*. He became argumentative and agitated when it was explained to him that his school records had been transferred when the school moved to new facilities. It was only through the intervention of Mr. Doe, who appears to have a fairly adaptive relationship with John Sample, that the client agreed to continue the interview. Mr. Doe stated that such behavior was frequent in his interactions with Mr. Sample and that he had attributed it to the difficulty in his and Mr. Sample's communicating without the use of sign. In fact, this sort of behavior characterized most of Mr. Sample's interactions throughout testing, regardless of the mode of communication or the partner in the communication.

Throughout the interviews, Mr. Sample was alert, coherent, and well-oriented in all spheres. Affect, though excessively variable, was appropriate to content. There was no evidence of hallucination, delusion, illusion, or bizarre ideation. His signing was generally well-formed, with rate and structure within normal limits; he did, however, seem to use a few signs repetitively and in an idiosyncratic fashion. Mr. Sample at no time exhibited any bizarre or otherwise remarkable behavior indicative of severe emotional disturbance. His level of motivation throughout the interviews and testing was questionable, and it may be that the current assessment does not represent Mr. Sample's optimal level of performance. Nonetheless, the consistency of test results suggests that the current assessment gives a reasonably accurate picture of Mr. Sample's current neuropsychological functioning.

Tests and Procedures Administered

Wechsler Adult Intelligence Scale-Revised (WAIS-R), Performance Scale

Wechsler Intelligence Scale for Children-Revised (WISC-R), Mazes Subtest

Lateral Dominance Examination

Sensory Perceptual Exam: Single and Double Stimulation

Wisconsin Card Sorting Test

Trail Making Test Part A & B

Bender Visual-Motor Gestalt Test

Knox Cubes

Luria-Nebraska Neuropsychological Battery, Motor Function Items, Tactile Subtest

Thematic Apperception Test

Rorschach Inkblots

Test Results

Attention, concentration, orientation, lateral preference. Most measures of attention and concentration were within normal limits. Mr. Sample was able to fingerspell the alphabet in 15 seconds and the numbers 1 to 20 in 10 seconds without omissions or sequencing errors. Results of the Trail Making Test Part A, which requires the client to draw lines connecting an array of numbers from 1 to 25 in order, were at the 40th percentile. Mr. Sample's performance on the Knox Cubes, which requires the client to repeat patterns of taps on four blocks, was markedly deficient. His performance was equivalent to that expected with a chronological age of 7 years, 6 months. Most of his errors were reversals of adjacent elements of the pattern or other sequencing errors. Errors of this type are more suggestive of problems in sequencing and planning than of attention deficits.

Mr. Sample was oriented to the year and month, but made an error of one day early in naming the day of the week and could not give the date of the month. He was oriented to place and person but was vague regarding his current problems and the reason for having testing done. Results of the Lateral Dominance Examination demonstrated that Mr. Sample is strongly right-handed, but that he has mixed eye preference.

Level of general intellectual functioning. Mr. Sample obtained a WAIS-R Performance Scale IQ score of 83, in the low average range of intelligence. This score represents a significant decrement in his current intellectual functioning compared to that in 1967 at age 10 (IQ 97). All subtest scores were in the low average range, there being no relative strengths or weaknesses in his performance. He persisted in inefficient and unsuccessful strategies, failing to learn from his errors.

Sensory and perceptual functions. Mr. Sample was consistently able to discriminate unilateral single and bilateral double simultaneous tactile stimulation to his hands. He could localize touch to different fingers and parts of his arms, but had mild difficulty with his left hand in discriminating one versus two points, and sharp versus dull or heavy versus light pressure. These latter findings may be related to peripheral damage to the nerves in his left hand during his recent job-related accident rather than brain-related phenomena.

Testing of visual fields was difficult as Mr. Sample often was unable to maintain a fixed focusing of visual attention. However, no consistent signs of a visual field defect or of visual neglect were noted. His ability to recognize objects and discriminate relevant versus irrelevant missing features visually was in the low average range.

Motor functions. Mr. Sample displayed mild to moderate deficits on motor speed and control tasks. Although gross motor control was adequate in simple movements, fine movements were impaired bilaterally, with mild deficits in the right hand and marked deficits in the left. This is expected given the client's work injury. More striking was Mr. Sample's difficulty in performing sequential or alternating movements. He was unable to maintain a tapping sequence of one tap with one hand, two with the other. He was also unable to maintain a finger touching sequence wherein he was to touch his thumb to each of his fingers consecutively. These deficits reflected problems in planning and executing more complex motor sequences than in ability to control any single fine movement. He was able to pantomime pouring coffee and threading a needle in the absence of the actual objects, indicating no significant apraxia.

Spatial organization and constructional skills. On the Block Design subtest of the WAIS-R, which requires the subject to build designs from blocks to match a picture, Mr. Sample placed blocks directly on the picture—a behavior suggesting "stimulus boundedness" and often seen in people with severe frontal lobe dysfunction. He also lost the square outer configuration of one of the designs—an error usually indicative of right cerebral hemisphere dysfunction.

Mr. Sample's Bender Visual-Motor Gestalt Test protocol (in which line drawings are copied using paper and pencil) revealed marked deficits in ability to organize visual perception. Designs were distorted and often rotated either 90 or 180 degrees. In his design distortions, Mr. Sample often lost significant gestalt features of the design, beginning with maintenance of the overall configuration, but losing it as design construction progressed, another sign of right hemisphere dysfunction.

Language and communication skills. Mr. Sample was able to produce signed discourse spontaneously when requested to describe his activities of the previous day. Consultation with the certified sign interpreter indicated that the client's signing was generally organized, fluent, and ASL-based with little English influence. He was able to produce, on confrontation, the signs for several common objects (i.e., paper, magazine, shoe, chair, cigarette, key) without hesitation or word finding difficulties. Although he could not produce the fingerspelled alphabet, he was able to produce the days of the week in proper sequence. He was able to complete one and twostep commands (i.e., give me the pencil; put the key on the paper and give me the cup), he could not reliably complete threestep commands. He was able to repeat sign sentences of up to five signs reliably, but would make frequent errors on sentences of greater length. No semantic or for6ational errors were noted in Mr. Sample's sign production. In general, results do not indicate aphasic disorder. Owing to Mr. Sample's known academic deficits, reading and writing skills were not assessed.

Calculation skills. Owing to Mr. Sample's known marked academic deficits, this area was not formally assessed.

Reasoning, abstraction, and cognitive flexibility. Mr. Sample was unable to maintain the left to right sequential ordering on the Picture Arrangement subtest, a test which requires the subject to arrange a series of pictures into a meaningful sequence, like a comic strip. He varied among right to left, left to right, and top to bottom ordering, suggesting that he has difficulty establishing and maintaining set for spatial sequencing. This type of problem is often seen in individuals with right anterior cerebral dysfunction.

Mr. Sample's performance on the WISC-R Mazes was also markedly deficient. While he had no difficulty with the early simple mazes, as they became increasingly complex, he became completely unable to trace the mazes without multiple errors. Even when he could see that his tracings were leading toward an error, he was unable to modify the course he had chosen. These results, together with the Picture Arrangement findings, suggest that the planning and sequencing deficits seen here and elsewhere are pervasive and not limited to complex motor movements.

Mr. Sample was unable to complete the Wisconsin Card Sorting Test. This task requires the subject to sort cards with figures on them according to a single dimension of the cards. The cards vary along the dimensions of type, color, and number of figures. The subject is not told which dimension on which to sort the card; he is only told whether he is correct or incorrect after he sorts each card. Mr. Sample initially sorted the cards by color, but was unable to maintain that set when cards matched by both type and number of figures, but not color. When the task was explained to him, and he was directed to put only cards of the same color into groups, Mr. Sample's performance improved. When he was directed to shift to sorting by type of figure, Mr. Sample made several perseverative sorts by color. Mr. Sample was also unable to complete the Trail Making Test Part B, which requires the subject to connect the numbers *1* through *13* and the letters *A* through *L* in order in an alternating sequence, first a letter, then a number. Mr. Sample required several trials before he could understand the task, and could not progress beyond the letter *C* without errors. Moreover, once his errors were pointed out to him, Mr. Sample was unable to proceed. These results suggest that Mr. Sample has significant deficits in set formation, maintenance, and shifting, and has difficulty altering his behavior to meet situational demands. Findings are consistent with marked frontal lobe dysfunction.

When asked to sign the months of the year backwards, Mr. Sample became confused, twice reversing to a forward sequence. This behavior suggest that Mr. Sample is easily pulled toward the more overlearned set and has difficulty reordering information once it has been learned—a finding typically seen in frontal lobe damaged individuals.

Memory functions. Mr. Sample was given four signs to remember (store, dog, black, train). On immediate recall, he remembered all without error. After a 15 minute delay, he could remember only one sign using free recall (i.e., with no cues or hints). With category cues, he recalled the other three. These results strongly suggest that Mr. Sample has intact immediate recall and intact ability to form and retain new memories. However, he has marked problems in retrieving the stored memories when he is required to organize a search strategy on his own. When the examiner provides a search strategy or organizing principle, he can successfully retrieve the newly learned data. This pattern of memory performance is most often encountered in people who have brain dysfunction which compromises the functioning of the frontal lobes.

Performance on the Benton Visual Retention Test, which requires that the subject draw replicas of geometric figures, contributed little to an understanding of Mr. Sample's memory problems. His severe spatial constructional difficulties involving rotation and loss of gestalt of the figures confounded performance on this task.

Personality features. Personality measures were not particularly remarkable. Mr. Sample appeared to have adequate defenses and sufficient energy to maintain them. Reality testing was appropriate, and there was no bizarre or otherwise remarkable content features in his responses. On the other hand, Mr. Sample was restricted and immature in his ability to evaluate social and emotional situations. He perceived situations almost entirely in terms of whether they were pleasant or unpleasant, and dangerous or benign. The subtlety and richness of human emotion did not seem to have much salience for Mr. Sample.

With respect to Mr. Doe's concern that Mr. Sample may be depressed over his physical damage and loss of functioning in his left hand, such does not appear to be the case. Rather, Mr. Sample exhibited behavior typical of an organic personality syndrome: He is generally apathetic, mildly euphoric, easily irritated, impulsive, and emotionally labile. It is doubtful that he fully appreciates the impact of his injury on his ability to function. He is more often responsive to the immediate inconvenience presented by his disabled nondominant hand.

Themes of importance to Mr. Sample involved dependency, comfort, and caretaking. He feels entitled to be cared for and becomes angry when others do not meet his needs. These feelings are not tempered by an internalized sense of social propriety or by ability to take an impersonal view of his environment. When Mr. Sample feels he has been slighted, or that his needs have not been met, his control decays and he displays inappropriately childlike tantrum behavior. At the same time, his behavior does not become disorganized, nor does he lose reality testing.

Summary Conclusions and Diagnostic Impression

1. Mr. Sample is presently functioning in the low average range of intelligence. His current functioning is significantly below that he displayed in the past (average IQ in 1967), suggesting the possibility of deteriorating neurologic status. He manifested cognitive impairments in almost every area of functioning assessed. Mr. Sample displayed mild to moderate deficits in ability to organize, plan, and execute tasks in all modalities, suggesting deficits in executive control over his behavior. Cognitive flexibility was markedly impaired. Mr. Sample demonstrated marked visual-spatial constructional deficits with perceptual rotation and fragmentation of designs. Memory deficits were noted in retrieval (not storage) of information following delay. Motor programming of complex sequential and alternating movement was impaired bilaterally. Simple motor control was markedly impaired for the left hand, probably as a result of his work injury. Mr. Sample displayed no evidence of depression or of a psychotic disorder. Rather, he is behaviorally dyscontrolled (i.e., impulsive, labile, and irritable), apathetic, and mildly euphoric.

2. Test findings are consistent with the presence of brain pathology. The pattern of results indicates significant dysfunction of the frontal lobes with dysfunction extending to the more posterior portions of the right cerebral hemisphere. Given the client's history of focal as well as grand mal seizures, and the CT scan findings from 1977, it is not surprising that neuropsychological testing indicates a similar localization of brain dysfunction. This lesion appears to be a long-standing residual of meningitis suffered in infancy and does not appear to involve a progressive disease process.

The overall decline in cognitive functioning since 1967 represents a clear deterioration that might be suggestive of a progressive dementing disorder. However, such slowly deteriorating patterns are also noted in people who suffer from poorly controlled seizure disorders.

3. Personality testing does not support diagnosis of a depressive or psychotic disorder. Rather, findings are very consistent with personality dysfunction noted in frontal lobe damaged individuals.

4. *DSM-III Diagnosis:*

Axis I: 310.10 Organic Personality Syndrome
Axis II: V71.09 No Diagnosis on Axis II
Axis III: 389.10 Sensorineural Hearing Loss, Unspecified
Axis IV: Severity of Psychosocial Stressors: 5—Severe

Axis V: Highest level of Adaptive Functioning
Past Year: 6—Very Poor

Recommendations

1. Mr. Sample is significantly impaired in his intellectual, social, academic, and personality functioning. These impairments all appear related to his brain dysfunction—not only to his significant right frontal lobe lesion, but to more diffuse dysfunction as well. Therefore, these deficits will be difficult to intrude upon and fairly unamenable to remediation.

2. More appropriate than remediation efforts would be an environmental approach. Mr. Sample can best maintain behavioral control in a highly structured environment where his behavior is monitored and guided so that he does not present a danger to himself or others. He is unable, and should not be expected, to maintain consistently appropriate behavior. Moreover, his judgment and memory are also impaired, and he will need continuing assistance in complying with his seizure medication regimen and in social interaction. While institutional care is probably not necessary at this time, a less restrictive, but highly supportive, structured, and involving group home may be necessary for Mr. Sample to function optimally. He cannot adequately function independently.

3. Mr. Sample is not a good prospect for intensive vocational rehabilitation. His vocational performance and skill level will continue to be variable and unreliable, despite training. More appropriate would be training and placement in low skill, simple, and repetitive work which is closely supervised. Mr. Sample's difficulty with maintaining appropriate social interaction will be troublesome in this regard. Most important is that Mr. Sample not be placed in employment where his work performance can present a potential danger to himself or others. Reduced cognitive functioning, lack of planning ability, and poor judgment make Mr. Sample an inappropriate candidate for all but the least dangerous jobs.

4. It is unclear whether Mr. Sample's present lower IQ represents a deteriorating picture. Although his currently measured level of cognitive functioning shows significant decrements from earlier measures, it is not possible to rule out motivational factors as governing the current results. Mr. Sample should be periodically reassessed in order to chart the course of any dementing illness that may be present. A two year schedule would be appropriate unless Mr. Sample displayed some sudden behavior change or rapid decrement in cognitive functioning. Such an event would indicate the need for immediate reassessment.

References

Benton, A. L., Hamsher, K., Varney, N. S., & Spreen, O. (1983). *Contributions to neuropsychological assessment: A clinical manual.* New York: Oxford University Press.

Chiarello, C., Knight, R., & Mandel, M. (1982). Aphasia in a prelingually deaf woman. *Brain, 105,* 29–51.

DeJong, G., & Lifchez, R. (1983). Physical disability and public policy. *Scientific American, 248,* 40–49.

Golden, C. J., Hammeke, T. A., & Purisch, A. D. (1980). *The Luria-Nebraska Neurological Battery manual.* Los Angeles: Western Psychological Service.

Goldstein, K., & Scheerer, M. (1941). Abstract and concrete behavior: An experimental study with special tests. *Psychology Monographs, 53*(2, Whole No. 239).

Goodglass, H., & Kaplan, E. (1979). Assessment of cognitive deficit in the brain injured patient. In M. S. Gazzaniga (Ed.), *Handbook of behavioral neurobiology* (Vol. 2, pp. 3–22). New York: Plenum Press.

Heaton, R. K., & Pendleton, M. G. (1981). Use of neuropsychological tests to predict adult patients' everyday functioning. *Journal of Consulting and Clinical Psychology, 49,* 807–821.

Isselbacher, K. J., Adams, R. D., Braunwald, E., Petersdorf, R. G., & Wilson, J. D. (1980). *Harrison's principles of internal medicine,* (9th ed.). New York: McGraw-Hill.

Lezak, M. (1983). *Neuropsychological assessment* (2nd ed.). New York: Oxford University Press.

Manning, A. A., Goble, W., Markham, R., LaBreche, T. (1977). Lateral cerebral differences in the deaf in response to linguistic and nonlinguistic stimuli. *Brain and Language, 4,* 309–321.

McKeever, W. F., Hoemann, H. W., Florian, V. A., & VanDeventer, A. D. (1976). Evidence of minimal cerebral asymmetries for processing of English words and American Sign Language stimuli in the congenitally deaf. *Neuropsychologia, 14,* 413–423.

Poizner, H., Battison, R., & Lane, H. (1979). Cerebral asymmetry for American Sign Language: The effects of moving stimuli. *Brain and Language, 7,* 351–362.

Poizner, H., & Lane, H. (1979). Cerebral asymmetry in the perception of American Sign Language. *Brain and Language, 7,* 210–226.

Reitan, R. M., & Davison, L. A. (1974). *Clinical neuropsychology: Current status and applications.* New York: John Wiley & Sons.

Schlesinger, H. S., & Meadow, K. P. (1972). *Sound and sign: Childhood deafness and mental health.* Berkeley: University of California Press.

Strub, R. L., & Black, F. W. (1981). *Organic brain syndromes.* Philadelphia: F. A. Davis Company.

Vernon, M. (1968). Current etiological factors in deafness. *American Annals of the Deaf, 113,* 1–12.

Wilson, J. J., Rapin, I., Wilson, B. C., & Van Denburg, V. (1975). Neuropsychologic function of children with severe hearing impairment. *Journal of Speech and Hearing Research, 18,* 634–652.

CHAPTER VI

Forensic Psychological Assessment

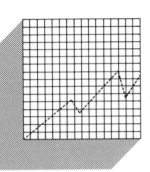

Larry G. Stewart
David A. Pritchard

Introduction

Rehabilitation and special education programs represent State/Federal/Local partnerships that are governed by a large number of statutes and regulations. The provision of services frequently entails collaboration and cooperation among many human service programs, each one having its own governing statutes and regulations. As a consequence, the work of the rehabilitation caseworker and counselor has extensive legal ramifications. These include agency regulations for the provision of various services, professional practices, and a host of other areas.

In addition to general and specific statutory and regulatory provisions that the counselor must work with on a daily basis, agency clients frequently bring specific conditions that have legal implications for the client and for the counselor and his/her agency. The Social Security recipient who has been referred to Vocational Rehabilitation for evaluation and possibly retraining, for example, brings specific legal requirements to the counselor which are defined by statutes and regulations. Other cases such as Workmen's Compensation, job discrimination, housing discrimination, civil commitment proceedings, and unfair labor practices may also become complicating factors in the rehabilitation process. Professional malpractice and illegal discrimination are growing areas of concern for counselors as well as other providers of human services. And, a number of clients come to rehabilitation programs with

a past record or current involvement with the criminal justice system, and this often has important implications for rehabilitation planning.

Recent years have seen the increasing participation of psychologists and psychiatrists in cases which involve legal issues, and from this the specialities of *forensic psychology* and *forensic psychiatry* have developed. These two specialities are concerned with the application of knowledge from the behavioral sciences in specific legal situations. As with other forensic fields, forensic psychiatry and forensic psychology attempt to provide assistance to legal decision-makers in complex cases where the evidence is not readily determined. Many of these cases involve clients in rehabilitation, education, and clinical programs.

The purpose of this chapter is to introduce the forensic psychological evaluation. The chapter attempts to define forensic psychology, the nature and scope of the forensic psychological evaluation are presented, and special issues in the forensic assessment of deaf persons are discussed. A sample forensic psychological evaluation concludes the chapter.

Forensic Psychology

Forensic psychology is a highly specialized field within the discipline of psychology which concentrates upon the use of psychological knowledge in answering specific legal questions. The forensic psychologist gathers information relevant to legal questions and interprets that information in a manner which is useful to legal factfinders (judge, jury, referee, mediator, etc.). Unlike other applied psychological specialties, forensic psychology is not aimed primarily at the treatment of needy persons and does not focus specifically on the general welfare of its clients. Rather, forensic psychology is concerned with objectively assisting a legal factfinder to make a legal decision—sometimes regardless of the consequences of the decision to the client. These decisions occur within municipal, state and federal court systems; in civil, criminal, and administrative law; and in juvenile delinquency/youthful offender courts (Rieber and Vetter, 1978). Forensic psychologists are called upon to participate in the legal system in a variety of roles (Monahan, 1980; Golbert, 1984), including conducting evaluations, submitting written evaluation findings, providing case consultation, serving as expert witness in court trials and hearings, in jury selection, and in victim evaluation.

Forensic psychology is concerned with knowledge from two highly complex and dynamic fields—psychology and the law. Many of the terms shared by both the law and psychology—such as insanity and incompetency, for example—are defined differently by each speciality. The forensic psychologist must interpret psychological findings in a manner consistent with the specific legal questions of the case at hand. Table 1 presents a listing of the legal questions frequently posed to forensic psychologists, along with the decisions that must be made in the legal setting. The examiner uses results from the psychological evaluation to arrive at an answer for each legal issue, and substantiates each answer with specific psychological knowledge and methods.

State of Nature. In any legal dispute, the factfinder is guided by statutes, administrative rules, constitutional provisions, and rulings in other cases (case law) to reach a decision in the instant (present) case. The relevant law in a case can be said to define a "state of nature" for positive action or a "state of nature" for negative action. For example, in an administrative law hearing involving a Workman's Compensation case the positive state of nature would justify a verdict of eligible (for compensation benefits) while a negative state of nature would justify a verdict of not eligible. In a criminal case, the positive state of nature would justify a verdict of guilty whereas the negative state of nature would justify a verdict of not guilty. The job of the legal fact-finder is to decide whether the defendant is in the positive state of nature or the negative state of nature.

The positive and negative states in each case are defined by applicable laws, statutes, and regulations. When a forensic psychologist is asked to assist a factfinder in reaching a legal decision, the forensic evaluation is designed to collect information relevant to the question of which state of nature best characterizes the client. In each case, the psychologist must understand the relevant states of nature as defined by applicable law. For example, in a personal injury case involving psychological harm, the forensic psychologist must understand what the law considers to be "an actionable psychological injury" and "an inactionable psychological injury". In a question of personal competency to make a contract, the forensic psychologist must understand the state of nature defined as "competent" by law and the state of nature defined as "incompetent" by law. In a Social Security disability determination case, the psychologist must understand how the law defines eligible and ineligible. Once the legal basis for resolving the dispute is understood, the psychologist can collect information relevant to the applicable states of nature.

Deciding what information is relevant to the disputed states of nature in a given case requires that the psychologist translate the *legal* descriptions of the applicable states of nature into *psychological* descriptions of the applicable states of nature. This translation requires a thorough understanding of both relevant law and relevant psychological knowledge. In some cases the translation is easily accomplished because the law is fairly specific and the psychological knowledge required in the case is also fairly specific. For example, the state of being eligible for Social Security disability income requires the presence of a disability which results in the ". . . inability to engage in *any* substantial gainful employment by reason of any medically determinable physical or mental impairment which can be expected to result in death or has lasted or can be expected to last for a continuous period of not less than 12 months . . ." (Social Security Administration, 1973, p. 3). Under this regulation, the psychological examiner needs to determine, first, whether the client has a mental disorder and, second, whether this disorder does or does not constitute a disability as defined by regulation. This determination is relatively straightforward. However, in other cases the translation of law into psychology is more difficult. For example, in deciding a child custody dispute, the fact-finder is to consider "the best interests of the child". It is often very difficult to define the best interests of the child since there are complex questions such as how, when, where, and by whom can the child's needs best be met. In such cases, there is considerable

Table 1

Legal Questions and Related States of Nature in Forensic Psychological Evaluation

Legal Issue	Positive State of Nature	Negative State of nature
1. *Professional Malpractice*	Negligent	Not negligent
	Psychologically injured	Not psychologically injured
2. *Personal Injury*	Psychologically injured	Not psychologically injured
3. *Personal Competency*		
a. To stand trial	Competent	Incompetent
b. To make a will	Competent	Incompetent
c. To marry	Competent	Incompetent
d. To make a contract	Competent	Incompetent
e. To manage one's affairs	Competent	Incompetent
f. To be responsible for a crime	Competent	Incompetent
g. To live outside a mental institution	Competent	Incompetent
h. To be a trial witness	Competent	Incompetent
i. To assert a timely claim	Competent	Incompetent
4. *Illegal Discrimination*		
a. Test bias	Biased	Unbiased
b. Selection or placement inequity	Discriminatory	Nondiscriminatory
5. *Child Abuse/Neglect*	Abusive	Nonabusive
	Neglectful	Nonneglectful
6. *Child Custody/ Visitation*	Custody	No custody
	Visitation	Nonvisitation
7. *Divorce/Annulment/ Separation*		
a. Insanity	Insane	Sane
b. Impotence	Impotency	Potency
c. Mental cruelty	Cruelty	No cruelty
d. Habitual intoxication/drug addiction	Habitual addiction	No habitual addiction
8. *Criminal Sentencing*		
a. Recidivism	Recidivism likely	Recidivism not likely
b. Mitigating/ aggravating circumstances	Mitigating	Aggravating
9. *Legal Procedure*		
a. Conviction-proneness of death-qualified juries	Conviction-prone	Not conviction-prone
b. Effect of jury size on verdicts	Effect	No effect

Legal Questions and Related States of Nature in Forensic Psychological Evaluation

Legal Issue	Positive State of Nature	Negative State of nature
10. *Evidence*		
a. Voluntariness of confession	Voluntary	Not voluntary
b. Credibility of eyewitness testimony	Credible	Not credible
c. Bias in person identification procedures (i.e., lineups, mug shots)	Bias	Not bias
11. *Administrative Law*		
a. Social Security disability	Eligible	Not eligible
b. Workman's Compensatioin	Eligible	Not eligible
c. Vocational Rehabilitation	Eligible	Not eligible
d. Parole release	Paroleable	Not paroleable

ambiguity in translating legal concepts into psychological concepts.

Examiner Qualifications. Forensic psychologists who are professionally prepared for their functions have received specialized preparation either during their doctoral studies or afterward. Some have degrees in both law and psychology. However, almost all practicing psychologists find themselves at one time or another involved in cases requiring some knowledge of specific laws. The difference between the forensic psychologist and other psychologists is that the former has received intensive training in applying psychological concepts to the legal area. Whenever the human services worker reviews a forensic psychological report, or needs to order one for his/her client, consideration must be given to the qualifications of the examiner. In preparing to make a referral, a discussion of the purpose of the evaluation with the prospective examiner will assist in determining whether the latter will be able to answer the legal questions of the case.

The involvement of psychologists and psychiatrists in legal proceedings as forensic experts is often subject to heated controversy and, at times, criticism. The methods and procedures upon which these behavioral scientists base their judgments are frequently attacked, with special criticism directed toward the reliability and validity of psychological tests (Ziskin, 1970). However, qualified psychologists have been recognized as capable of rendering expert testimony on mental disorders in court since *Jenkins v. United States* (1962).

Whether the legal states of nature are clear or ambiguous, the usefulness of a forensic evaluation to a legal fact-finder is determined by the clarity with which the forensic psychologist communicates the basis for his legal opinion. It is useless for the forensic examiner to summarily conclude that a client is ineligible for SSDI or Workman's Compensation, or is or is not competent to manage his own affairs, without also presenting to the fact-finder the specific reasons for the reported state of nature. A summary judgment without substantiating details is essentially an attempt to substitute the psychologist's judgment for the fact-finder's judgment. In all legal disputes, the ultimate resolution is always made by the fact-finder. The forensic expert is simply a consultant to the fact-finder and the value of the consultant rests solely in an ability to explain clearly and factually why a client is in one legal state of nature and not the other. Once the consultant has done this, the fact-finder is able to take the consultant's judgment into consideration along with all other case information and reach an independent conclusion regarding the legal dispute. Thus, the fact-finder can either accept the consultant's opinion or reject it, in whole or in part.

Nature and Scope of the Forensic Psychological Evaluation

Referral. A forensic consultation begins with a referral from some party to a legal dispute or from

74

a service program. The referring person may be aligned with the client (e.g., defense counsel), opposed to the client (e.g. prosecuting counsel), or neutral (e.g., court or service agency). The first step in the consultation process is to clarify the applicable states of nature. What is the dispute (or issue) about? How does the applicable law or regulation define the states of nature at issue in the case? Through communication with the referring party, the specific issues to be investigated in the forensic evaluation are clarified. In this process, too, questions which are not at issue but which are relevant to the main issues are also clarified. This is crucial because the forensic evaluation is designed to focus only on the relevant issues while questions not at issue are excluded. Because of this, the forensic evaluation should never be used as the sole basis for treatment planning or clinical intervention. The forensic evaluation is not designed nor is it intended to be broad, and it is not intended to include all the areas that are in most psychological evaluations. However, the forensic evaluation goes into great depth in the area of the legal dispute.

PreEvaluation Preparation. After the relevant legal states of nature are defined, the forensic psychologist must translate these legal categories into psychological terms. What are the psychological parameters present in a biased test? What psychologial criteria separate the person whose mental disorder precludes employment from the person whose mental disorder does not preclude employment? There are no standardized procedures for making these and other translations. Reasoning by induction and deduction is required. The forensic psychologist is aware of the many personality variables which have been reported through psychological research; he/she is aware of research on perception, memory, cognitive functioning, and emotion; and, he/she is aware of research on dysfunctional human behavior which arises from mental disorders and other disabilities. Using all of this information selectively, the forensic psychologist must decide which variables and processes are relevant to the specific legal issues at hand. In selecting and in excluding psychological variables, the examiner must strive to be comprehensive yet economical. Inclusion of irrelevant variables lengthens the evaluation process and introduces information which is confusing to the legal fact-finder. Excluding relevant information results in depriving the fact-finder of knowledge which may be decisive in the case and may leave the examiner open to an indefensible professional opinion. In a Workman's Compensation dispute, for example, the issue is whether a job-related accident produced a disabling psychological or neuropsychological injury. In this case, it is relevant to collect information on the existence of any psychological and/or neuropsychological disorders, their time of onset and duration (pre- and postaccident), the causal connections between the disabling condition and the time of onset, and the degree of disability caused by the injury. It would be irrelevant to collect information on ability to stand trial or competency to manage one's own money.

The Forensic Examination. Once the examiner has identified the types of information needed to provide an opinion on the legal issues raised, a decision must then be made regarding the means for obtaining this information.

1. *Background, Collateral Information.* While the evaluation itself is crucial, other information is almost always required. Reports from and interviews with third parties, police reports, prior examination and evaluation reports, and work performance reports are examples of other sources the examiner often must rely upon. Such information is useful for many purposes, including assessing the client's credibility, identifying malingering, and determining dangerousness, for example.

2. *The Examination.* The psychological evaluation of a client in a forensic assessment proceeds much in the same manner as for a general psychological evaluation (see Chapters II and III). Tests of intelligence, abilities, personality, psychopathology, and neuropsychological functioning are administered, scored, and interpreted.

a. *Malingering and Dissembling.* One major difference between a forensic evaluation and a general psychological evaluation is that the former is far more attentive to the possibility of malingering and dissembling. Legal situations frequently prompt the involved individual to pretend to be ill or otherwise incapacitated in order to avoid work or responsibility, or, on the other hand, to attempt to hide real problems behind a facade of wellness. During the evaluation, the *malingering client* consciously attempts to convince the examiner of the presence of problems (feigning depression, amnesia, etc.), while the *dissembling client* attempts to mask problems and appear normal or well in order to escape negative consequences. In most legal disputes the client has much to gain (such as monetary gain, benefits, freedom) from persuading the examiner that a certain state of nature exists. In other situations, the client will gain from appearing better adjusted than he is (for example, a prisoner applying for parole or a VR client who wishes to qualify for a training program when actually he desires only the support funds—such as SSDI—that accompany training). There are varied means for identifying malingering and dissembling.

Inconsistencies among various test scores as well as background information, for instance, provide clues to the presence or absence of these traits. However, it is the examiner's ability to synthesize and accurately interpret all of the available evaluation information that most often leads to accurate findings.

b. *Focus of Examination.* Another important difference between the general psychological evaluation and the forensic psychological evaluation is to be found in the narrow focus of the latter. The forensic examination is not a comprehensive evaluation; rather, it focuses upon identifying information relevant to the specific legal issues in the instant case. Less attention is given to considerations regarding treatment or remediation of identified client problems except when these are among the relevant case issues.

Analyzing and Interpreting Evaluation Findings. Following the collection of relevant information in the instant case, the forensic psychologist evaluates this information for its *reliability, consistency,* and *probative value. Reliability* refers to the credibility of the obtained information; *consistency* refers to the extent to which the information obtained from various sources reinforces an interpretation; and, *probative value* is the degree to which the information points toward one state of nature over the other. In a child abuse case, for example, a reliable eyewitness' account of having observed physical abuse has more probative value than a psychological test result which was in the normal range. The forensic psychologist weighs all of the information and, where feasible, decides whether the information is more consistent with one state of nature than the other. In reaching this professional opinion, the forensic psychologist does not have to exclude all reasonable doubt, nor does the evidence have to clearly and convincingly point to one state of nature to the exclusion of other states of nature. Rather, the forensic psychologist must have the professional opinion—or "professional certainty"—that the evidence supports one state of nature over another. In this case, "professional certainty" is usually translated to mean "more likely than not". Stated another way, if the forensic psychologist believes that it is more likely than not that a given state of nature exists, then a professional opinion to this effect may be rendered. However, if the examiner is unable to make such a statement, then no opinion can be rendered.

The Report. When a professional opinion can be rendered in a case, the forensic psychologist is usually, but not always, asked to write and submit a report presenting the information obtained, describing how the information was obtained, presenting interpretations of the information, and stating the examiner's professional opinion concerning the state of nature. In writing the report, the examiner includes all relevant information on both sides - positive and negative - of the legal question; evaluates the information for its reliability, consistency, and probative value, and renders a professional opinion in terms which are understandable to the legal fact-finder. In cases where a professional opinion one way or another cannot be rendered, the reason(s) for this are usually specified in the report (e.g., uncooperativeness on the part of the client, unavailability of crucial information).

The Forensic Examiner as a Witness. A written report of a forensic psychological evaluation in some cases cannot be introduced as evidence unless the examiner is available as an expert witness. The reason for this is that cross-examination is sometimes essential in establishing the evidential value of the contents of the report. Thus, in order to assure both sides in a legal dispute an equal opportunity to argue their case, witnesses must be available for both examination and cross-examination. The forensic psychologist is frequently subpoenaed to testify regarding forensic evaluation contents, interpretations, findings, and professional opinions rendered. During expert witness proceedings, the questioning attorney may ask the forensic psychologist to describe the evaluation, to state the results, to render a professional opinion, and to state the bases for the opinion. On cross-examination, the questioning attorney usually attempts to show that some important information was omitted, that inappropriate or incorrect emphasis was placed on some information compared to other information, that the witness' opinion is incorrect or biased (or both!), that the procedures used to collect the information (especially tests) are unreliable and invalid, that authorities in the field of psychology disagree with the procedures or tests used, or that the witness does not understand the legal question at issue. This adversarial questioning is a regular feature of judicial proceedings, and serves to ensure that the fact-finder (judge, jury, mediator, etc.) has the opportunity to hear both sides to the dispute prior to making an independent decision.

Special Issues in the Forensic Psychological Evaluation with Deaf Persons

General Issues. Persons who are deaf or otherwise seriously hearing-impaired are subject to the same wide range of legal proceedings enumerated in this chapter for the general public (see Table 1).

However, hearing-impaired persons encounter special challenges in legal proceedings and sometimes pose unique problems to legal fact-finders due to communication-related barriers. Interpreters play a vital role in helping to overcome these communication barriers, and in recent years the judicial system has increasingly relied upon interpreters for deaf persons. Yet, important problems remain, including those of (a) unavailability of suitably qualified interpreters at the right time, in the right place; (b) the difficulty of interpreting legal terminology and concepts; (c) the relatively large proportion of deaf persons who have significant English language comprehension limitations; and (d) the unfamiliarity of legal proceedings participants—judges, juries, attorneys, witnesses—with deafness and interpreting issues.

There is a small but growing body of knowledge concerning deafness and the law (see, for example, Myers, 1964; National Center for Law and the Deaf, 1984). However, with few exceptions, the professional literature in the area of forensic psychology has given little attention to deaf persons. Exceptions include Vernon and Coley (1978), who, after analyzing the contents of the Miranda Warning (*Miranda v. Arizona*, 1966), concluded that 90 percent of prelingually deafened adults fall below the minimal reading comprehension level required for understanding the warning. In another article, Stewart (1985) presented the basic concepts of forensic psychology in relation to the needs of the adolescent deaf population, and recommended studies of forensic psychology and forensic psychiatry practices with the deaf population. Again, however, the field of forensic behavioral science has largely bypassed deaf children and adults as a special needs group up to the present time. Because of this, much needs to be learned concerning the forensic assessment of deaf persons.

Ironically, however, forensic assessments of deaf persons occur with regularity throughout the country. These are conducted by psychological examiners who have varying levels of expertise in the area of deafness and varying levels of expertise in forensic psychology. Most forensic psychologists have received no preparation to interview and test deaf individuals, and most psychologists who work with deaf people have received no preparation in the area of forensics. Specialists in the area of deafness such as Levine (1960, 1981), Moores (1982), Rainer and Altshuler (1967), Vernon (1967), and Vernon and Ottinger (1981) have presented convincing evidence of the need for special competencies on the part of psychological and psychiatric examiners in the evaluation of deaf persons. These special competencies are found in their application

in understanding client background information, in interviewing, in test selection and administration, in interpretation of test results, and in making appropriate diagnoses and recommendations. We see, essentially, the need for three bridges of understanding: the bridge between psychology and the individual, the bridge between psychology/the individual and the law, and, the bridge between psychology/the individual/the law and deafness.

Thus, the forensic psychologist who works with deaf persons must relate to not two but three complex and changing fields—psychology, the law, and deafness. A deficiency in preparation in any one of these fields on the part of the psychologist lessens the reliability, consistency, and probative value of any forensic evaluation report on a deaf individual. Interpreting, for the deaf person, helps to bring forensic psychological evaluation services closer to the deaf population, but it can never replace the forensic examiner who is fully prepared to directly serve deaf persons.

Special Issues. The forensic psychological evaluation with the deaf person is conducted in a manner similar to what has been described above for other clients. The same areas covered in the general psychological evaluation (see Chapters II and III) are a part of the forensic evaluation, and the same considerations applicable to evaluating deaf clients are germane to the forensic assessment. Appropriate review of client background factors and developmental history, current circumstances, and elements relevant to the legal issues at hand are contingent upon examiner-client communication variables and examiner understanding of the implications of such factors as age at onset of deafness, family circumstances, educational experiences, language development, and multiple disabilities. Assessing the client's self-perceptions and understanding of his/her legal situation is contingent upon the examiner's interviewing expertise, which includes skill in following up on statements made by the client. Test administration issues remain those of appropriate test selection, appropriate test administration, and appropriate interpretation of test results.

Assessing such variables as malingering and dissembling is as much an art as a science. The examiner's ability to do this with a deaf client centers around his/her expertise in communicating with the client, all other factors (expertise as a psychologist, knowledge of symptoms of malingering and dissembling, etc.) being equal. This is based partly on the fact that many of the tools available to the forensic examiner with hearing individuals are ruled out with the large number of deaf persons who have significant English language deficiencies.

In the authors' experience, *by far the greatest issue in the forensic assessment of deaf clients is the attitude on the part of many examiners that they are able to evaluate deaf persons adequately without special preparation*. In a recent court case which is all too typical, the authors witnessed a psychiatrist present testimony on a multiply handicapped, language-impaired deaf adult male charged with a major crime. The examining psychiatrist was unable to use sign language and had had no previous experience in examining deaf persons. Yet, the psychiatrist confidently provided a report which contained specific diagnostic findings which included (a) no mental disorder, (b) able to stand trial (able to understand the nature of the charges against him and able to assist his lawyer in his own defense), and (c) malingering. When asked for the evidence which would support his findings and professional opinion, the psychiatrist specified two main sources of information: (a) the client's "confession" to the police at the scene of the alleged crime, and (b) the client's daily conduct in the security ward at the state hospital while living there over the period of the evaluation; specifically, the client was "able to do his daily janitorial duties in a responsible fashion, unlike most of the other clients there." This evidential basis for a professional opinion was found by the presiding judge to be unacceptable based on findings reported by the authors which were: (a) the client had reading ability below the fourth grade level, and could not understand most of the words in the Miranda warning the police read to him at the time of his arrest; (b) the client did not understand the nature of the legal proceedings being taken against him, and was in no position to assist his counsel in his own defense (even through the use of an interpreter who used American Sign Language); (c) the client's measured IQ was in the low normal range, his education had been mediocre, and he had spent many years in jail on other offenses. His level of insight was such that it was judged impossible for him to malinger in the fashion cited by the psychiatrist; and (d) a personality disorder was evident, with features of Atypical Personality Disorder, DSM III code 301.89 (American Psychiatric Association, 1980).

In judicial proceedings, it is not at all uncommon for two forensic examiners to report contradictory findings on the same individual. However, the ability of an examiner to qualify as an expert witness with the court should certainly, in the case of deaf clients who do not possess effective English language and/or oral communication skills, include consideration of qualifications to evaluate a deaf person. At this time, however, it appears that it is up to the opposing counsel to bring out during cross-examination any deficiencies in the forensic examiner's qualifications to evaluate a deaf person. Questions that should be asked in establishing qualifications for evaluating a deaf person should include, at least, the following:

1. Ability of the examiner to use sign language (how long used, what form, at what level of expertise?;
2. If an interpreter was used, what was the interpreter's level of certification, what has been the examiner's experience in using interpreters (how many times used, in what circumstances, over how many years, what selection criteria were used in selecting the interpreter in the instant case, how did the examiner evaluate the effectiveness of communication through interpreting); what is the name of the national interpreter's organization;
3. What type of training has the examiner received in evaluating deaf persons, where obtained, dates of training, name(s) of training supervisor(s);
4. Number of deaf individuals evaluated during the examiner's professional career and how many were evaluated for forensic purposes;
5. Titles of current authoritative textbooks, and names of authors, in the area of psychological evaluation of deaf persons;
6. Names of tests typically used in the evaluation of deaf persons for intelligence, academic achievement, personality, and neuropsychological screening;
7. What are the major effects of prelingual deafness on human development;
8. Names of authorities in the area of forensic assessment of deaf individuals.

The examiner's answers to these questions will provide a more objective basis for the fact-finder in his/her weighting of the probative value of the examiner's professional opinion in the case of a deaf individual.

Sample Forensic Psychological Evaluation Report

As Table 1 shows, there are many different types of legal issues that may lead to a forensic psychological evaluation. These issues are so wide ranging that it is not possible to provide the reader with a representative evaluation report. Each legal issue has its own states of nature, and the evaluation is always focused to provide answers to the specific issues in the instant case. However, the illustrative report presented below will serve the purpose of demonstrating the legal focus of a forensic psychological evaluation, or how the psychological evaluation findings are related to specific legal issues with a deaf individual. As with other sample reports, the one that follows is fictitious but based on several actual evaluations.

CONFIDENTIAL: FOR USE BY COURT ONLY
Report of Psychological Evaluation

NAME OF CLIENT:	PUBLIC, John Q.
HOME ADDRESS:	9876 N. West Circle, Apt. 1
	Downtown, Upstate 01234
BIRTHDATE:	_____
CURRENT AGE:	23 years
EXAMINATION DATES:	_____ and _____
REFERRED BY:	The Superior Court of Midcounty, Upstate, Criminal Division, and Deputy Public Defender, Midcounty Public Defender's Office
EXAMINER:	_____

I. **Referral Information**. JOHN Q. PUBLIC is currently in the Midcounty Jail as a result of alleged violation of Section _____ Penal Code, and has been referred to me for an examination under Section _ Evidence Code. A professional opinion has been requested from me regarding several specific legal issues which will be detailed in Section III below. Deputy Public Defender _____, Midcounty Public Defender's Office, contacted me to arrange for this examination through an order from the Honorable _____, Judge of the Superior Court of Midcounty dated _____. The Deputy Public Defender provided me with a copy of several documents related to the case, which will be cited in Section VII below.

II. **Charges Against Defendant**. According to Court documents, the defendant was arrested at 7:05 p.m. on _____, after being found inside the _____ Quick Market, _____ East North Street, Downtown, Upstate, after closing hours. The police report for the alleged violation indicated that the defendant had broken a glass in the rear door of the market, unlocked the door, and entered, and was attempting to take 8 boxes of cigars. The police entered at that point and arrested the defendant. Subsequently, the defendant was jailed on a charge of burglary (_____ P.C.). The Crime Report for the violation (# _____), City of Downtown Police Department, prepared by Officers _____ and _____, states: "On (date) at approximately 1850 hrs. Downtown Officers received a R/B of a (burglary) in progress. Prior to any Officers arriving at the scene dispatch had confirmed that the R/P had observed a subject entering through the rear window of the location. Dispatch further related that the subject was entering a cash register store and that he was still inside of the location. Upon the arrival of Officers, Officer _____ and Officer _____ responded to the front of U/S, Officer _____ and Officer _____ responded to the rear of the location. Officers observed the rear window to the location at _____ East North Street to be broken, with a hole approximately 9" long and approximately 7" wide. Officers further observed the latch to the window to be ajar. At this time Officer _____ looked in through the opening at which time he related to the other Officers that he observed a trash can propped up against the door barracading the rear door shut. Officers then heard the sound of footsteps and the sound of somebody bumping into miscellaneous items coming from within the location. Officers believing that the suspect was still inside the location then forcibly gained entrance through the rear door. Upon Officers checking the location, U/S and Officer _____ observed a subject later identified as Public, John Q. in a crouched position at the end of a deli counter. The subject was kneeling in an apparent attempt to hide from Officers at the north end of the counter. U/S then apprehended the suspect and placed him under arrest for _____ P.C. Officers then checked the interior of the location for possibly other outstanding suspects with negative results. Officers observed the floor directly behind the counter where the suspect was kneeling to have 8 miscellaneous brands of cigar boxes scattered around the floor. The cigars were later recovered by Officer _____ and booked into evidence by Officer _____ . . . during the booking search, Officer _____ found a small pocket screwdriver in suspect Public's right front pocket . . . On _____ at 0900 hours R/P responded to station to claim cigars. Photo was taken as evidence and R/P and retained as evidence. R/P related he was also missing $10–$15 in change from the cash register and $152.00 from a zippered cash bag beneath the counter."

III. **Purpose of Assessment**. As detailed in Judge _____ 's Court Order dated _____, the purposes of this evaluation were to examine the defendant and report my professional opinion in a written report to the Court and to the Public Defender's Office regarding (1) the defendant's sanity/insanity: (2) the defendant's dangerousness (dangerous/not dangerous), (3) competency to stand trial (competent/incompetent), (4) mental capacity to be responsible for a crime (mental capacity to form the specific intent/lack of mental capacity to form the specific intent), and (5) nature of possible treatment for defendant.

IV. **Location of Interviews/Testing**. My interviews and testing sessions with defendant John Q. Public were held in an interview room within the Midcounty Jail, Downtown, Upstate.

V. **Date, Time, Length of Interview, Testing Sessions**. Two interview/testing sessions were held with Mr. Public. One was on _____ beginning at 1:00 p.m. and ending at 4:30 p.m., and one was on _____ beginning at 8:00 a.m. and ending at 12:30 p.m. These sessions involved a total of 8 hours of testing and interviewing. Additionally, transportation time between the jail and my office on these two dates totaled 3 hours.

VI. **Psychological Tests Administered**. The defendant was administered the Wechsler Adult Intelligence Scale Revised (Performance Scale only), the Vocabulary Test of the WAIS-P Verbal Scale, the Bender Visual Motor Gestalt Test, the House-Tree-Person Test, portions of the QNST (Quick Neurological Screening Test) and Eisenson's "Examining for Aphasia" test. Also, several arithmetic problems were presented to screen defendant's basic skills in arithmetic.

VII. **Documents Reviewed**. One letter (2 pages) from Deputy Public Defender _____ dated _____ was reviewed in this case, along with an 8 page Booking and Property Record and Crime Report # _____ prepared by Officers _____ and _____, dated _____; _____ and Associates Reporter's Transcript of Preliminary Examination, County of Midcounty, State of Upstate, before Honorable _____, Judge, Division _____, Superior Court, dated _____; and, an order of Psychological Evaluation Appointment, Criminal Division, Midcounty Upstate Superior Court, dated _____, signed by Honorable ., Judge of Superior Court. Total time used in reading and studying these specific documents totaled approximately one hour over several separate days.

VIII. **Collateral Interviews**. No others were interviewed during the course of this evaluation. However, three brief consultants over the telephone were held with Deputy Public Defender _____ to clarify several aspects of Mr. Public's circumstances.

IX. **Notification of Rights**. The defendant was notified of his legal rights in this case (i.e., the right to refuse to answer any and all questions asked, the right to refuse to take any and all tests), and was informed of the purposes of the evaluation, the fact that evaluation findings would have to be reported to the Court and to the Public Defender's Office and might be used against him, and that I might be subpoenaed to present testimony in open Court concerning the evaluation. This explanation was presented in as elementary fashion as possible to Mr. Public, and he appeared to understand the basics of this explanation although it was my impression at the point the explanation was given that the defendant has a significant limitation in his ability to understand the full nature of the information he was given, as most others of this circumstances would (this is discussed further later in this report).

X. **Interview Behavior, Mental Status**.

1. *How Arranged, Delivered*. John Q. Public was brought by a jail guard to where I was waiting in the interviewing room within the Midcounty Jail, on both days of the two interviewing/testing sessions. All interviewing and testing took place in this room.

2. *General Appearance*. On both testing and interviewing days Mr. Public was observed to be quiet and compliant when brought to the examining room by the guard. He is a tall, gaunt, somewhat stooped young Caucasian male with dark blonde hair worn shoulder-length. He is light complexioned, with acne-scarred facial skin. He had a drooping moustache, but was otherwise clean-shaven. He appears to be about 6' tall and of good nourishment, weighing, he stated, 175 pounds. He was dressed in a jail jumpsuit which was slightly rumpled and lightly soiled in places. Dirty white tennis shoes were worn. His teeth were noted to be uneven in front and unbrushed, and his fingernails were noted to be soiled. Thus, grooming and personal hygiene were neglected. His gait was unremarkable and no overt signs of any physical abnormalities were present. Physical coordination seemed normal. Eye contact was minimal but appropriate to the circumstances. No unusual bodily movements were present. He sat slumped during most of the two sessions, and gave a general appearance of low energy level, shyness, and sombreness. His face was typically inanimated, and unless questioned he was silent. Mr. Public was reported prior to this evaluation to be deaf, to not have intelligible speech, and to rely upon written notes and sign language for communication purposes. His behavior during the evaluation was consistent with this report.

3. *Communication, Affect, Mood*. Mr. Public communicated with me in sign language, using no speech or lip movements. His sign language was primarily American Sign Language but with some

signed English, typical of deaf young adults in this part of the state and reflecting the signs used in the educational system he attended. He expresses himself readily in this mode, and was able to understand my questions fairly well once our level of understanding of one another was reached. He had difficulty with fingerspelling, often stumbling over the spelling of many words. My own use of fingerspelling had to be limited since he had difficulty understanding spelled words other than the most elementary ones. He stated that he could speak a little and read lips a little, but depends on sign language for good understanding. He has in the past used a hearing aid but did not use one at the time as he felt it doesn't help him.

Defendant's mood was cooperative, non-defensive, docile, quiet, slightly bored, polite, cautious, sober, serious, even, consistent. No anger, hostility, rudeness, arrogance, or passive aggression was noted. Very mild depression was noted, but this was appropriate to his situation. No anxiety was in evidence. Affect was somewhat controlled but not in a pathological fashion. No mood swings occurred. No autonomic hyperactivity (sweating, yawning, upset stomach, etc.) was in evidence. No inappropriate or incongruent thoughts were verbalized nor were any bizarre behaviors exhibited. No malingering or dissembling was evidenced.

4. *Sensorium/Intelligence*. Mr. Public was alert and attentive, exhibiting clearness of thoughts, without indications of clouded consciousness, drowsiness, or other indicators of loss of ego boundaries. His orientation to time, place, and person was excellent. He reported that he was in jail because he had been caught involved in stealing. His attention span was intact, good, sustained. His concentration was good. Immediate, short-term, and remote memory functions were normal within his circumstances. He was a good historical informant, able to furnish general information about himself, and he was limited only by communication and comprehension factors in furnishing details about his life. He does exhibit limitations in language use and understanding, and does exhibit deficits in his knowledge and understanding of his world; these, however, are judged to reflect, in part, his congenital deafness (which he reported; he does not know the cause of his deafness) and impoverished background. His ability to understand abstract concepts was limited due to English language factors. He knew no proverbs, could not respond to open-ended questions, and was able to reply only to concrete, specific, and simple questions. His fund of general knowledge was limited and relatively impoverished. On the WAIS-R Performance Scale, his intelligence was found to be in the average range

(IQ of 98, with all subscale scores even except for Picture Arrangement, where the scaled score was 6—one standard deviation below the mean). His test performance was unremarkable; however, his deficiency on Picture Arrangement suggests a weakness in the area of sequential planning and reasoning. Mr. Public had no education until the age of 10 years, then attended day school classes for the deaf until he dropped out at the age of 16. Hence, his education has been very limited. On the WAIS-R Verbal Scale's Vocabulary Test, Mr. Public obtained a raw score of 9 and a scaled score of 3, which is more than two standard deviations below the mean. This confirms the impression of severely limited English language skills. His arithmetic skills are also severely limited; on an informal screening procedure, he was able to successfully work only simple addition, subtraction, division, and multiplication problems at approximately the third–fourth grade level. He was unable to present reasoned ideas for his future, and I would place his judgment at a rather immature level, effective in simple situations but deficient in demanding or difficult situations. His stream of thought is simple and clear in nonstressful situations, but somewhat slowed and superficial.

5. *Abnormal Mental Trends*. No hallucinations or delusions were reported or implied. No mental or emotional conflicts were evidenced. Mr. Public stated he had never heard voices, did not think he had any special powers, had never had any unusual feelings, sensations, or experiences. No suspiciousness was noted, and no neurotic symptoms were present. Sexual abnormalities were denied. No temper difficulties were indicated. No suicidal thoughts were present, and defendant states he has never thought of killing himself or anyone else. Mr. Public does exhibit strong dependency features and a rather gullible predisposition.

6. *Insight*. Defendant understands why he is in jail and the charges against him. He seems normally aware of himself and his circumstances, at his level of maturity and judgment. He states that he was forced at knife-point to enter the store where he was caught stealing, by another Caucasian male, a stranger, who had walked up to him on the street, spoken to him, learned of his deafness, and then pulled a knife and forced him to follow him to the back of the store. This stranger, allegedly, had disappeared in the darkness shortly before the police had arrived. Mr. Public did not malinger or dissemble at any other point during this evaluation, and on this basis I would judge this account of being forced into the store to steal as more likely than not to be true.

7. *Personal Background*. Mr. Public is not now

married nor has he ever been. He states that he has a deaf girlfriend, age 26, but it is a casual relationship. He has dated since age 18, and hopes some day to marry and have a family. He is not now employed, and has never held a job in competitive employment. He lives with his mother and stepfather, Mr. and Mrs. _____, along with a brother, _____, age ____, and a sister, _____, age ____. They live in a four bedroom apartment in a lower-middle socioeconomic class part of the city. He is attending _____, an adult education program for deaf adults who have poor language and communication skills. He hopes to complete this program within one year and then take vocational training. He is not sure what job he would like in the future. He has never learned to drive and gets around the city via public transportation. He attended the _____ Day Classes for the Deaf in Downtown from the age of 10 until 16, then left due to lack of interest. Since then he has stayed at home until six months ago, when he started his adult education classes. His father died when he was eleven, for reasons unknown to him, and his mother remarried one year later. He states that his mother and stepfather are good to him and he has always felt comfortable with them and his siblings. He learned to sign at age 10, but his family members do not sign and communication within the home appears to be minimal for him. He watches TV, does chores such as dishwashing, cleaning his room, running errands, and sweeping the floor, and likes to spend time at _____, a neighborhood videogames arcade. His only source of monetary support is his family. He does not receive any government subsidy. His stepfather is employed as a construction laborer, his mother as a cook in a cafe. Mr. Public also likes to draw, read comics, and be with his family. He appears to have no peer friendships, does not attend social activities in the deaf community, and has no TTY or closed captioning decoder for TV.

8. *Life-Threatening Behavior.* When questioned, Mr. Public reported once having thrown a large rock at a neighbor who had been very rude and threatening to him, and this resulted in an arrest. This occurred when he was 18 years old. Aside from this, he could not cite any threatening behavior to others. He stated he had never gotten into a fight since school.

9. *Military History.* None. Mr. Public is disabled and exempt from military service.

10. *Criminal Legal History.* Mr. Public could not furnish dates, but he was in jail for a short time for the rock-throwing incident when he was 18, and was also jailed for "a week or two" when he was about 21 for having a radio in his possession which the police said was stolen. A casual friend gave it to him as a gift, Mr. Public states. The current instant offense is the third one for him.

11. *Substance Abuse History.* Mr. Public denies having ever used tobacco, alcohol, marijuana, or any other illegal substance.

12. *Sexual History.* Defendent appears naive in the area of sexual behavior. He denies having had any prior sexual experiences with women or men, and states he would like to have sex with a woman some day.

13. *Medical History.* Defendant states that his health is "O.K.". He has never had surgery, can remember no serious illnesses or accidents in the recent past.

XI. ***Psychological Test Results, Interpretations***. Mr. Public cooperated readily with this examiner and understood test directions without difficulty. He attended well to all test tasks and seemed to be comfortable and at ease. There were no distractions. Thus, the results are considered to be reliable and valid.

A. *Intelligence.* As stated earlier, Mr. Public scored in the normal range on the WAIS-R Performance Scale, with a relative weakness in the area of sequential planning and reasoning. Otherwise, his performance was within the normal range. The WAIS-R Verbal Scale was not used since the results would have been invalid due to his poor language skills.

B. *Visual Motor Coordination Skills.* On the Bender Visual Motor Gestalt Test, Mr. Public's drawings of the designs were within the average range. He was slightly careless, but otherwise his productions were accurate. The conclusion suggested is that his visual motor coordination skills are intact.

C. *Basic Academic Skills.* The results of the WAIS-R Verbal Scale Vocabulary Test indicate that Mr. Public has severely restricted English vocabulary skills. This is consistent with his congenital deafness and relatively poor educational background. His arithmetic skills are also restricted to approximately third–fourth grade level, computation-wise. Poor communication within the family structure also contributed to these deficiencies. His relative social isolation since age 16 is also viewed as a contributing factor. These results suggest that the defendant is seriously handicapped where English language and arithmetic are concerned.

D. *Personality.* On the House-Tree-Person Test, Mr. Public drew a neat, well-proportioned, and detailed house in freehand that would impress anyone. However, his tree drawing was done quickly and without detail. The human figure was drawn even more quickly and without much detail. Taken as a whole, the drawings suggest that this man relates primarily to his physical environment and has accurate perceptions in it, with good awareness, discrimination, and alertness. However, his attention and understanding of other people and social contexts is much lacking. He is shy with others and seems to have a poorly developed sense of self. He is somewhat passive and dependent in social and interpersonal relationships. Generally he is able to relate to his world with equinamity when he is not expected to participate actively, but when stress is present he will tend to become insecure and frustrated. He may be expected to express this frustration through withdrawal from the source of stress or, if this is not possible, mild to moderate behavioral expressions of frustration. In relations with others, he can be expected to be dependent and lacking in self assertiveness. He is concrete in his orientation, relating to activities that he can control (videogames, books, household chores, relations with close family members). He does not have an antisocial personality, and evidences no psychopathology. He is, however, very lonely and isolated, and this more than anything else may be said to explain his lack of social sophistication. "Immature personality" would best describe his current personality structure, marked by slight passive dependency.

E. *Neuropsychological Factors.* Utilizing the QNST (Quick Neurological Screening Test) for screening purposes, the following was ascertained. Olfactory, taste, and tactile senses are within normal limits. He has some hearing in his right ear, none in the left. He is able to walk with normal balance with eyes open. With eyes closed, he is unable to balance himself on one leg and leans, then begins to topple to one or another side. He is able to walk in a straight line with eyes open. When eyes are closed, he is unable to take even one step without toppling to the side. The direction of this topple is variable, sometimes to the left and sometimes to the right. There is no letter agnosia, no word agnosia, no sentence agnosia, no number agnosia. He is able to recognize the primary colors. He can read and understand very short, simple statements but has significant difficulty reading and comprehending sentences at and above third/fourth grade level. Eisenson's Examining for Aphasia procedures results indicate significant difficulties with verbal materials, and moderate receptive and expressive aphasia-like disturbance in written language functions and reading. Defendant spells words on fingers before attempting to write them down on paper. Summatively, these screening procedures indicate the defendant has impaired hearing, impaired vestibular (balancing) function, and central nervous system-based disturbance in the language function. These difficulties have important implications for educational and personal growth, for they present a serious communication deficiency and, hence, interpersonal interaction barriers.

F. *Understanding of Legal Issues, Proceedings, Assisting Counsel.* A discussion with Mr. Public at his level of understanding resulted in my impression that he understood his legal situation, was aware of possible consequences, understood the role of judge and jury, understood the job of his counsel, and understood generally how he would need to assist his counsel in his own defense. This discussion proceeded slowly, and it must be emphasized that Mr. Public's understanding is at a very rudimentary level. It is crucial that an appropriately qualified interpreter assist Mr. Public at all stages of the legal process if he is to participate equitably in his own defense.

G. *Psychological Diagnosis.* Based upon this current assessment and background information, the following diagnostic impressions are offered (DSM-III diagnostic nomenclature is used):

Axis I: V71.01 Adult antisocial behavior
V62.30 Academic problem
V62.20 Occupational problem
V62.81 Other interpersonal problem (lack of friends and social participation with peers)

Axis II: (1) Immature, dependent personality traits (not covered by other DSM-III categories);
(2) Developmental language and communication impairment associated with etiology of prelingual deafness and developmental experiences (no DSM-III category to cover this).

Axis III: (1) Congenital profound sensorineural bilateral hearing loss (etiology unknown). (By report).
(2) Central nervous system impairment affecting verbal language processing (possible etiology associated with hearing loss). (By testing).
(3) Impaired vestibular function (poor balance) associated with etiology of hearing loss. (By testing).

XII. **Professional Opinions on Legal Issues**. Based upon this evaluation of Mr. John Q. Public, I offer the following professional opinions in response to the legal issues presented to me by the Superior

Court of Midcounty, Upstate in the Court Order dated _____.

1. *Sanity/Insanity.* Based on the information available to me, it is my professional judgment that it is more likely than not that John Q. Public was sane at the time of the alleged commission of the crime of which he has been charged;

2. *Dangerous/Not Dangerous.* Based on the information available to me, it is my professional judgment that it is more likely than not that John Q. Public is not now a danger to himself or to others and will not pose a danger to himself or others if released into the community.

3. *Competency/Incompetency to Stand Trial.* Based on the information available to me, it is my professional judgment that John Q. Public has a basic understanding of the nature of the charges against him and the purposes of the proceedings against him, and is able to cooperate at a basic level with counsel in his own defense *provided a skilled interpreter for the deaf is present to assist him in all court proceedings and in all consultations with his defense counsel.* On this basis it is my opinion that it is more likely than not that John Q. Public is competent to stand trial.

4. *Competent/Incompetent (Responsibility for a Crime).* Based on the information available to me, it is my professional opinion that it is more likely than not that John Q. Public does have the mental capacity to form the specific intent to break into a building with the intent to commit a theft.

5. *Nature of Treatment Needed.* Based on the information available to me, it is my professional judgment that John Q. Public needs a treatment program consisting of the following elements:
   (a) Vocational Rehabilitation referral and VR services consisting of a psychological evaluation for rehabilitation planning purposes, a vocational evaluation, independent living training, personal and social adjustment training and participation, economic assistance for self-support purposes during training, personal counseling and guidance directed at assisting him to develop a plan for his personal and vocational life, and basic adult education training to strengthen his communication skills, knowledge of the world around him, and basic survival language skills and arithmetic skills;

   (b) Supervised probation which ensures Mr. Public's participation in his Individualized Written Rehabilitation Plan, over a two year minimum period;
   (c) Guidance for Mr. Public's parents provided by the VR counselor to enlist their understanding, support, and cooperation in the implementation of his rehabilitation plan;
   (d) Encouragement of Mr. Public to participate in social and recreational activities in the deaf community on a regular basis. In this regard, the _____ Center on Deafness in Downtown can provide Mr. Public with a monthly listing of deaf community activities.

Thank you for this referral. Please contact me if I can clarify any part of this report or if I can provide additional information.

Respectfully submitted,

_____

Psychologist

References

American Psychiatric Association (1980). *Diagnostic and statistical manual of mental disorders. (3rd ed.)* Washington, D.C.: Author.

Golbert, J. (1984, February). Can psychologists tip the scales of justice? *Psychology Today.* Washington, D.C.: American Psychological Association, pp. 1–8.

Jenkins v. United States, 307 F2d 637, D.C. Circuit Court (1962).

Levine, E. (1960). *Psychology of deafness.* New York: Columbia University Press.

Levine, E. (1981). *Ecology of early deafness.* New York: Columbia University Press.

Miranda v. Arizona, 384 U.S. 436 (1966).

Monahan, J. (1980). *Who is the client?* Washington, D.C.: American Psychological Association.

Moores, D. (1982). *The education of the deaf.* Boston: Houghton Mifflin.

Myers, L. (1964). *The law and the deaf.* Washington, D.C.: U.S. Department of Health, Education, and Welfare.

National Center for Law and the Deaf (1984). *Legal rights of hearing-impaired people.* Washington, D.C.: Gallaudet College Press.

Rainer, J., & Altshuler, K. (1967). *Psychiatry and the deaf.* New York: New York Psychiatric Institute.

Rieber, R., & Vetter, H. (1978). *The psychological foundations of criminal justice, Volume 1.* New York: The John Jay Press.

Social Security Administration (1973). *Disability evaluation under Social Security.* Washington, D.C.: U.S. Department of Health, Education, and Welfare, Author.

Stewart, L. (1985). Implications of forensic psychology with deaf adolescents. In G. Anderson, & D. Watson (Eds.), *Proceedings of the National Conference on Habilitation and Rehabilitation of Deaf Adolescents.* Washington, D.C.: Gallaudet College Press.

Vernon, M. (1967). A guide to the psychological evaluation of deaf and severely hard-of-hearing adults. *Deaf American, 19,* 15–18.

Vernon, M., & Coley, J. (1978, April). Violation of constitutional rights: The language impaired person and the Miranda warning. *Journal of the Rehabilitation of the Deaf,* 11(4), 1–7.

Vernon, M., & Ottinger, P. (1981). Psychological evaluation of the deaf and hard-of-hearing. In L. Stein, E. Mindel, & T. Jabley (Eds.), *Deafness and mental health* (pp. 49–64). Chicago: Grune and Stratton.

Ziskin, J. (1970). *Coping with psychiatric testimony.* Beverly Hills, CA: Law and Psychiatric Press.

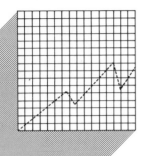

CHAPTER VII

Psychiatric Assessment

Bernard M. Gerber

Introduction

An understanding of the psychiatric evaluation of the deaf person calls for a discussion of psychiatric assessment in general and special considerations of work with deaf people in particular. This chapter will describe the use of psychiatry in evaluating deaf rehabilitation clients in terms of the referral process, the format of the evaluation itself, and unique considerations related to the assessment of deaf clients. In addition, a sample report of a psychiatric evaluation is provided to illustrate appropriate communication between psychiatric consultant and rehabilitation counselor.

The Psychiatric Assessment Referral

The referral for psychiatric assessment originates with the rehabilitation counselor. It is vital to appreciate the initial reasons for this referral, since they help to define the approach to the client and frame the specific questions to be answered by the evaluation. Initial reasons often are based more on impressions and concerns about the client than on particular clinical questions, and these need to be addressed by the counselor and the psychiatric consultant. The counselor, for example, may be worried about the emotional maturity of the client, based on his or her behavior in the office; or he may notice unusual behavior or mannerisms or ways of communicating that tell him that this client requires further study. Past history of psychiatric or behavioral problems can alert the counselor to the possibility of continuing difficulties, requiring further assessment. And the counselor may be following pre-set guidelines which mandate psychiatric evaluation due to recommendation from others, or to satisfy inquiries from supervisors or other consultants.

These initial reasons for the referral are often different from the purpose or goals of the evaluation, which are usually stated in a more formal question format. For example, the counselor's formal request may be for the consultant to determine the client's mental status and make specific diagnostic statements about the client's condition. In addition to diagnostic findings, the consultant may be asked to state his conclusions about prognosis and to list any recommendations regarding appropriate use of rehabilitation services. These more formal questions may vary from client to client, but the general outline of goals for the psychiatric evaluation remains fairly standard.

It is very important for the counselor and the consultant to discuss the case prior to the evaluation. As stated above, the counselor often has reasons for the referral which are not easily stated in formal requests or questions, but which can yield much valuable information to the consultant about the client. "Gut" feelings and impressions of the counselor count as vital pieces of information to the consultant, since the counselor often knows or has worked with the client. Also, many important issues need to be discussed prior to the evaluation, including the client's previous evaluations or tests, medical consultations obtained, language skills, and the need for an interpreter. The problem related to language and communication, and the use of interpreter, will be dealt with in more detail later.

The Psychiatric Evaluation

Background. A significant amount of information can be collected by the consultant prior to the actual clinical encounter with the client. As mentioned above, the consultant should discuss the case with the referring counselor to obtain needed insight into the problems which led the counselor to request an evaluation. In addition, the rehabilitation record can detail the client's training and employment history, including any important problems faced by the client, his/her co-workers or employers.

Other information which should be obtained by the consultant prior to the interview with the client includes results of previous psychological, medical, or other testing, as well as records, if available, from previous psychiatric assessments. At some point, either before or after the interview with the client, data from friends or family members should be sought. This information can expand the consultant's awareness of the client's social and family relationships and the status of his/her interpersonal functioning. Of course, any discussion with outside parties, even family members, is dependent on the permission of the client, since confidentiality is a critical part of the relationship with the client. It must be understood by the client that the consultant will be talking with the rehabilitation counselor about the results of the evaluation, as part of the client's rehabilitation program. However, any discussions about the client must take place with the client's permission.

The Clinical Interview. In the actual interview with the client, a generally standard format is used as a guide to obtain assessment information. Due to the limitations of time, this format follows an accepted medically-oriented approach to the interview (Kolb, 1977; MacKinnon & Michels, 1971); however, since each individual presents with different issues, personality styles, and language levels, the flow of the interview will need to be molded to the individual client. This semi-structured approach will be outlined and discussed more fully below. As will be evident in reading the appended sample consultation report, the basic categories of the material covered in the interview are reflected in how the report is written.

At the start of the interview, the consultant asks the client about the reason for the interview, in the client's own words. At times, the client does not know the reason for the appointment; he was told by his counselor to come to a particular office to see a certain doctor, and he did so. He may know that the meeting is part of his overall rehabilitation assessment, along with many other evaluations he knows he must go through to get desired training or schooling from the rehabilitation agency. In fact, he may tell the consultant this, especially if he is unaware of, or hiding, behavioral problems which prompted the consultation in the first place.

If the client is aware of personal difficulties, or has had prior psychological or psychiatric help, he may tell the consultant that he is there for the evaluation because he has problems which need attention so that he can profit from his rehabilitation program. This statement from the client is, in my experience, rare. The average rehabilitation client, when asked why he is in my office for the evaluation, states that he is there because his counselor told him to come. This initial inquiry into the reason for being at the evaluation is often labelled the "chief complaint" in the interview format. The client, or patient, states in his own words what is bothering him and why he has come to the evaluator.

The next section of the interview is usually labelled the "present illness" in a standard medical/psychiatric report. In the case of the rehabilitation psychiatric evaluation, this section usually delves into the recent life of the client, how he came to be involved in the rehabilitation process, what school or job experiences he has had lately, and what he wants to get out of his rehabilitation efforts. When emotional problems or behavioral troubles mark the history, questions are asked about these problems, especially as they relate to interference with school or job activities and with social and family relationships. The client's own sense of the origins of these problems is explored and compared with the findings or impressions of others, when appropriate. Much information about the client's level of insight and social judgment is obtained from his responses in this section of the interview. In addition, underlying issues become more evident, such as the client's communication style and language skills, his personality, as demonstrated by the way he interacts with the interviewer, his thought processes, and his ability to concentrate and remember. Many of these features will be discussed further in the section on the mental status examination, but it must be mentioned that data about a person's mental status are not collected separately from the rest of the interview, but are noted throughout the exchange.

The section which usually follows this "present illness/situation" is the "past history". Here, the evaluator is interested in various aspects of the client's past life, including family and developmental history, school and language training experiences, sexual and relationship/marital history, social activities and friendships, work history and behavior, and the use of drugs, alcohol, and tobacco. In addition, questions are asked about the client's medical background, including any major illnesses or surgery, any medications taken for current medical problems, any allergies, especially to medicines, and any prior psychological or psychiatric illnesses and treatment. In this section the consultant looks for contributing events, whether social, medical, or psychological, which may have influenced the client's behavior and his current level of functioning. In the case of the client with significant behavioral or emotional problems, it is important to explore medical/biological factors, as well as social/psychological issues, since many medical conditions and medications can influence behavior and mood to a large degree. Obviously, past history carefully explored can yield vital information about the client's personality and coping skills, information which can help in understanding his current situation and the promise for future growth and advancement.

The final section of the interview/evaluation report is the mental status examination (Manschreck & Keller, 1979). As mentioned above, much of the data reported in the mental status exam is gleaned throughout the interview and is not elicited separately. How the client behaves during the evaluation, how he communicates, how he expresses his feelings and thoughts—all are used as data in describing his mental status. In addition, body language, ability to concentrate and remember, and the presence or absence of unusual or odd behaviors or mannerisms are noted during the entire interview. Some questions, however, are asked in a separate section of the interview, if the information is not obvious from other parts of the exchange. For example, the client may be asked more specific questions about his mood and the content of his thoughts, such as whether he ever feels confused or has strange feelings or thoughts, whether he feels he hears voices or sees things others do not see, or whether he has ever contemplated suicide. Questions to test memory, concentration, abstracting abilities, and cognitive skills are asked in this section, such as digit span, recall, fund of general knowledge, understanding of proverbs or common sense sayings, simple arithmetic problems, and general orientation to time, place, and person. The sample report will show how this material is presented in the overall context of the evaluation.

Formulation and Diagnosis. In this section of the evaluation and the report, the consultant lists his diagnostic findings, along with descriptive language regarding his conclusions and how he arrived at the diagnoses. Often the diagnostic labels themselves are not sufficient, and may be misleading if not accompanied by explanatory discussion qualifying the terms used. The psychiatric nomencla-

ture involves technical terms as well as new categories of disorders and the rehabilitation counselor should not be expected to be versed in the subtleties of the latest psychiatric jargon. The labels themselves, though important to list as diagnostic findings, need to be explained and related to the individual client being assessed. It is expected that the consultant will relate the client's past history and current behavior to the diagnoses listed, in order to justify these findings.

Diagnoses are listed as described in the *Diagnostic and Statistical Manual, 3rd Edition*, of the American Psychiatric Association (DSM-III) (1980). Multiple levels of findings are listed, defined as axes I through V, including (I) major mental disorders, (II) personality disorders, (III) physical disorders, (IV) current level of stressors in the patient's life, and (V) highest level of functioning within the past year. A complete description of these axes and the details of each diagnostic category are available by referring to the DSM-III.

Recommendations. Finally, the consultant lists his recommendations to the counselor regarding a variety of issues. Usually, these suggestions follow the purpose and goals of the evaluation. The consultant was asked to answer specific questions about the client and his mental condition, his potential for using rehabilitation services, and/or his overall prognosis. These specific questions should be addressed in the recommendation section of the report.

The evaluator, therefore, gives his impressions about how the client's mental and emotional status may affect his use of rehabilitation services, including schooling, job training, or job placement. In addition, suggestions can be made about the client's use of ancillary or supportive services, and about whether the client could benefit from psychiatric treatment, including medication or psychotherapy. For example, if a client has shown significant immaturity in his behavior, with impulsivity and a tendency toward angry outbursts correlated with communication frustration, the consultant might recommend extended social education counseling, preferably in a group setting. Evidence of depression, psychosis, or other major mental disorders would lead to recommendations for psychiatric treatment, often with medication and follow-up sessions. Such problems can clearly interfere with the client's ability to take advantage of rehabilitation services until they are properly treated.

It should be understood that the consultant makes recommendations only, and that these suggestions are offered to the rehabilitation counselor for his review and decisions. It is often necessary for the psychiatric consultant and the counselor to discuss the report after it is submitted, so that all the findings and recommendations are clearly understood. Each report to the counselor ought to state the consultant's readiness to confer with the counselor and to answer any questions which may arise. No action should be taken regarding recommendations by the consultant until discussed and agreed on by the counselor, unless there is an acute emergency.

Psychiatric Evaluation with Deaf Clients: Special Considerations

Factors Relating to the Client. A number of factors related to the conditions of hearing impairment itself have significant impact on the deaf person's development and ultimate psychological status, as well as on the process of assessment should the person present for psychiatric evaluation. For example, issues such as severity of hearing loss and age of onset are clearly critical in determining future language development, family and social consequences. There is a great deal of evidence which points to clear differences between prelingual and postlingual deaf persons; that is, between persons who were born deaf or suffered profound hearing losses prior to age 2–3 years, and those deaf persons who lost their hearing after normal auditory-verbal means of communication were established (Schlesinger & Meadow, 1972). These differences are observed in areas of family and social development, language development, educational achievement, and preferred means of communication. The "correctability" of the hearing loss through use of hearing aids obviously affects the consequences of the loss on development.

In addition, a major contribution to variance in developmental and educational outcome is the presence of coexisting multiple handicapping conditions (Chess, Corn, & Fernandez, 1971; Vernon, 1969). Many causes of deafness also cause a variety of other physical problems, especially neurological deficits. As an example, the rubella syndrome commonly presents with many complicating conditions, including cardiac, ophthalmological, and neurological disorders, in addition to deafness (Chess, Corn, & Fernandez, 1971). Organic brain disorders often are present among deaf people who have other handicapping conditions, and affect development and ultimately, emotional and psychological status.

For those who lose hearing postlingually, it is important to be aware of the course of that loss. There are major differences between those who lose hearing gradually over a period of time and those who lose hearing acutely and traumatically. Those whose loss is gradual, especially the elderly, experience depression often mixed with paranoid features. Those who suffer acute losses tend to experience similar reactions to others who live through traumatic losses, including shock, denial, anger, depression, and disturbances in body image and self-esteem. The problem of dealing emotionally with acute hearing losses obviously has rehabilitation and vocational implications, especially for the young to middle-age adult, who may have already embarked on an educational or career course. A fuller discussion of these issues can be found elsewhere (Gerber, 1984).

Negative or misguided attitudes on the part of the deaf client can interfere in the evaluation process. Inexperience and/or ignorance about what a psychiatrist is or what he does may contribute to a feeling of mistrust or fear. Past negative experiences with the hearing-controlled health care system may also play a role in the development of negative attitudes (Vernon, 1965). For many deaf people, as is true in the hearing community, there is a stigma associated with the use of mental health care and a concern that they will be labelled as "crazy" by friends and family. Many deaf persons are also fearful about their talk with the doctor becoming public knowledge within the deaf community. The issue of confidentiality often needs to be openly discussed with the client at the start of the interview.

Factors Relating to the Evaluator. What the evaluator brings to the assessment situation is also of critical importance to an understanding of the evaluation process and the factors which can complicate its successful application. This question will be discussed in two sections: the consultant's knowledge of deafness and its consequences, and the language/communication barrier and how it is dealt with in the evaluation itself. These concepts are closely interconnected, but will be discussed separately for the purpose of clarity.

In my view, nothing is more essential in the proper psychiatric assessment of the deaf rehabilitation client than a knowledge of deafness and its consequences. At a minimum, the consultant should know basic information about the causes of deafness and how the severity of hearing loss and its age of onset affect the person's development. The consultant needs to be aware of the family, social, and educational implications of early deafness, and the way that language and communication are influenced by severe hearing loss. Without this knowledge, it is probable that differences in communication, behavior, emotional expression, especially body language, and social interactions will be misinterpreted.

All too often, psychiatrists and other mental health

professionals interpret in pathological terms what are essentially normal communication and social patterns for the deaf person under observation. For example, in order for the evaluator to understand the relationships in the client's family, he must know how families deal with deafness in a child, what difficulties they and the child face and how these struggles evolve through the developmental stages. To understand why a particular client feels as he does about authority, the consultant must understand the educational and social experiences of most deaf persons and the role they play in influencing attitudes about authority. Without some knowledge of sign language (a topic to be covered more in the next section), the consultant might easily misinterpret facial expressions, mistaking a gesture meant to show linguistic emphasis to be a look of anger, for example.

These situations are further complicated by tendencies toward bias and stereotyping common among those unknowledgeable about deafness or any other minority group (Nash & Nash, 1981). Any prejudgment, such as seeing all deaf people as mentally retarded or language deficient, obviously hinders the evaluator's capacity to assess the person objectively, and will make his conclusions invalid. At the least, ignorance about basic knowledge of deafness will reduce any empathic relatedness between evaluator and client and will decrease the accurate assessment of affective states and subtle shades of meaning. At its worst, such ignorance may allow for conclusions and diagnoses which are not only incorrect, but harmful.

The second area deals with the language/communication barrier inherent in the interaction between deaf client and hearing consultant. Obviously, the situation would be quite different if the evaluator were deaf and shared common language and background factors with the client. There is some clinical evidence that deaf clinicians bring with them a very different point of view from that of a hearing therapist in working with deaf patients, based on the opportunity for both to use a "native" language (sign language) and for the clinician to use empathic responses born out of sharing similar life experiences (Brauer & Sussman, 1980). However, I know of no deaf psychiatrists currently functioning in this field, so this discussion of the language/communication barrier remains relevant. Perhaps with more liberal policies in medical education, and the interest of capable deaf persons, deaf psychiatrists will appear on the scene. For now, though, we must assume that we are dealing with hearing consultants working with their deaf clients.

Interviews and assessments can be divided into two groups: language-shared and interpreter-facilitated. In language-shared evaluations, the consultant is skilled in using sign language or any other mode of communication preferred by the deaf client. This skill usually means skill in American Sign Language, in addition to signed English, gesture, pantomime, and other communication systems. These situations have the advantage of avoiding third-party (the interpreter) involvement in the interview, and maximizing relatedness between the participants. Unfortunately, very few psychiatrists have such language skills and must rely on interpreters in doing psychiatric evaluations.

In the context of quality clinical work, the use of an interpreter requires a professional, certified interpreter with proven skills in sign language interpreting. Top levels of skill certification would be needed in clinical settings because of the need for accurate and objective language translation. Vital issues regarding physical setup and psychological/dynamic factors relating to interpreter use in psychiatric evaluation and treatment have been discussed in detail elsewhere (Gerber, 1983). Many consultants have never before used an interpreter in doing evaluations, and may require preparation regarding the appropriate interpreting process. This type of professional education can be provided by the interpreter or the referring agency or counselor. The consultant and the interpreter must also be aware that many deaf persons are not familiar with using interpreters, and this may interfere with communication flow in the interview. Hopefully, as more interpreting services become available to the deaf community, fewer deaf people will be inexperienced in the use of interpreters.

Another area of special consideration in the evaluation of deaf clients is the need to modify many diagnostic criteria for major mental disorders because of the language factor. Many criteria listed for the diagnosis of such major disorders as schizophrenia, manic-depressive illness, anxiety states, and some organic brain disorders involve the observation and analysis of speech. The structure and flow of speech patterns, the interplay of speech with other nonverbal behaviors, the content of the speech itself—all are important factors in assessing the client during the psychiatric evaluation (MacKinnon & Michels, 1971). For example, rapid, pressured speech, along with a "flight of ideas" which are hard to keep up with, and hyperactive behavior, are components of the diagnosis of mania. Slow, quiet speech, with long time delays in response to questions and little eye contact, are key parts of the diagnosis of depression. Of importance here is that more than the ideas, thoughts, or content of language are under observation; the structure and patterns of speech themselves are key factors in diagnostic assessment.

Evaluating the non-speaking deaf client, therefore, presents the consultant with the need to modify the use of standard diagnostic criteria. Experience and knowledge of sign language is needed to correlate signed behavior with speech behavior in the hearing client. Unfortunately, research is lacking to validate such correlations. For example, what is the signed behavior equivalent to rapid, pressured speech in the hearing manic, or to the slowed, quiet speech of the hearing depressed patient? And how do we make sense of "auditory" hallucinations described by a deaf client with almost no functional hearing? In the absence of much-needed research into these and many other questions, the evaluator is left to use his clinical experience and knowledge of deafness and sign language to properly assess the client. If the psychiatrist lacks such experience, he must rely on the skills of the interpreter to help him fit the client's thoughts, feelings, and behaviors in the interview into the diagnostic criteria which are available. To be avoided is the use of writing to perform these evaluations. All too often, the consultant is unaware of the differences between English and American Sign Language (ASL), and the average deaf person's underdeveloped skills in English. ASL grammar in written form can be misinterpreted by the unknowledgeable consultant as evidence of mental retardation or psychosis, with dangerous consequences.

This next section provides an example of a psychiatric report to the rehabilitation counselor regarding a client evaluation. The client described is a fictitious case drawn from the author's experience of assessing a number of deaf clients. It is meant to serve as an illustration of the material covered in a good psychiatric evaluation, as well as the style and format of a desired report. It is recommended that the report be compared to the discussion near the beginning of this chapter covering psychiatric evaluation, its format and report style.

Sample Psychiatric Report

Mr. John Smith
State Rehabilitation Agency
Main Street
State

Re: Mr. Charles Doe
    Psychiatric Evaluation

Dear Mr. Smith:

This letter represents a report of my psychiatric evaluation of Mr. Charles Doe done on April 16,

1984. He is a 23 year old congenitally deaf man who was seen in your office requesting help to get a job or training for improved trade skills. Psychiatric evaluation was requested to assess the client's mood problems in light of a past history of behavioral disturbances, to recommend any necessary treatment or follow-up, and to provide conclusions about his prognosis and capacity to make use of additional rehabilitation services. The interview was conducted with an interpreter, since my sign skills are only moderate.

Mr. Doe stated in the interview that he had come to see me because his VR counselor had set up the appointment. He said the evaluation was needed to help him get more services from VR, but that he also knew he had "problems" and was in a "bad mood" a lot lately, recognizing that he might need help to deal better with his difficulties.

He said that he had not been sleeping well, and sometimes drank alcohol or smoked pot to help him feel better when he was "down", or to sleep. He often wakes early, unable to go back to sleep. His appetite has been low, and he said he has lost 10 pounds over the past two months. Mornings seem worse, as he feels a little better later in the day. He feels angry frequently, often without knowing why. He gets into arguments and fights easily, with family, friends, and co-workers. He occasionally has thought of suicide, but knows he would never try it. He said he has "always" felt depressed, but that things seemed to get worse a few months ago, when he broke up with his girlfriend. He denies experiencing bizarre thoughts or having hallucinations or memory lapses.

Since graduating from the state school for the deaf at age 19, he has worked at a variety of odd jobs, none lasting more than six months due to his own impatience, reduced tolerance for frustration, and tendency to get into altercations with supervisors and co-workers. He lives with his mother, father, and 17 year old sister, all hearing. The mother is the only one who signs, and her skills are minimal. Conflicts in the family are frequent, occasionally marked by angry outbursts. There is no history of violence. Mr. Doe knows he has trouble getting along with people, but feels that he is often the victim of others who take advantage of him or treat him unfairly. On the other hand, he was able to express feelings of poor self-esteem, seeing himself as a failure, as inferior, especially compared to hearing people. With his permission, I spoke after the interview with Mr. Doe's mother. She said that communication has always been a problem in the family, that Mr. Doe and his father act cross with each other "constantly", and that her son often loses his temper over "little things". She has noticed that he has been moody lately, keeping to himself more, and walking around during the night, which often wakes her.

Past History

Psychiatric: There has been no prior psychiatric evaluation or treatment, despite a long history of school and work behavior problems. Psychological testing done two weeks ago showed average intelligence with some deficits in visual-motor performance and signs of diminished self esteem and inner turmoil. He had good reality testing.

Medical: He appears in good health, with no known history of significant illness. Deafness is believed to be related to maternal rubella. He smokes 1 ½ packs of cigarettes a day, and uses alcohol and marijuana on a frequent basis. He has no known allergies.

Family and developmental: Mr. Doe's background, school, and work history are familiar to you. Of note are his frequent problems in school with unruly behavior, often requiring disciplinary action. In addition, many family members have suffered from depression, including his mother and maternal grandmother, and a paternal uncle, who required long-term hospital care many years ago.

Mental Status Exam

Mr. Doe was oriented to time, place, and person, and was alert. He was generally cooperative in the interview, though he tended to look toward the interpreter when he had trouble answering a question, even when it seemed clear he understood. His signs were clear but slowly done, and his response time was delayed. His mood was described as "down", and "angry". His affect was constricted, in that he showed the same demeanor at all times, appearing sad and slowed-down. In talking about his girlfriend, he was teary-eyed, but did not cry. There was no evidence for psychotic signs or symptoms, hallucinations, or delusions. He was not fully cooperative in testing detailed cognitive skills, such as arithmetic and digit span. He was able to give simple but abstract meanings to common proverbs. Remote and recent memory were intact. Social judgment was impaired, since he showed a diminished understanding of how his behavior affected others and an immature sense of empathy with others' feelings. Insight was fair since he knew he had problems and seemed ready to get help for them.

Formulation and Diagnosis

The client has both longstanding characterological problems and an acute illness. It is clear that years of behavioral problems, school and work difficulties, immature social relationships and judgment, and a tendency to externalize blame are markers of personality disorder. On the other hand, he also shows evidence of a more recent psychiatric disorder, namely major depression, marked by mood disturbance, psychomotor slowing, sleep trouble, weight loss with decreased appetite, suicidal thoughts, and use of drugs to combat uncomfortable symptoms.

DSM-III diagnoses, therefore, are:

1. Major depressive episode, with probable chronic depression as an underlying problem;
2. Mixed personality disorder with immature and passive-aggresive features.

Recommendations

1. Psychiatric treatment, to include use of antidepressant medication; behavioral and social-educational psychotherapy or counseling is indicated, to be done by the treating psychiatrist or by a therapist skilled in working with deaf clients.
2. Once symptoms of the acute depression are controlled, and the client shows a willingness to work in therapy on the social/behavioral problems, then he could be evaluated for further rehabilitation efforts, including job training. I would estimate that the first phase of treatment would take about two months, but would depend on the client's cooperation and efforts.

   If the acute depressive symptoms resolve, but the client is unable or unwilling to profit from outpatient therapy in improving his frustration tolerance, controlling his angry behavior, and learning more about the world of work, then you might consider the advantages of a residential job training and counseling program. A group program with other deaf young adults would offer Mr. Doe a chance for more appropriate peer relationships under supervision, more intense educational and training opportunities, and more on-the-site counseling to deal with behavior problems.

Thank you for referring this interesting young man to me for psychiatric evaluation. If you have any questions about my assessment or this report, please feel free to call me to discuss them. It would be a good idea for you to contact me after you have read this report, so that we can further discuss my findings and recommendations.

Sincerely yours,

Psychiatrist

References

American Psychiatric Association (1980). *Diagnostic and statistical manual of mental disorders, third edition (DSM-III).* Washington, D.C.: Author.

Brauer, B., & Sussman, A. (1980). Experiences of deaf therapists with deaf clients. *Mental Health and Deafness,* National Institute of Mental Health, Experimental issue no. 4:9–13.

Chess, S., Corn, S., & Fernandez, P. (1971). *Psychiatric disorders of children with congenital rubella.* New York, Brunner/Mazel.

Gerber, B. (1983). A communication minority: Deaf people and mental health care. *American Journal of Social Psychiatry,* 3(2), 50–57.

Gerber, B. (1984). Psychosocial and rehabilitation aspects of hearing impairment. In D. Krueger (Ed.), *Emotional rehabilitation of physical trauma and disability.* New York: Spectrum.

Kolb, L. (1977). *Modern clinical psychiatry.* Philadelphia: W. B. Saunders.

MacKinnon, R., & Michels, R. (1971). *The psychiatric interview in clinical practice.* Philadelphia: W. B. Saunders.

Manschreck, T., & Keller, M. (1979). The mental status examination: General considerations. In A. Lazare (Ed.), *Outpatient Psychiatry,* (pp. 172–177). Baltimore: Williams and Wilkins.

Nash, J., & Nash, A. (1981). *Deafness in society.* Lexington: Lexington Brooks.

Schlesinger, H., & Meadow, K. (1972). *Sound and sign: Childhood deafness and mental health.* Berkeley: University of California Press.

Vernon, M. (1965). Interpreting in counseling and psychotherapeutic situations. In S. Quigley (Ed.), *Interpreting for Deaf People.* Washington, D.C.: U.S. Department of Health, Education, and Welfare.

Vernon, M. (1969). *Multiply handicapped deaf children: Medical, educational, and psychological considerations.* Washington, D.C.: Council for Exceptional Children.

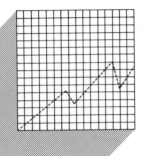

CHAPTER VIII

Vocational Assessment

John W. Shiels

Introduction

This chapter presents a perspective on vocational evaluation within the rehabilitation process, with a particular focus given to the assessment of deaf persons. A sample evaluation report is included to illustrate many of the points discussed in this chapter and to provide the counselor with a point of reference; the report is focused on the vocational evaluation done in the rehabilitation facility.

Vocational Evaluation: Some Parameters

What is a "vocational evaluation" and what does it encompass? This term has been defined in a number of ways, but unfortunately, there still appears to be a variety of ways in which this term is used in various contexts. More than 10 years ago Hoffman (1972) suggested there was much confusion in the field because terms associated with this process were ill-defined and lacked standardization. For example, some practitioners used the terms "vocational evaluation" and "work evaluation" interchangeably, while others noted important differences between the two. Additionally, terms such as "prevocational evaluation," "situational assessment," and "work adjustment" were used loosely but defined differently. Whether such terms are any more standardized today than they were a decade ago might be open to debate. While there is possibly more agreement within rehabilitation academia, it is the author's experience that definitions—and thus perhaps expectations—continue to vary among service providers and counselors in the field.

A popular definition of vocational evaluation is given by Nadolosky (1971), who describes it as a "process which attempts to assess and predict work behavior primarily through the application of practical, reality-based assessment techniques and procedures." There are many other definitions available which may be more elaborative or more esoteric but in the end mean essentially the same thing. It might even be said simply that a vocational evaluation addresses an individual's ability and potential "to work." What differentiates among definitions and causes confusion among practitioners is not so much concerned with the concept, but rather what the implications are in practice in the way of service provision. There are many agencies and facilities for example, that offer a "vocational evaluation" to the rehabilitation counselor, but the scope of these assessments might range from a few hours of GATB testing at one extreme, to a month or more of assessment within a rehabilitation workshop. Both of these services address some vocational factors related to the client's ability "to work," and both may play an important part in the rehabilitation process, yet obviously the scope of these two evaluations is much different. (Additionally, the relative value each might have for the client and counselor in facilitating the client's progress through the rehabilitation process could be much different as well. Conceivably, the GATB testing might generate precisely just the case decision-making information both the client and the counselor need; conversely, the client and counselor might find that an entire month's assessment in the rehabilitation workshop has done next to nothing in the way of furthering the rehabilitation process).

The author favors the broader definition of vocational evaluation which encompasses an assessment of relevant medical, psychological, social, vocational, educational, cultural and environmental factors. A "work evaluation" is perhaps best thought of as something more limited in scope. In Hoffman's (1972, p. 189) words:

> Work evaluation is never defined as the broad concept that was mentioned for vocational evaluation but as an evaluation of vocational strengths and weaknesses of the handicapped and disadvantaged through the utilization of some specific methodologies, mainly the utilization of work, real or simulated.

An even more limited endeavor is GATB testing, which is most accurately "vocational testing." This is where test performance alone is the basis of any recommendations given.

If this all seems confusing, then the need for better standardization of terms becomes all the more apparent. In the meantime however, the prudent counselor will not become preoccupied with academic definitions so long as he or she can decide what services are needed, whether simply some test scores, or something more comprehensive in scope. Once this is decided, the terms used to market those services become of little importance.

Objectives. Vocational evaluation is a process that, compared to the psychological evaluation, for example, has no easily definable beginning and end. Indeed, at one conceptual level, the psychological evaluation is part of the "vocational evaluation." There is no set formula for determining how comprehensive in scope services must be, or how many days or hours the assessment should be, but in most cases, the evaluation should achieve at least the following objectives:

1. *Provide a judgment or prognosis of rehabilitation potential.* In many cases the rehabilitation counselor will make a referral for evaluation in order to determine whether the client can benefit from VR services, or whether he or she would be more appropriately served by some other state agency. Even if this is not stated as a reason for referral, the evaluation report should, if only implicitly, achieve this objective.

2. *Identify direct vocational assets.* Particular attention should be given to outlining aptitudes, work skills, and positive work-related behaviors, and especially those related to any goals the client might express. In a broad sense however, anything that is not a limitation is an asset.

3. *Identify vocational barriers and limitations.* These will be both global and specific. Global employability factors could include such things as attendance, lack of motivation, interpersonal problems, and other factors which act as employment barriers to any occupation. Specific barriers might be related to certain skills and aptitudes, and are especially important when the client expresses a particular vocational objective. A lack of clerical aptitude for example, is a limitation for a client who expresses desire for bookkeeping work, but not for a client who is interested in groundskeeping work.

Limitations are best stated in measurable terms (Couch and Freeman, 1976). When this is done, progress in work adjustment training can be measured against evaluation baseline data. Evaluation done over a period of one month in the rehabilitation workshop offers a good opportunity for quantifying some of the more global factors, but this is much less easily done in a more clinical and shorter assessment such as a one week evaluation done in the rehabilitation facility. At the very least however, limitations should be substantiated with specific examples.

4. *Provide recommendations for subsequent planning.* This is where the evaluator, taking into consideration all evaluation data (referral information, test data, observations, interactions with clients, impressions, and everything else), recommends a plan of action for the VR counselor and the client.

The best recommendations are those which are specific and realistic. There is sometimes a fine line between making ideal recommendations on the one hand, and on the other, those capable of being readily implemented. It is of little help to make recommendations for services that do not exist.

Another school of thought however, is that the evaluator should recommend that which he/she feels is best for the client, regardless of how difficult it might be to carry out that recommendation. Under this viewpoint, after identifying employment barriers, the evaluator simply recommends methods and services for circumventing and/or ameliorating those barriers; it becomes the counselor's problem to figure out how to implement recommendations for services that might not then exist. One value this has is that when nonexistent services continue to be recommended, documentation builds up that can be powerful when used to substantiate "the need" in the fight to establish services where none exist.

The thoughtful evaluator will make reality-based recommendations that the counselor can use, but at the same time—perhaps in the "discussion" section of the report—can reflect upon theoretical and ideal plans.

Achieving Evaluation Objectives. In the same way that there is no standard number-of-days to an evaluation, there is no single or standard system for achieving objectives that will be appropriate with all clients. Some evaluation facilities may lean heavily toward psychometric, paper and pencil testing and interviewing, while others may be more oriented toward situational techniques, and still others may depend heavily on work sample testing. There are various pros and cons; any one of these approaches might be effective for some clients, but none will be sufficient for all clients. A counselor in need of a vocational evaluation for an educationally-retarded cerebral-palsied person for example, is not likely to get much help from an evaluation which emphasizes psychometric testing, nor would evaluation in the rehabilitation workshop be the best approach for an honor-roll student requesting VR support for a liberal arts education. In the attainment of evaluation objectives, two critical elements can be identified: 1) assessment tools and techniques, and 2) the skill and flexibility of the evaluator.

1. *Tools/techniques*: In apparatus, these can range from a variety of psychometric instruments, standardized paper and pencil tests such as scholastic achievement measures, interest inventories, occupational exploration kits and related materials, to commercial work samples, facility-developed work samples, and most recently, computer terminals. Process techniques may include integration of biographical and referral data, focused interviewing (e.g., initial interview, end-of-day feedback interview, a mock job interview, etc.), systematic behavioral observation and use of situational assessment methods. Tools are more objective and "hard-data" oriented, while techniques are more subjective.

2. *Skill of the Evaluator*: How the evaluator goes about achieving assessment objectives will depend on his/her training background, tools available, individual preferences for various techniques, and other factors. The more training and experience the evaluator has, the less likely he/she will depend on any particular test battery or process techniques. The hallmark of the skilled evaluator is flexibility; to be able to adapt, to improvise, and to proceed competently in the absence of "standard procedure."

To use a modern analogy, if evaluation tools are "hardware," and process techniques are "software," then it is the evaluator who combines them and sets them into the motion needed to attain the evaluation objectives. Even the most sophisticated computer is useless until it has the software necessary to put it to work; and even then, the two together have limited value still if the operation performed is not related to the user's goal. In this respect, no amount of sophisticated evaluation hardware will help a person who does not know how and when to put it to use, and how to apply whatever data it may generate to original objectives.

The Evaluation Process: A Reference Point

The above discussion of various definitions and the summary of evaluation objectives has been generalized and presents more of a conceptual framework. As can be seen, some of the terminology used can be misleading; further, it has been indicated that "vocational evaluations" can take place in a variety of settings, are done with various kinds of equipment, and can vary in length from hours to months.

The following presents an overview of the evaluation process as it might occur within a rehabilitation facility, and will provide the counselor with a general understanding of what takes place and what the counselor might expect from this assessment. The sample report at the end of the chapter will serve to illustrate many of the points discussed below. Represented is an evaluation of approximately one week in length.

1. *Referral Process.* How the referral is handled will have a critical impact on the evaluation. The relative benefits the assessment will have for the client and counselor are often closely correlated to the time and care that the counselor gives in making the referral. The counselor will not only be able to have a clear idea as to why the evaluation is being requested, but will need to concisely state those reasons as specifically as possible on the referral form.

A part of the referral process is also preparing the client for the evaluation. The evaluator should be able to assume that the client clearly understands why the evaluation is being done and what benefits can be expected. On the first day of the assessment, the evaluator will clarify to the client the referral reasons as he/she (the evaluator) understands them and will discuss some of the specific things that will take place during the assessment, thus supplementing the counselor's original explanation.

With some clients, the counselor may want to enhance evaluation preparation by taking the client to the assessment locale for a pre-eval visit. Most evaluation centers would be happy to make such arrangements, and many actively encourage it.

Other things being equal, the most successful evaluations tend to be those where the client is an active, enthusiastic participant. At the other extreme is the passive, unmotivated "test subject." How much care and effort that goes into the referral and client preparation by both the counselor and evaluator can make a significant difference in the client's level of participation.

2. *Biographical Information/Referral Material.* As noted in earlier chapters, biographical data and the utilization of this information on the part of the evaluator is an important aspect of the assessment. The referring counselor will want to provide the evaluator with all pertinent background information available including, but not limited to, medical, psychological, and social work reports, school transcripts and scholastic testing results, reports of previous vocational testing, employment record and related information.

The evaluator will carefully review and perhaps make working notes of this data prior to the client's arrival, and thus the assessment has already started even before the client sets foot in the evaluation center.

In some cases the evaluator will acquire additional information on his/her own—assuming signed consent is in hand—such as via phone calls to previous employers, teachers and others, however this is more an exception than the rule.

Some counselors may fear that providing the evaluator with full background information may lead to "self-fulfilling prophesies"; that is, that the evaluator will go through the assessment with preconceived notions based on referral material which may jeopardize an unbiased assessment. The trusting counselor however, will put these fears to rest with the realization that background data will help the evaluator do a better assessment than he/she otherwise could. One difference between vocational *testing* and a vocational *evaluation*, for example, is that the former provides recommendations based almost solely on objective tests results, while the latter will attempt to encompass and integrate all known information into final prognoses and recommendations. The evaluation process entails much more than simply test results, and the qualified, professional opinion and judgment of the evaluator—although subjective—will usually provide the counselor with more direction than what could be generated through a "blind" assessment.

The counselor who carefully prepares and furnishes the evaluator with salient background information should fully expect—indeed, demand—that this information be utilized and integrated into evaluation findings.

3. *Initial Interview.* The first impressions the evaluator forms upon meeting the client are important and usually noted in the evaluation report, since these impressions are likely to be similar to the impressions prospective employers will form. Other early impressions will be obtained through the initial interview. During this interview, the evaluator will orient the client to the evaluation environment, may explain rules and clarify attendance expectations, review referral reasons, and clarify biographical data. The evaluator will be taking note of appearance and grooming, behavioral idiosyncracies, observed levels of anxiety, motivation, self-confidence and other factors which individualize the client. Of particular importance, the client will be given the opportunity to talk about his/her disability, with apparent adjustment level noted. Also during the initial interview, the client will normally be asked about vocational interests and goals.

The information and impressions derived from the initial interview and integrated with other background information will help set the stage and direct the future course of the assessment. At this juncture the evaluator will have working hypotheses to test throughout the remainder of the evaluation, but at each subsequent phase of the process initial hypotheses may be modified or new ones developed and the course of evaluation activity adjusted accordingly to best achieve assessment objectives.

4. *Standardized Testing.* Early in the evaluation the client will normally take several standardized tests such as short measures of general intellectual ability, spatial and clerical aptitudes, and instruments designed to measure basic scholastic skills such as reading and mathematics. Results of these tests will help the evaluator in selecting other tests and work samples during the assessment. If initial standardized testing indicates that the client's arithmetic skills are limited to simple addition and subtraction for example, the evaluator will most likely avoid later administering a work sample requiring multiplication skills.

The extent and nature of standardized testing will depend on referral questions, reports of previous testing done, nature of client's disabilities and other factors, but in short, the purpose of this phase of the assessment is to provide some initial objective baseline data.

5. *Interest Testing Exploration.* The evaluation will normally include vocational interest testing, which may be done prior to other psychometric testing, afterward or mixed within, depending on evaluator preference. In many cases interest testing will be valuable in identifying interest patterns not readily apparent in manifested interests such as previous employment and avocational activities, and not easily articulated by the client. Sometimes interest test results will show glaring conflicts with expressed interests, and thus prompt further investigation.

There is a huge variety of interest tests and inventories available, ranging from sophisticated computer-assisted inventories to informal checklist approaches, and from verbal tests to pictorial inventories.

After interest testing is completed, the evaluator might use the results to stimulate an in-depth discussion of goals and aspirations of the client. This might lead to further exploratory activity through the use of various occupational guidance books and other exploration materials that are available in the evaluation center.

One point to keep in mind that clients sometimes have difficulty with is that interest tests make no attempts to measure *skill* levels, nor are they predictive of vocational *success/failure*.

6. *Work Sample Testing/Physical Capacities Assessment*. Whereas psychometric aptitude tests usually attempt to isolate a single cognitive or psychomotor function, work samples are normally multi-factor tasks designed not so much to replicate tasks involved in a specific job, but rather to approximate worker tasks inherent in various occupation clusters. An advantage often cited is that work samples often look like real work. Because of this "face validity," client motivation might be much easier achieved than in the case of the more abstract nature of psychometrics. Additionally, work samples offer a broad range of opportunity for observation of worker traits and temperaments, and are also frequently valuable as exploration tools, since the client is able to sample a variety of work tasks.

Although there are few work samples that even begin to approach the thoroughness in research and the validity of popular psychometrics used in vocational assessment, work samples can be just as valuable—if not more so—in their role as evaluation tools. Subjective observation of client performance and reaction is often more useful information than the objective performance score.

Physical capacities can be observed and quantified over work sample performance and nonstandardized techniques. Some work samples are specifically designed to assess certain dexterities and range of motion. The evaluator will be taking note of any complaints the client makes in regard to physical pain and/or fatigue. How much a focus is directed toward physical capacities testing will depend on the client's expressed goals and referral questions. In some situations, physical capacities testing may be a primary reason for the assessment, and in other situations, represent a relatively minor consideration.

7. *Behavioral Observations*. Throughout the assessment the evaluator will be recording a good deal of behavioral observations. Some evaluators may use structured systems for this while others might rely on a personal, internalized system developed through experience. Among observations of worker behaviors would include approach to tasks, planning and task conceptualization skills, perseverance and frustration tolerance, ability to follow instructions (written, oral/manual, diagrammatic, etc.), ability to maintain concentration on task, ability to ask questions and request assistance when necessary, ability to maintain motivation on disliked tasks, appropriate response to supervision, quality of interaction with co-workers, and many others.

These observations are a critical element of the evaluation process since successful employment depends not only on work skills and qualifications, but also on appropriate work-related behaviors. Many people who lose their jobs do so for reasons other than skill factors. Thus, an important part of the evaluator's work is to be able to recognize and describe work-related behaviors that may need modification before competitive employment is feasible.

8. *Exit Interview*. At the conclusion of the assessment the evaluator will normally engage in a somewhat formal feedback session with the client where evaluation results are summarized and related to original referral reasons, expressed goals and other considerations. This interview tends toward more of a "re-cap" or closure nature since the client has been receiving performance feedback on specific activities throughout the evaluation process.

For many reasons these sessions can sometimes tax the skills of even the most experienced evaluator. Clients will have varying levels of comprehension and ability to accept information that may touch sensitive areas. Because the client has been involved in a week or more of activity which will likely have significant impact on his/her future, it is normal to expect the client will want to know "the results," and indeed, this information must be imparted to the client since the concept, one of the primary purposes of evaluation, is to help the person achieve a better understanding of skills, limitations and potential. Some evaluators may feel that this responsibility belongs to the counselor, and that it is unwise—if not potentially harmful—to provide any feedback that will encourage or discourage the client one way or the other since the evaluator can only make recommendations and has no decision-making role in the client's rehabilitation process.

Another reason why this session might be rather generalized and non-commital is because the evaluator might simply not be prepared to provide an adequate summary and to talk in "wholes." A considerable amount of data has been generated throughout the assessment which may require additional time in analyzing and synthesizing before the evaluator is willing to present it. Another reason still is that the client may be involved in other evaluations at the same time (e.g., psychological, psychiatric, social work) and thus the evaluator will not want to suggest any plans that might be contraindicated by other assessments.

How this exit session is handled then, will depend on a number of variables the evaluator will want to consider. In rare situations it might best be scheduled at a later time when the counselor and perhaps others can be present.

The Evaluation Report

After the client leaves the assessment center, a major part of the evaluator's job still lies ahead in writing the evaluation report. As mentioned above, a vast array of test data, observation notes, and referral and biographical data will need to be analyzed, synthesized and summarized into a cohesive document. The report may be the only tangible product of the evaluation process. It is not uncommon that an evaluator will invest four or more hours in report preparation.

Just as evaluations differ in length, equipment used and process techniques, so do evaluation reports. Some are rather lengthy, heavily-narrative affairs, while others are of a "fill-in" or checklist format. Recently, more and more evaluation reports are done on word processing equipment. No single method or format in inherently any better than others so long as it provides the counselor with the information needed and expected. The individual counselor will have his/her own preferences. With respect to quality assurance, the following points may be helpful, some of which are general and would apply to nearly any kind of professional reports:

1. *The report should be personalized.* The client should be identified by name rather than referred to as "client." Using the person's name does not necessarily imply of loss of "objectivity"; on the contrary, it lends an individuality to the report and recognizes the client as an unique person with individual strengths and weaknesses. With reports that use the word "client" instead of the person's name, the counselor might understandably wonder if the evaluation center simply "processes" people. As mentioned, subjective observations and impressions are an important part of the assessment; the client is more than simply a "test subject" and the report should so evidence.

2. *The report should be readable.* Counselors will have varying degrees of familiarity with theory and terminology associated with psychometric and work sample testing, but the experienced evaluator will assume very little and present the report in language readily understood. As is common in other disciplines, the recently-graduated evaluator will often write a report that looks as though it were intended to impress the professor and other evaluators rather than to impart useful information to the referring counselor. In some cases, a highly technical, jargon-filled report might be little more than an intellectual smoke-shield that avoids addressing referral issues. The assertive counselor will refuse to be intimidated by this and will demand a readable report.

3. *The report should reflect integrated information.* There is little point of the counselor taking the time and effort to furnish the evaluator with background data if the latter chooses to ignore it, or is unable to recognize the implications suggested therein. The evaluator who makes recommendations for services already attempted, or who suggests placement options incompatible with biographical data (e.g., groundskeeping work for a client with a severe hay fever condition) has been less than thorough.

4. *The report should not avoid subjective opinion.* Evaluation is an art as much as a science, and the trained evaluator is qualified for professional judgment and opinion. Evaluators are sometimes called to the courtroom to make testimony, and although this happens relatively rarely in state VR cases as compared to industrial rehabilitation, the possibility is always present. This is threatening to some evaluators, and in response they may adopt in practice a report style which "over-anticipates" legal scrutiny. As a result, the report may end up being rather bland and evasive. Recent information disclosure laws might also contribute to an over-cautiousness on the part of evaluators. To be sure, evaluators must recognize and respect client rights and the bounds of ethical and professional standards in regard to report information, but when this is taken to an unwarranted extreme, the counselor will be deprived of valuable information and insight.

As a summary, the report should be a personalized, readable and integrated document that will further the counselor's understanding of the client both as a worker with individual strengths and weaknesses, and as a unique person.

The Deaf Evaluation Client

The unique communication and knowledge requirements associated with deafness are viewed as requiring modifications in instrumentation, techniques, and methodologies, but not the goals and objectives of vocational evaluation (Watson, 1976, p. 4).

The *assessment objectives* and the *evaluation process* as described above then, are essentially no different for the deaf client than with rehabilitation clients with other disabilities. Adequate assessment of the deaf person however, imposes special knowledge and skill demands on the part of the evaluator different from those needed for the normal-hearing VR client: communication skills, and knowledge of deafness.

1. *Communication Skills.* When the reader understands that the evaluation as stated several times previously is more than a set of test and work sample scores, then perhaps some appreciation can be held for the importance of the communication factor in the evaluation process. The rapport and quality of dialogue between the evaluator and client will be significant evaluation variables. The poorer the communication, the more the evaluator will have to depend on objective test data. Where there is not good communication, behavioral observations will lack insight, interviewing will be difficult and likely quite artificial, and obtaining all-important client reactions to various activities will be hard to do. In such cases, the evaluation report is more apt to be describing a "test subject" rather than a person.

The evaluator who regularly assesses deaf clients will need a broad range of manual communication skills, including the ability necessary for working with clients having severe communication limitations. Basic skills with manually-coded English alone will not be sufficient.

To be sure, there will be some occasions when an evaluator with even the most proficient manual ability will find it nearly impossible to establish sufficient communication with the client. In recent years for example, evaluation centers serving deaf clients are seeing a substantial increase in foreign-born deaf persons whose expressive communication is essentially via crude gestures. Although the assessment of such persons may suffer for lack of good communication, the evaluator's skills in deafness should still result in a better evaluation than what could normally be achieved by the evaluator uninitiated in deafness.

The importance of the communication factor in the assessment cannot be overstated. As Watson (1976) points out, "Communication comprises the foundation of the evaluation process. Without evaluator-client communication, appropriate vocational assessment . . . . (is) simply not possible" (p. 4).

2. *Knowledge of Deafness.* The trained evaluator will have a basic knowledge of human development and behavior. Counseling and interviewing skills, teaching and training skills, knowledge of research principles, statistics, and developmental psychology are among the knowledge and skill requirements of the evaluator. However, unless the evaluator also is well-versed in the psychosocial/vocational implications of deafness, appropriate assessment of the deaf rehabilitation client becomes nearly impossible, and the risk of misdiagnosis runs high.

In most cases, the deaf client brings to the evaluation center a set of life experiences and communication abilities which present rehabilitation implications more complex than what the generalist evaluator is prepared to readily identify. Even a basic orientation to deafness will not be enough: evaluators who regularly assess deaf clients will need to strive for an awareness intimate enough to allow a diagnostic recognition of individual differences among deaf people.

As stated, the basic process of the assessment is not different in the case of the deaf client, but methods and techniques will be modified. Obviously, test and work samples instructions will usually need to be presented manually and will often be simplified. On some instruments, extra practice items might be included. While these deviations from standard administration procedures technically invalidate the obtained test data, the experienced evaluator will not let this technicality stand in the way of the assessment.

In reviewing the above description of basic elements within a vocational evaluation done in the rehabilitation facility, some special considerations for the deaf client need to be mentioned. In the referral process for example, the counselor will want to take special care in preparing the client. The concept of "vocational evaluation" is somewhat abstract, and with many deaf clients, the counselor may have considerable difficulty trying to explain what it is, and what it's all about. Use of analogies and other creative techniques may help, and of course, a visit to the evaluation center may prove most effective. In the author's experience, far too many deaf clients arrive for the assessment relatively unaware of why they are there, and what to expect. Some clients arrive presumably just because "my VR counselor told me to come here." Because the client's attitude upon arrival may dictate to a large extent the obtained assessment benefits, the counselor will want to prepare the client in such a way as to maximize motivation. Ideally, the client should regard the evaluation as an opportunity for self-discovery, as opposed to viewing it simply as another VR rule to follow. In the same vein, the evaluator will want to make certain during the assessment that he/she does nothing to lend the impression that the evaluation is being done for the benefit of the VR counselor rather than the client.

Comprehensive biographical data on the deaf client will provide the evaluator with important information on which to establish some early, if tentative, hypotheses. This information when carefully reviewed may be extremely valuable in alerting the evaluator to both specific and global characteristics which might otherwise have gone unrecognized but which present important implications in rehabilitation programming. A more obvious example would be in the case of the young deaf adult whose background in both objective and subjective measures indicates well above average potential, yet whose transcripts and achievement scores show performance levels below his/her deaf peers. This would immediately bring to mind the possibility of adjustment and/or neurological factors which would need careful scrutiny before specific vocational training becomes feasible. In this respect, to the evaluator trained in deafness, biographical data can sometimes suggest the presence of secondary disabilities not previously diagnosed.

Biographical data/referral material can also suggest functional limitations and lack of potential which might be altogether misleading. The seasoned counselor will undoubtedly be able to recall cases where his/her clients were underestimated or misdiagnosed by previous persons lacking familiarity in deafness. Because biographical data on deaf clients can often be inaccurate, the experienced evaluator will learn to consider it in a tentative fashion only, and to the extent possible, verify this information with the client.

Another process consideration in the assessment of deaf individuals is related to evaluation interviews. Compared to other rehabilitation clients, these interviews might be less formal and less structured. Even when the evaluator is fluent in manual communication methods, structured interviewing might be perceived as threatening to many deaf clients, and even more so when the client has not been adequately prepared for the assessment.

Extremely important in interviewing—and at a more general level, evaluator-client communication—is the confidentiality factor. Because evaluators often work with more than one client at a time, the visible nature of manual communication imposes considerations the evaluator must constantly keep in mind. Depending on the physical environment of the evaluation center, it might become necessary to retreat to another room for interviewing. This is not advisable in the sense that it serves to formalize the process and therefore may increase client anxiety; however the confidentiality factor must take precedence, and the evaluator may have no other choice.

As mentioned above, the testing process differs from other evaluations in the sense that administration procedures will normally be modified to reduce the language barriers, but the order of testing might differ as well. Standardized testing normally precedes work sample assessment, however the evaluator of deaf clients might often choose to intersperse where possible. The consideration here is that paper and pencil "school-type" tasks tend to be the most threatening for deaf clients, and too much of this done early in the assessment process may alienate all but the most motivated and self-confident clients and jeopardize the development of rapport. Thus, the evaluator may wish to carefully space out standardized testing and include simple hands-on, "face-valid" tasks early in the process.

Vocational exploration done in the evaluation process with deaf clients will normally be less formalized, and more generalized, especially within the representative one-week evaluation as described above. Although exceptions abound, the implications of growing up deaf and thus communicatively isolated—and often coupled with the sheltered nature of the state residential school—have a significant effect on the process of vocational development. The deaf client typically has less work experience and occupational knowledge/awareness than normal-hearing age peers. Expressed vocational goals, if any, often lack an experiential base and evidence of any realistic appraisal of self-skills/limitations and how they relate to preparation, training and skill requirements of actual jobs. Of late, for example, many young deaf adults are expressing desire for "computer jobs", yet even the most casual questioning often reveals an obvious lack of any real understanding and appreciation for the many different kinds of computer jobs and the various skills they require. This relative vocational immaturity is easily understood when popular theories of vocational development are reviewed (McHugh, 1976), but the effect is that it limits the amount of directive, specific occupational exploration done during the assessment.

As a rule, vocational interest testing with deaf persons has questionable benefits. When shared with the client, the results may sometimes stimulate and provide clues for further exploration; however as prescriptive instruments, their validity is considered negligible. Studies have indicated that the vocational interests of young deaf clients differ significantly from hearing groups of similar age (Farrugia, 1982). There are no interest tests standardized on a deaf sample other than one outdated inventory with norms for deaf males only. Verbal inventories are largely inappropriate because of the language factor; pictorial interest tests may be unbiased in the sense they are non-language, however the experiential bias may be severe.

Through observations and obtaining client reactions to various work samples and other activity, some information regarding interests and temperaments can be compiled. A client's interest and orientation to the broad "data-people-things" categories will often be apparent via observations (Cheung, 1983) and in many cases, these interests will need to be further explored through situational techniques, job-tryouts and other methods more appropriate for the deaf client. When there is a lack of vocational experience, awareness and goals, it will be far too premature for the evaluation to establish a specific vocational training objective.

The process of making behavioral observations is no different in the evaluation of deaf clients, but here the evaluator's knowledge and familiarity with deafness becomes crucial. Lack of test sophistication, impulsiveness, passivity, dependency and immature social skills for example, are generally considered to some extent characteristic in many deaf rehabilitation clients. The evaluator lacking experience in deafness may be apt to regard the manifestations of these behaviors as suggestive of "dullness" or significant emotional disorder. Certainly some of these behaviors will need to be modified through personal and work adjustment services, however the experienced evaluator will be less likely to exaggerate their significance through suggesting underlying pathology where there is otherwise no evidence.

The report in the evaluation of deaf clients will usually give some focus to at least two elements normally receiving cursory if any attention in the evaluation of other clients:

1. *Method and Quality of Communication.* What was the primary mode of communication during the assessment, and how effective was it? Secondary mode? Did communication factors significantly impact the evaluation process, and if so, in what specific ways?

2. *Integrity of Test Results.* In spite of the fact that test administration procedures were modified, how much confidence is there in the test results as being indicators of abilities? This section or paragraph in the report is intended to substantiate that test procedures were in fact modified, and to comment on the estimated effects this had on obtained scores, where applicable.

Closing Comments

As discussed earlier, the nature and scope of vocational evaluations will differ from one facility to another. The one-week evaluation as represented here has some obvious limitations with respect to the assessment of deaf rehabilitation clients and should not be considered the first and last word on evaluation services needed. In many cases, this one-week assessment should represent a small part in what is actually a much more comprehensive "vocational evaluation" process which should be integrated with a number of other evaluations such as psychological, social work, educational, independent living skills, medical/opthalmological, audiological, speech and sometimes psychiatric. Even with these, the one-week vocational evaluation will frequently need to be supplemented with off-site approaches such as the use of community job sites and/or the rehabilitation workshop, especially in the case of the more severely disabled deaf client. In this respect then, the one-week evaluation may be considered more of a first-step rather than a "complete" vocational assessment, but in any case the results and recommendations should assist the counselor in planning for further evaluation services where needed.

Questions Often Asked By Counselors

1. *What can be done to best prepare the client for the vocational evaluation?* As stated earlier in this chapter, preparation of the client for the assessment is an especially important part of the counselor's role in making the referral because the client's attitude will be a key factor in obtaining maximal benefits. The following are some suggested points the counselor might keep in mind when trying to explain what the assessment is, and what it's all about:

A. Maintain a positive orientation. The evaluation is not being done because there is something "wrong" with the client; on the contrary, it is to help identify assets and what's "right" with the client.

B. Explain that there will be many things for the client to do. Some things will be like school tests, but most things will usually be different from anything the person has done before. Some things will be challenging, and some easy; some will be enjoyed, and some probably disliked. All will help the person learn more about himself/herself. Especially, be sure to mention that there is no "pass" and "fail." Every person is different—some people are naturally better than others at math, or working with small things, or dancing, etc.,—no one is expected to do well on all the tasks in the evaluation.

C. Emphasize that the assessment is being done for the client, not just for the counselor's benefit.

When the counselor is successful in getting this point across, the observed behavior when the evaluator asks "why are you here?" will be to the effect, "I want to learn more about my interests and skills," as opposed to, "my counselor said I had to come."

D. It might be helpful to explain the assessment through use of analogies when the client appears to have difficulty conceptualizing the nature of the evaluation. Would the client buy a used car without trying it out ("evaluating it") first? How is it decided who will "make" the team, and play in which positions? Etc.

In some cases a visit to the evaluation center will prove most beneficial, and give the client a first-hand look. The client may see other deaf clients there, which might either serve to reassure or threaten, depending on the client's attitude. The counselor will be alert to the client's reactions and should encourage him/her to ask questions and express feelings. Certainly the counselor will want to remind the client that evaluation findings will be kept confidential.

Many clients will express a good deal of resistance, and here the counselor's creativity and skills in modifying the client's attitude will be important. Even the best of counselors may occasionally have to apply some leverage, e.g., remind the client that further VR services will be withheld until evaluations are completed. However, the counselor who does this is as a matter of routine needs to reconsider the advisability of this in terms of how it may affect the client's attitude toward the evaluation.

2. *When is referral for a vocational evaluation appropriate?* Unfortunately, there is no simple, black and white answer to this question. The variables to consider would include the scope and quality of vocational assessment services available to the counselor, the availability and quality of other evaluation services, policies and guidelines used within the counselor's state VR system, individual preferences of counselors, and of course individual client considerations.

In many cases, the vocational evaluation will be done pretty much as a routine for deaf clients entering into VR services. Work history will usually be limited if not entirely nonexistent; goals may be absent or lacking realism. In such cases, the assessment will be beneficial in providing immediate direction for further rehabilitation services.

The homemaker who is years out of school and seeking to enter or reenter the labor market through VR assistance and the older deaf adult with a faulty work history will also benefit from evaluation services. The more severely disabled the client, the longer the client is apt to be receiving VR assistance, and thus the more important diagnostic services become in the beginning of VR services. Like the psychological evaluation then, vocational assessment services are indicated when long-term services are anticipated.

The case of the recent graduate seeking VR support for a four-year college program will need careful consideration. In some cases, the counselor may conclude that a psychological evaluation is sufficient, especially when the client has a history of good academic adjustment and when there is a lack of any other evidence suggesting that college might not be appropriate. In such cases, the counselor might feel lengthy vocational assessment services would be redundant. To be sure, if done, the evaluation may only offer an endorsement that college indeed is most appropriate. On the other hand, considering the high dropout rate among preparatory and freshman deaf students at many colleges, the "insurance" of a vocational evaluation will be a relatively small, yet perhaps very valuable investment.

3. *What is the feasibility of interpreter services in Vocational Evaluation?* In some situations, an interpreter may be necessary to facilitate the communication between the evaluator and the client. As a regular practice however, this is not advisable. Prerequisites would include the use of an interpreter with special training and an unusually high degree of skill; also, both the client and evaluator will need to be fully cognizant of the interpreter's role and function. Even so, the "third-party" factor is rarely desirable and introduces variables with immeasurable effects. Too often the evaluator may end up evaluating the interpreter's skills more than the client's.

Locating an interpreter with the skills necessary will often be quite difficult for counselors, and the expense involved will be considerable. In some cases the counselor might find it both cheaper and more desirable to send the client to the nearest city where there are vocational assessment programs specifically for deaf persons.

It has been suggested that regular interpreter services in vocational assessment should be considered more a "last resort" after other options are exhausted. Those options include training the evaluator in deafness/manual communication, use of an evaluation assistant skilled in deafness, and training a person skilled in deafness in evaluation (Watson, 1976).

Final Report of Vocational Evaluation

Client: M-----   Date Staffed: N/A
DOB: Date of Report:
Eval Period: 7–11 198   Examiner:

104

Referral/Background

M----- is an 18 year old hearing-impaired male referred for a vocational evaluation by P-------, 'DVR in _____ . The purpose of this referral was to assist rehabilitation planning by outlining M-----'s interests, skills and aptitudes, and especially to assist in determining if M-----'s interest in attending college is appropriate.

M-----'s hearing impairment is attributed to maternal rubella. Audiology reports indicate he is profoundly deaf in his right ear, with the left side showing a moderate-to-severe loss. Speech discrimination scores have been tested to range from 50–70% in open sound field testing. There is some evidence that his hearing ability deteriorated somewhat during his early teens.

He recently was graduated from L------- High School, and although L------- has a number of other deaf and hard-of-hearing students receiving special services, M----- participated in only a few special classes; in the regular classroom he did not use an interpreter. M----- was to some extent active in school affairs and generally socialized with normal-hearing students, having only brief and superficial acquaintances with the other hearing-impaired students.

Other referral material indicates an approximate 3.0 accumulative GPA. Reading skills are at the 8th grade level, and math skills at the 7th. Of particular interest, Wechsler testing done a year ago shows both verbal and performance IQ in the upper part of the average. The verbal IQ being what it is seems to confirm that his hearing loss has not substantially interfered with language acquisition. Most notable of his performance IQ is the considerable variability among subtests. Visual memory and perceptual motor speed are areas of apparent weakness, with strengths in part-whole assembly tasks.

M----- lives at home with his parents and a younger normal-hearing brother. His father is an instructor in a local community college. Both his parents and an older brother are college graduates. Interviews with M----suggested there is a good deal of tension between him and his mom, and in fact that's one reason he said he was looking forward to going away to college.

Most reports in referral material describe him as a very polite, well-liked young man. He exhibits a lot of ambition, and one comment made was that he "seems driven to succeed."

General Description/Behavior

M----- is a well-groomed, clean-cut looking young man of average height and build. He kept all of his scheduled evaluation appointments and except for this first day when he apparently had some problems with the bus, he was punctual in arriving. His attire consisted of blue jeans, sportshirts and athletic shoes and seemed quite typical of his age peers. His dark brown hair is styled and kept relatively short. Personal appearance is further highlighted by his fashionable glasses.

Communication throughout the evaluation was through a mixture of manual and oral methods. M----- has only basic manual communication skills and seems more comfortable with oral methods. In one-to-one oral situations he appears to function very much as a normal-hearing person. His speech is reported to be fully intelligible in spite of a prominent lisp. The examiner is also severely hearing-impaired but with normal speech, and communicated with M----- using speech and signs simultaneously. Expressively, M----- used speech and his limited sign skills, but often would revert to speech alone. He was very patient in repeating himself when requested, and otherwise sensitive to communication issues. Rapport was easily established, and in general there were no significant communication problems affecting the assessment.

M----- wears an ear-level hearing aid on the left side and says he depends a great deal on it for communication purposes. He said he can use the telephone with good success and therefore sees no reason for getting a TTY, especially since he doesn't have any close deaf friends. He neither feels a television caption decoder would be worth the expense.

In talking about his hearing loss, M----- generally denied that it poses any significant limitations. Only reluctantly did he admit that group situations sometimes present difficulty. At some points he was so emphatic in dismissing his hearing loss as a major concern, that one starts to get the opposite impression. He said most of his friends are normal-hearing, and when this subject was pursued, the impression was that he has many acquaintances, but few real friends. He is interested in the opposite sex, but to date this interaction has been casual and at the group level.

Initial impressions were of a very motivated, energetic young man. Indeed, upon being greeted in the waiting room on the first day he literally leaped out of his seat and extended his arm in a warm, firm handshake. He preceded the examiner and walked rapidly into the evaluation unit as if he were already very familiar with the building and eager to get started, until he finally realized he would have to stop a minute and await further direction. This behavior was characteristic throughout; M----- would exit rapidly when leaving for lunch or at the end of the day, and altogether gives one the impression there is a sense of urgency about him.

His motivation for the testing was intense, and

he later admitted that he was so concerned about doing well that he felt a lot of nervousness. During the evaluation exit interview he was visibly anxious, sitting on the edge of his chair listening intensely to various feedback given. Even though it was made clear to him at the beginning of the evaluation that he was not expected to do well on all tasks, he had some difficulty accepting some of his poorer performances when discussed at the exit session. For a minute he thought this meant that perhaps VR would not support him then in college.

Vocational History/Interests/Goals

Last summer M----- worked at a daycare center where his duties included preparing food, planning activities and supervising children aged two to six. This job paid him a minimum wage and was obtained through a summer work training program.

The previous summer he worked at a medical institution as a laboratory assistant preparing slides, cleaning animal shelters and operating a centrifuge. This was also part of a youth work training program. He said he enjoyed this experience very much.

In addition to the above, M----- has carried a paper route off and on for the past three years.

When asked about vocational goals, he explained that he plans to attend college to study business administration. He feels this work will involve travel, working with people, prestige, and have high income potential. He is hoping to earn $50,000 to $90,000/year. He has done some self-directed exploration regarding this goal and feels that it offers him an exciting and secure future.

Vocational interest testing done through a non-verbal inventory produced a profile showing average to above average interests in the liberal arts, business, services and science clusters. Manual and mechanical-related activities are strongly rejected. His highest interest scale was in management, followed closely by sales and music.

Supplementary scales indicate a strong preference for sedentary work, very high "ambition" and a desire to perform challenging work required advanced skill levels. Although the high score in the sedentary scale does not seem consistent with the restless, "on-the-go" behavior one sees in M----- the profile as a whole seems compatible related to his expressed interests.

Performance Data

NOTE: Instructions for work samples and other tests were of necessity presented in manual communication—including the Language of Signs and fingerspelling—because of the communication factors and language deficiencies associated with early severe deafness. While it is understood this deviation from the standard administration procedures in theory may have affected the validity of comparing this client's scores with those in the normative group, experiences has shown that under most circumstances the obtained scores can be used with confidence. Scores and rankings mentioned below and on appendices are considered good estimates of relative ability unless otherwise noted.

On a paper and pencil test of nonverbal abstract concept formation, M-----'s 73rd percentile score is generally consistent with previous intellectual testing and indicates relatively good ability in perceiving and conceptualizing the essential differences among objects and events in his nonverbal environment. This test is often considered a measure of general learning ability.

A psychometric test of ability in what is commonly called spatial relations shows a below average score, however M----- completed only two-thirds of the items within the time limits. Allowed to complete the test, his nonstandard score rose to the top of the average range.

On the other hand, he did poorly on a test of speed and accuracy in performing tasks related to clerical work where he was demonstrating his ability to rapidly compare sets of names and numbers for similarity. He performed with good accuracy on this, however his slow pace rendered 01st percentile scores when compared to employed male bank clerks. His poor performance here seems consistent with previous testing suggesting deficits in visual memory and psychomotor speed.

An industrially-normed reading test shows a slightly below average score when M----- is compared to semi-skilled workers, but this score becomes very poor when using a norm group composed of office and technical workers. This score does not seem consistent with a high school GPA of approximately 3.0 and for a college bound liberal arts major.

Arithmetic testing shows average skills when using the office and technical workers norm group but shows marked weakness in using fractions, decimals and percentages.

Work sample testing shows mixed results, although there was a clear tendency for M----- to achieve better accuracy ratings on "data" tasks than on manipulative/mechanical work. His work speed on JEVS work samples was generally satisfactory with few exceptions, however these are rather "generous" norms. On Valpar tasks his speed was below competitive levels and appears more representative of his work pace in general than what is indicated on other work samples.

Among his best performances was a task on which he was demonstrating his ability to work accurately using a tenkey to total long columns of figures. On this he made no errors. (He mentioned that in his office machine classes at school, he was always accurate but criticized for being slow). He also did relatively well on a payroll task where he was required to compute wages, including overtime rates at time-and-one-half.

On the other hand, he was not successful in putting together a door lock he had taken apart, nor assembling some small pipes and unions according to a diagram. He did correctly get together a leather belt after taking it apart, but not without considerable trial and error behavior which resulted in a poor rating for time.

From an occupation experience kit M----- had the opportunity of assuming the manager role of a hypothetical business and was faced with making decisions and judgments related to advertising, finance, staff management and treatment of patrons. He scored 30 points of 46 possible, and the booklet states that a score above 30 indicates some potential for this line of work. Thus, M-----'s score was on the borderline and is neither very encouraging nor discouraging.

Physical capacities were not comprehensively tested but were observed over a number of work samples. Gross movement and manual abilities seem within average limits, however bi-manual coordination appears below average. For example, on a repetitive assembly task requiring rapid use of both hands M-----'s productivity level was measured at 37% of competitive standards. He greatly disliked this task and his score likely reflects this, but nevertheless observations did suggest some difficulty with bimanual coordination.

Fine eye-hand coordination was tested to be poor on both subtests of the Crawford Small Parts Dexterity Test. M----- appeared anxious to do well on this and nervousness may have been an interfering factor, but he later admitted that "I've always had a problem working with small things."

He made no significant complaints of pain or fatigue during the assessment, nor were any restricted ranges of motion noted. Given his expressed desire for white-collar work, the evaluation did not focus heavily on physical skills.

Significant work behaviors observed included that M---was very eager to get started on tasks and often had difficulty in patiently listening to instructions first, a behavior sometimes associated with "test anxiety." Once getting started on a task though, he would place emphasis on accuracy frequently at the expense of the time factor. Another observation was that he rarely displayed much in the way of planning skills. It was as if his desire to "get on with" the task prevented him from some initial reflection in conceptualizing the goal and then structuring his material for maximal efficiency. For example, on a work sample where he was required to count and place 100 nuts into each of 15 jars he would grab a handful from the bin and count them one-by-one into the jars, keeping count in his head. The majority of subjects will make groups of 10 or 25 on the table before placing the nuts in the jars, and others will start in a manner like M----- but soon change to a more efficient method. M----- however, persisted through the entire task with his original approach. Not surprisingly, he lost count several times and thus had to empty the jars and start again. This kind of rigidity was also noted to some degree in his trial and error problem-solving on other tasks.

On the plus side, his cooperation is easily obtained and he interacted very well with the other deaf evaluees. He strives for accuracy in his work and will follow instructions to the letter once he understands them.

A summary of vocational assets would include good physical appearance, acceptance of supervision, basic math skills, ability to attend to details and work accurately, and positive motivation for training and further vocational development. He has limited, but apparently successful work experience. M----- definitely seems a "people-oriented" person who is pleasant, cooperative and very polite, which certainly is an asset in many occupations.

In terms of his expressed vocational goal, math abilities will need significant improvement and is an area which transcripts suggest has been a traditional weakness. He generally works accurately with data, however he is very slow at this. Planning and organizational skills as observed through hands-on testing seem below average and would appear a major limitation in mechanical and technical work. Observations hint that he becomes so absorbed in the immediate that he may lose sight of the larger picture. At a more general level, there appears obvious deficits in visual memory and fine visual motor skills. (See IVEP and appendices for further assets/limitations).

This evaluation is not particularly designed to assess specific neurological functioning, however as mentioned above, there are hints that M----- has some impairments.

Impressions and Recommendations

Evaluation data, observations and referral material suggest that M----- is a young man with average to above average learning abilities in most areas. There is no question that he possesess good rehabilitation potential and will benefit from further VR services.

M----- expresses interest in attending H---- State University in the fall. He has had to work especially hard during his senior year to achieve a high school accumulative GPA of 3.0. Language arts, history classes and social studies have been his most successful classes, while math and science have been relative weaknesses.

His goal of business administration work is not wholly unrealistic in terms of skills, interests, temperaments and potential, however there is reason to believe that M----would have a very difficult time succeeding in an academic major related to this work. As mentioned, math abilities are a question mark. According to the State Pre-College Test/Student Guidance report, the probability of M---- obtaining B or above grades at a four-year college in subjects related to his expressed goal does not look optimistic. There's a 15% chance in business administration for example; 14% chance in mathematics, and 04% chance in economics. He would thus need to sustain much more than average motivation, but on the plus side, he is already doing this.

Indeed, M----- has been described being "driven" to succeed, and this was apparent from observations and interaction with him during this assessment. He talks about the future and his desire "to succeed" with uncommon intensity. He explains that he and his parents have had considerable financial problems, and that he is tired of pinching pennies and wants a secure future with high income potential. Although this is certainly understandable, the examiner cannot help but suspect this compulsion goes deeper. The anxiety related to the intensity of this motivation was readily apparent during the exit interview. As mentioned earlier, when confronted with some of his poorer scores, M----- seemed to think for a minute that college support would not be recommended, but when it was finally made clear to him that the examiner did not necessarily feel college was inappropriate, M----- heartily pumped the examiner's hand and became smothering with thanks in a display of emotion unlike this examiner has ever encountered.

On the surface, M----- seems a well-adjusted hard-of-hearing person, yet he becomes so emphatic in his denial that his hearing loss is of any great concern to him, that one starts to suspect the opposite. It has been the examiner's experience for example, that some young persons with hearing losses and educational backgrounds like M-----'s display a similar kind of intensity in motivation and compulsion for perfection. It's almost as if high achieve-

ment and superior performance become necessary for self-acceptance to make up for the inadequacy the individual feels because of the hearing loss. It is beyond this examiner's qualifications to make diagnoses of emotional status however, and whether or not this is true in M-----'s case is best left to be addressed in the psychological evaluation.

In the sense that M----- has expressed interest in several other occupations within the past year and a half-such as history professor and counselor— his present goal should be considered tentative. He well understands that he is not required to select a major until after his sophomore year and readily admits the possibility that he will change his mind between now and then. In any case, he definitely appears headed toward a liberal arts education and "people" oriented work such as education and allied fields. Business administration and related occupations remain questionable, while mechanical and technical areas seem clearly contraindicated.

If results of other assessments are in agreement, the examiner would support M-----'s interest in attending college, however HSU is a highly questionable choice. M--appears to be going all out in achieving a 3.0 GPA, and, like other young hard-of-hearing students have discovered, may find an institution like HSU much more difficult than expected. He should be encouraged to think more about attending a school offering a full range of support services for hearing-impaired students, such as CSUN. Gallaudet would also seem appropriate, however M----- mentioned that he would dislike living on the East Coast.

Recommendations

1. College support is recommended. The chances of success in college will be improved if he were to attend a college with support services for deaf students. Consideration should be given to starting at the community college level in a transfer program.

2. The above recommendation is made contingent upon the results of a psychological evaluation. Particular attention should be given to assessment of neurological functioning. A rubella victim, M----- runs a relatively high risk of neurologic damage, which could have important vocational implications. A personality assessment will be valuable in gaining insight into emotional status, particularly related to adjustment to hearing loss. The evaluation will be best done by a clinician well-experienced in assessing hearing-impaired persons.

3. M----- will benefit from vocational exploration and guidance counseling in helping him firm

up a vocational goal and deciding on a realistic college major. This counseling should include some values clarification exercises, since his motivation for business administration work seems rooted in a desire for high income more so than any intrinsic interest for the work.

4. M----- gave the impression there was a considerable amount of tension in the home, and as such, support counseling for both him and his parents might be indicated.

References

Cheung, F. M. (1983). Vocational evaluation of severely disabled deaf clients. In D. Watson, (Ed.), *Vocational evaluation of hearing-impaired persons: Research and practice*. Little Rock, AR: University of Arkansas, Rehabilitation Research and Training Center on Deafness and Hearing Impairment.

Couch, R. H., & Freemen, E. R. (1976). Vocational evaluation of deaf clients: Objectives and processes. In D. Watson, (Ed.), *Deaf evaluation and adjustment feasibility: Guidelines for the vocational evaluation of deaf clients*. New York: New York University.

Farrugia, D. L. (1982). Deaf high school students, vocational interests and attitudes. *American Annals of the Deaf, 127*(6), 753–762.

Hoffman, P. R. (1972). Work evaluation: An overview. In J. G. Cull, & R. E. Hardy (Eds.), *Vocational rehabilitation: Profession and process*. Springfield, IL: Charles C. Thomas.

McHugh, D. F. (1975). A view of deaf people in terms of Super's theory of vocational development. *Journal of Rehabilitation of the Deaf, 9*(1), 1–11.

Nadolosky, J. N. (1971). *Development of a model for vocational evaluation of the disadvantaged*. Auburn, Alabama.

Watson, D. (1976). *Deaf evaluation and adjustment feasibility: Guidelines for the vocational evaluation of deaf clients*. New York: New York University.

CHAPTER IX

Evaluation Recommendations and Rehabilitation Outcomes

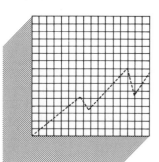

Michael D. Bullis
Paula A. Marut

Rehabilitation counselors often base case practice decisions upon the findings and recommendations from a variety of evaluation procedures. Determination of program eligibility, identification of client problems and needs, and selection of services to be provided are but a few of the kinds of decisions that are directly influenced by recommendations from such diagnostic procedures. Accordingly, a central question to be addressed is, "How effective or useful are evaluation reports in predicting actual rehabilitation outcomes?"

The purpose of this chapter is to address one aspect of the general usefulness of such evaluation findings. More specifically the utility of *vocational evaluation* recommendations that are made in the rehabilitation process will be examined for deaf persons. In order to structure this treatment, the manuscript consists of three sections. Relevant research studies that have been conducted to evaluate the relationship of vocational evaluation recommendations to rehabilitation outcomes will be reviewed in the first section. In the next section, a study conducted by the authors that addresses the subject area will be discussed. Finally, implications of the study for the evaluation of deaf persons will be presented.

Literature Review

Vocational Evaluation (VE) is a widespread diag-

nostic procedure in the field of rehabilitation. Essentially, this type of evaluation involves the use of vocationally-oriented assessment instruments to assess handicapped persons to aid in the development of an appropriate habilitation/rehabilitation plan. This assessment approach is structured to address the following issues: ". . . whether a client will be able to work, what kind of work he will be able to do, and what types of training are necessary to enable him to work" (Gellman, 1968, p. 99). The worth of VE, then, can be ascertained by examining the extent to which these issues are answered correctly. The literature that is available on this topic, however, is sparse and provides only inconsistent evidence for the efficacy of the VE approach.

Several research projects provide evidence in support of the validity of the VE process and its subsequent recommendations. One study, conducted with mentally retarded persons (Apprell, Williams, & Fishell, 1964), found that VE reports effectively differentiated subjects who became successfully employed from those subjects who did not become employed. Rosenberg and Usdane (1963), in a followup of 534 subjects who were evaluated through the TOWER system, found that 70% of 132 subjects who were recommended for immediate placement were successful in that endeavor. Also, 8% of those persons who were recommended for long term training became employed three months after completing the designated training programs. Thus, it was concluded that VE with the TOWER system is a valid and useful assessment technique for planning rehabilitation programs. In a third study (Handelsman & Wurtz, 1971) demographic variables (e.g., age, sex), work experience, education, and VE recommendations were correlated with the employment outcomes of 29 subjects. It was found that the VE recommendations were highly related to employment and, of the factors included in the research, the recommendations were the strongest predictor of rehabilitation outcomes. Finally, in a study by Hallenbeck and Campbell (1975) 70% of the VE recommendations for 200 disabled subjects were actually implemented in the rehabilitation process. It was also found, however, that the vocational evaluators in the investigation had difficulty in predicting the subjects' tenure in training endeavors.

On the other side of the ledger, Cook (1978) and Cook and Brookings (1980) conducted two penetrating studies that were less than supportive of the validity of VE recommendations. In the first investigation, Cook (1978) found that VE recommendations in three areas (work adjustment, direct vocational training, and long term evaluation) were statistically unrelated to rehabilitation program completion ($X^2 = 2.98$, df = 2, p. = 25). A similar analysis was also conducted to compare VE staff expectations of program completion in the three areas with actual client outcomes. There was reasonable congruence between staff expectations and actual outcomes in the category of long term evaluation ($X^2 = 2.08$, df = 1, p<.15) and considerable congruence between staff expectations and work adjustment training outcomes (Yates corrected $X^2 = .38$, df = 1, p<.001). Conversely, there was little relationship between staff expectations and program completion in the area of direct vocational training. Finally, it was found that there was a statistically significant relationship between program completion and eventual employment (Yates corrected $X^2 = 2.08$, df = 1, p<.05). This study, and the results, were later replicated (Cook & Brookings, 1980).

The results of Cook's research indicate that VE recommendations may be accurate, but only for certain questions. For example, there was little overall relationship between recommendations in three program categories and program completion, but moderate congruence was found between staff expectations of program completion and actual outcome in two categories (long term evaluation and work adjustment). Since it can be reasoned logically that persons recommended for such placements would be most in need of services and aid to become employable, it would appear that evaluators can identify persons who possess obvious vocational shortcomings. Next, and perhaps the most crucial point of the two studies, is that program completion was found to be significantly related to work outcomes. In short, persons who complete training programs are more likely to become employed than those persons who do not complete such training.

The general implication of these studies is summarized by Cook and Brookings (1980):

> . . . in assessing vocational potential, it would be efficacious to assume that the state-of-the art is such to preclude an isomorphic relationship between training and employment, to realize the importance of external factors and to move from global to specific prediction classifications.
>
> (p. 53)

Consequently, it would appear that recommendations that focus on classifying subjects as program completers or dropouts are more helpful in the rehabilitation process than recommendations for actual placement (i.e., training or vocational). In line with this conclusion it is suggested (Cook, 1978, Cook & Brookings, 1980) that recommendations should be based on such variables as the client's finances, living situation, and support system in developing a plan to maximize the probability that the subject will complete a training program.

In summarizing data from both groups of investigations, it can be said that evidence for the efficacy of the VE appraisal system is moderate—at best. This conclusion is based on variable and sometimes conflicting results. Further, it is difficult to draw inferences from these studies for the field of deafness since none of them included an identifiable population of deaf persons. Hence, we have as yet no evidence concerning the validity of vocational evaluation practices with deaf persons.

The study described in the next section was designed to examine this issue. Specifically, the following research questions were addressed and served to guide the investigation:

Question: To what extent are VE recommendations actually implemented?

Question: What is the relationship of VE recommendations that are followed to actual employment outcomes?

Question: What is the relationship of specific categories of implemented VE recommendations to employment outcomes?

Research

Sites

Two agencies were involved in this study: The Southwest Center for the Hearing-Impaired (SCHI) and the Arkansas School for the Deaf (ASD). These facilities are described below.

SCHI is a comprehensive rehabilitation center located in San Antonio, Texas that serves multiply disabled hearing-impaired young adults. Referrals are accepted from across the United States with the majority coming from Texas and Louisiana. The vocational evaluation is used primarily by SCHI for individualized program planning within the facility itself; in some instances individuals are referred for the evaluation only.

ASD is a residential institution located in Little Rock, Arkansas. The school has a student population of approximately 240 and serves students from birth to 21 years of age. The Arkansas Rehabilitation Services, Office for the Deaf and Hearing-Impaired, houses a vocational evaluator at the school. Students are routinely evaluated at entry into junior high school (about the 7th grade) and again during their senior year. The initial evaluation is intended to aid the school in placement of students in appropriate vocational training areas, and the exit evaluation is used by rehabilitation for postsecondary training selection and/or job placement.

Data Collection

The data for the study was collected at two stages: during the initial evaluation and during the follow-up evaluation. For both phases the vocational evaluators at each site assisted in collecting and checking the information that was gathered. For the initial stage of the data collection, sheets were designed to match the organization of the client files at both facilities and included the following variables: date of birth; sex; age at onset of the hearing loss; etiology of the hearing loss; severity of the hearing loss; secondary disability; date of entry into evaluation; date of exit from evaluation; race; list of recommendations made; R-300 (a set of information routinely collected on VR clients) or its equivalent; and a description of the employment outcomes for the subject.

Approximately one year after the initial data collection, follow-up information was collected on all subjects. Information included: current Vocational Rehabilitation status; a listing of VE recommendations generated; indication of whether the listed recommendations were followed; entry and exit dates of the recommendations followed; employment status of the client; relevant anecdotal information;

and weekly salary at follow-up.

Several decisions regarding the coding of variables were made by project staff. For example, subjects were categorized as successfully employed (full or part-time work in either a competitive or sheltered setting), unemployed, or indeterminate (still in training or unknown). Other specific coding decisions will be described at appropriate points in this chapter.

Subjects

The population from SCHI consisted of 99 subjects. The average age was 26 years, with a range of 20 to 54, and 60.6% of the subjects were male. Ninety-eight percent of the clients sustained hearing loss before the age of 5 years, or in the prelingual stage of development. The severity of hearing loss for the subject's best ear was profound (85 dB and above) in 70 percent of the cases. In the remaining 30 percent of the cases hearing loss for the best ear was in the moderate to severe range. Finally, 49% of the cases had secondary disabilities in addition to the hearing impairment.

The population from the ASD consisted of 105 cases. The average age of this group was 21 years, with a range of 15 to 46, and 50.5% of the sample were male. The age at onset of the hearing impairment for this group also was prelingual, with 98% of the cases incurring hearing loss before the age of 5 years. The severity of the hearing loss in the best ear was profound in 70% of the cases, and 35% of the population reported having secondary disabilities.

Analyses were conducted across the two groups to ascertain if they were comparable. It was decided that if the groups were reasonably similar they would be aggregated to create a larger subject pool. Univariate statistics (independent t-tests and chi-square) were conducted on the following variables: sex, presence of a secondary disability, educational level, hearing level in best ear and age at onset of the hearing loss. These comparisons are summarized in Table 1.

As shown in Table 1 the only statistically significant differences (at the .05 alpha level) between the two groups were for the variables of age and education. These differences are explained by the fact that SCHI serves adult clients whereas ASD serves a younger population. Given the results it was decided that, from a statistical standpoint, the groups were reasonably similar and that it would be appropriate to aggregate the subjects for subsequent analyses. A rational defense for the aggregation is also available in that subjects in both sites are evaluated and recommendations are usually

Table 1
Comparison of the Two Subject Pools

Variable	SCHI	ASD	Statistic	P
Age	X=26.44	X=20.98	+ =6.61	.00
Sex	male-60	male-53	X^2=1.73	.19
	female-39	female-52		
Secondary Disability	yes-48	yes-37	X^2=3.26	.08
	no-51	no-68		
Educational Level	X=8.94	X=10.16	+ =2.71	.01
Hearing Level in the Best Ear	X=3.79	X=3.67	+ =.85	.40
Age at Onset	X=1.03	X=1.04	+ = −.35	.73

Table 2
Recommendations Made and Followed

Type of Recommendation	No. Made	No. Implemented	Percent Implemented
Academic Training	85	69	.85
Vocational Training	105	66	.62
Direct Job Placement	25	18	.72
Work Adjustment	94	89	.95

implemented within the agency. Hence, the VE practices are reasonably similar at SCHI and ASD.

Analyses and Results

In this section the statistical analyses that were used to address each of the research questions are described and the results of the study are presented.

Question: To what extent are VE recommendations actually implemented?

Table 2 provides a descriptive presentation of the number of recommendations made and later implemented in four broad categories: academic training, vocational training, direct job placement and work adjustment training. Inspection of the table reveals that, overall, there is a relatively high level of congruence between recommendations made and those that are eventually implemented.

In order to establish the statistical significance of this congruence (or, percentage of evaluation recommendations actually followed versus the percentage of recommendations expected to be fol-

lowed), evaluators were asked to estimate the percentage of recommendations, for each of the four categories, that they believed would be followed in the subjects' habilitation/rehabilitation plan. These estimates were as follows: academic training—95%, vocational training—90%, direct job placement—90%, and work adjustment—95%. Using this information, one-sample chi-square tests were computed. These analyses are presented in Table 3.

It may be seen that significant values (at the .05 alpha level) were obtained for academic training, vocational training and direct job placement. The percentages of recommendations followed in those areas were different from the estimated percentages with fewer recommendations being followed in those areas than the evaluators expected. Reasonable congruence was found between the expected and observed frequencies in the work adjustment category. In other words, staff could estimate accurately the percentage of recommendations that would be followed in this category but not in the other three areas.

Table 3
One Sample Chi-Square Tests

		Followed	Not Followed	
Academic Training	Observed	69	12	$X^2 = 16.43$ (df = 1) 81
	Expected	76.95	4.05	p = .001

		Followed	Not Followed	
Vocational Training	Observed	66	39	$X^2 = 85.96$ (df = 1) 105
	Expected	94.5	10.5	p = .001

		Followed	Not Followed	
Direct Job Placement	Observed	18	7	$X^2 = 9.09$ (df = 1) 25
	Expected	22.5	2.5	p = .01

		Followed	Not Followed	
Work Adjustment	Observed	89	5	$X^2 = 2.21$ (df = 1) 94
	Expected	89.3	4.7	p = .70

Question: What is the relationship of VE recommendations that are followed to actual employment outcomes?

In order to address this question two variables were created by the authors. First, the number of VE recommendations made for each subject was listed and the number of recommendations implemented was counted. It was found that there was a natural division in the percentage of recommendations that were followed in the rehabilitation process. For many clients few, if any, recommendations were implemented. In most cases in this group fewer than half of the VE recommendations were followed. For a second group of subjects it was found that most of the VE recommendations were implemented. In order to quantify this difference it was decided to code subjects in one of two ways:

1. 50% or less of the VE recommendations were followed, or

2. 75% or more of the VE recommendations were followed.

Individual two by two chi-square statistics were then conducted between each of these variables and employment outcome. These analyses are presented in Table 4.

It may be seen that a stronger relationship was found between employment and the second variable (i.e., 75% or more of the VE recommendations followed) ($X^2 = 3.48$, df = 1, p. = 06) than between employment and the first variable (i.e., 50% or less of the VE recommendations followed) ($X^2 = .52$, df = 1, p. = .47). In other words, more of the variance of the employment outcome variable is explained when 75% or more of VE recommendations are implemented than when 50% or less of the VE recommendations are implemented. Thus, it seems that the more closely VE recommendations are followed the closer those recommendations will reflect the ultimate employment outcome of the subject.

Table 4
Chi-Square Tests of the % of VE Recommendations Followed to Employed Outcomes

			Employment		
			No	Yes	
50% of VE	NO	Observed	32	4	36
Recommendations		Expected	30.07	5.93	$X^2 = .52$ (df = 1)
Followed	YES	Observed	120	26	146
		Expected	121.93	24.07	p = .47
			152	30	

			Employment		
			No	Yes	
75% of VE	NO	Observed	55	5	66
Recommendations		Expected	55.12	10.88	$X^2 = 3.48$ (df = 1)
Followed	YES	Observed	97	25	122
		Expected	96.88	19.12	p = .06
			152	30	

Question: What is the relationship of specific categories of implemented VE recommendations to employment outcomes?

Investigation of this question was hindered by the fact that multicollinearity existed between the four recommendation categories. For example, it was entirely possible for a subject to receive a vocational training recommendation and a job placement recommendation. Such interdependency of variables violates the assumptions of the chi-square test and invalidates the use of the statistic (Siegel, 1956). Consequently, it was reasoned that the best way to address the question was to recode the data into discrete and independent categories and, then conduct a chi-square analysis between the employment outcomes and the recommendation categories. Review of the data set revealed that there were three discrete categories: l) training (including both academic and vocational training); 2) direct job placement; and 3) work adjustment. Unfortunately, it was found that only four subjects were recommended for direct job placement. This number was too small for inclusion in the proposed two by three chi-square table. Cells with expected frequencies of less than five would be produced in such a design and invalidate the chi-square analysis (Siegel, 1956). Thus, individual two by two chi-square tests between the training category and employment outcome and the work adjustment category and employment outcome were used. These analyses are presented in Table 5.

As shown in Table 5, no statistically significant relationships were found between each recommendation category and employment outcome. This indicates that there was no meaningful relationship between the type of VE recommendation made and the employment of subjects.

Discussion

The analyses in this study led to three primary conclusions. First, it was found that while a good percentage of VE recommendations were followed at the two study sites, the percentages actually differed significantly from staff expectations. Fewer recommendations were followed than expected by the staff for academic training, vocational training and direct job placement. The only category in which significant congruence between recommendations and outcomes was found was in the area of work adjustment. Thus, at the sites in this study rehabilitation professionals had an inaccurate perception of the actual implementation of VE recommendations in these categories. Specifically, fewer recommendations were implemented than the staff believed would be followed. However, congruence was found between staff estimates of work adjustment recommendations being followed and the actual completion of these recommendations. It is probable that persons recommended for work adjustment are the most vocationally deficient and, thus, are easy to identify. Further, given that many of the subjects in this study were located at a sheltered facility and were severely handicapped, it is logical to assume that such recommendations would be followed. These results are consistent with those of Cook (1978), Cook and Brookings (1980), and Hallenbeck and Campbell (1975).

116

Table 5
Chi-Square Tests of VE Recommendations Categories to Employment Outcomes

			Employment No	Employment Yes	
Training Recommendations	NO	Observed	78	26	104
		Expected	75.15	28.85	$X^2 = 1.10$ (df = 1)
	YES	Observed	21	12	33
		Expected	23.85	9.15	p = .30
			99	38	

			Employment No	Employment Yes	
Work Adjustment Recommendations	NO	Observed	41	16	57
		Expected	42.02	14.96	$X^2 = .05$ (df = 1)
	YES	Observed	63	21	84
		Expected	61.96	22.04	p = .83
			104	37	

Second, it was found that as the percentage of VE recommendations that are followed increases, the relationship between VE recommendation and employment outcomes improves in a statistically significant manner. In other words, the closer the VE report is followed in the habilitation/rehabilitation process, the more likely it is that correct decisions regarding the subjects' employment will be made. This result is supportive of the criterion validity of the VE process in this study; or, it appears that completion of VE recommendations relates favorably to employment outcomes. This is also consistent with Cook's work (Cook, 1978; Cook & Brookings, 1980) and with other studies (Hallenback & Campbell, 1975; Handelsman & Wurtz, 1971).

Finally, in this study there was little relationship between VE recommendation category (i.e., training and work adjustment) and employment outcome. It apppears that at the two study sites, it made little difference what kind of placement recommendation was made in relation to eventual employment. This result, too, is consistent with Cook's research (Cook, 1978; Cook & Brookings, 1980).

Implications for Practice

In this section the results of the study will be discussed in relation to the practice of VE in the field of rehabilitation of deaf people. This discussion must be tempered by at least two factors. First, the study was retrospective in nature and did not provide the experimental control necessary to make clear assumptions about relationships between variables. Second, only two sites were involved in the study. Thus, it is difficult to generalize the results of the study beyond these agencies or similar types of agencies.

The results of the present study indicated that evaluators tended to overestimate the level of adherence to evaluation recommendations. This indicates a need for evaluators to become more realistic as to the difference between the number of recommendations made and the number actually followed, particularly if the evaluee will not be receiving services from the same facility where the evaluation took place. Attention should be given to the relative importance of each recommendation as well as the feasibility of its being implemented. Cost and availability should be taken into consideration when generating a recommendation as to its contribution to the rehabilitation of the individual being evaluated. Explanations as to how each recommendation contributes to the successful rehabilitation would be in order so as to improve the consumer's understanding of the plan outlined in the VE report.

Next, from the significant relationship between number of recommendations followed and eventual employment, it follows that professionals should carefully consider the possible losses when deciding to follow only selected recommendations rather than the entire plan as outlined by the evaluation. The fact that the incidence of employment increased with the percentage of recommendations followed gives support to the validity of the VE recommendations. It also points to the advisability of following these recommendations as completely as feasible.

The third issue in this study relates to the VE recommendation categories and their connection to employment outcomes. The results of this study, and of others (Cook, 1978; Cook & Brookings, 1980), suggest that VE appears to be better suited to assessing individual skills and attributes than recommending that subjects be placed into discrete training or placement categories. In short, it would appear that VE should not be structured to make grand assumptions regarding subjects' vocational placement. The data from this study, and from the research cited previously, leads us to believe that all too often such recommendations fail to lead to successful employment.

Finally, it should be noted that the basic research model presented in the study can be applied to assessment questions in other fields. For example, it would be entirely possible to evaluate the validity of other evaluation decisions in terms of a contingency table analysis. Such an approach is recommended to investigate evaluation issues in rehabilitation (Cook, 1980), psychology (Wiggins, 1973), personnel selection (Cronbach & Gleser, 1965), and medicine (Sevenson & Pearson, 1964).

Summary & Conclusion

The purpose of this study was to examine the validity of VE recommendations that were made for deaf subjects at two sites. Three primary results were reached. First, rehabilitation professionals in this study had an inaccurate perception of the actual implementation of VE recommendations. In general, fewer recommendations were implemented than were expected by the staff. Next, it was found that as the percentage of VE recommendations that were followed increased, a stronger relationship existed with employment outcomes. Finally, it was found that there was only weak congruence between the type of VE recommendation that was made and employment outcome. In line with these results, it would seem that rehabilitation professionals should pay close attention to implementing VE recommendations and that the focus of VE should shift from designating a specific vocational or training category to the one that emphasizes social and individual variables.

As mentioned previously, it is difficult to generalize the results and implications of the study to other settings. However, the investigation does provide an important "first step" in the validation of the VE process for the deaf population. Perhaps most important, a viable research strategy to investigate the VE process in other arenas was employed.

Validity of assessment for deaf persons rests upon the accumulation of evidence from a series of investigations and not just from data generated through one effort. Thus, it is hoped that this study will serve to instigate further research on this topic and, perhaps, serve as a blueprint for other investigations. It is only through such empirical inquiry that VE and other types of assessments with deaf persons will become effective tools for the rehabilitation professional.

References

Apprell, M., Williams, C., & Fishell, K. (1964). Factors in the job-holding ability of the mentally retarded, *Vocational Guidance Quarterly, 130,* 127–130.

Cook, D. W. (1978). Effectiveness of vocational evaluation training recommendations. *Vocational Evaluation and Work Adjustment Bulletin, 11,* 8–13.

Cook, D. W. (1980). Clinical vs. statistical prediction: Issues in building rehabilitation diagnostic capability. *Rehabilitation Counseling Bulletin, 24,* 151–160.

Cook, D. W., & Brookings, J. B. (1980). The relationship of rehabilitation client vocational appraisal to training outcome and employment. *Journal of Applied Rehabilitation Counseling, 11,* 32–35.

Cronbach, L. J., & Gleser, G. C. (1965). *Psychological tests and personnel decisions (2nd ed.).* Urbana, IL: University of Illinois Press.

Gellman, W. (1968). The principles of vocational evaluation. *Rehabilitation Literature, 29,* 98–102.

Hallenbeck, P. N., & Campbell, J. L. (1975). Evaluator recommendations and subsequent performance: A followup of work evaluation clients. *Vocational Evaluation and Work Adjustment Bulletin, 8,* 21–27.

Handelsman, R. D., & Wurtz, R. E. (1971). The validity of prevocational evaluation predictions in the community workshop. *Journal of Applied Rehabilitation Counseling, 2,* 15–16.

Rosenberg, B., & Usdane, W. (1963). The TOWER system: Vocational evaluation of the severely handicapped for training and placement. *Personnel and Guidance Journal, 42,* 149–152.

Sevenson, W. M., & Pearson, J. S. (1964). Automation techniques in personality assessment: A frontier in behavioral science and medicine. *Methods of Information in Medicine, 3,* 34–36.

Siegel, S. (1956). *Nonparametric statistics for the behavioral sciences.* New York: McGraw Hill.

Wiggins, J. S. (1973). *Personality and prediction: Principles of personality assessment.* Reading, MA: Addison-Wesley.

The preparation of this manuscript was partially supported by Grant No. G008103980 from the National Institute of Handicapped Research.

We would like to thank Dr. Larry Stewart for his helpful comments in the development of this chapter.

CHAPTER X

Innovations in Assessment Strategies: One Approach

Lois A. Shafqat

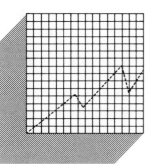

Introduction

The use of the Sixteen Personality Factor Questionnaire with deaf persons is not a new concept; however, translating it into their native language is. This chapter proposes a rationale for the need of a significant proportion of the deaf population to be presented test items in American Sign Language (ASL) on videotape, thus allowing for a test profile which may be more reflective of the individual deaf client's personality. This will be possible due to the fact the client will not also inadvertently be tested on his/her ability to read and comprehend English, the second language of many deaf people. At the end of the chapter are samples of both a 16PF narrative report and a Personal Career Development Profile.

An Overview of the 16PF

The Sixteen Personality Factor Questionnaire (16PF) is an objectively scoreable test devised by basic research in psychology to give the most complete coverage of personality possible in a brief time. The test was designed for use with individuals aged sixteen and above. Form A, which is discussed in this chapter, was written in newspaper English (roughly seventh grade) and is composed of 187 test questions.

The personality factors measured by the 16PF are composed of sixteen dimensions or scales which

are theoretically independent of one another. Each item on the test loads on only one of the sixteen factors so that no dependencies were introduced at the level of scale construction (16PF Manual, 1972).

Administration of the 16PF leads to the individual's being assigned a source-trait score (in standard scores stens - ranging from one to ten) on each of the sixteen factors. The resulting profile of source-trait scores is potentially usable in an almost infinite number of specific behavior predictions. When coupled with a knowledge of the individual's current life situation, the ability to predict future behaviors becomes more accurate (Cattell, Eber, Tatsuoka, 1970).

Norms for the 1967–68 edition of Form A were established through the testing of more than ten thousand individuals. Two principal criteria employed in selecting data were race and geographical location, with as broad a sampling as possible being used. Separate normative tables were also developed on the basis of sex and age. The final norm group included individuals from 15 to 70 years old (16PF Handbook: Tabular Supplement No. 1, 1970).

With respect to consistency in the form of reliability, the most important of the reliability coefficients is the *dependability coefficient*, which is the correlation between two administrations of the same test *when the lapse of time is insufficient for people themselves to change* with respect to what is being measured. It has been found the *dependability coefficient* seems to rest more on the effectiveness of test administration and the rapport of the subjects with the tester (in this case the interpreter on the videotape) than with the nature of the factors.

Separate from *dependability* is the test of the stability of the coefficients which would be obtained from a retest after a two month or longer interval. It should be pointed out that the difference between dependability and stability is not a property of the test, but of the various traits being tested. One can expect changes to take place due to learning or maturation as well as fluctuations which will be due to the varying psychological states of the subject over time (Cattell, Eber, Tatsuoka, 1970).

It is felt the reliability of the ASL videotape version of the 16PF will be affected by similar variables as the written forms.

Background of the Use of the 16PF with Deaf Persons

In 1967 Eber and Cattell developed a low-literate form of the 16PF (Form E) which was written at a third to sixth grade reading level. Form E was a forced-choice questionnaire rather than the multiple-choice of Forms A, B, C, D. It contained only 128 items versus the 187 items of the Forms A, B. Trybus (1973) established separate norms for this form on a group of 142 female and 138 male entering students to Gallaudet College. By 1974 additional data had been collected on similar students, refining the normative data even further (Jensema, 1975).

Over the past decade the 16PF proved to be a valuable instrument for college counselors and became increasingly so since the entrance onto the market of the 16PF Personal-Career Development Profile (Walter, 1977).

The 16PF PCDP (Personal-Career Development Profile) is a computer generated report which uses data extrapolated from the 16PF responses. It includes information relative to a person's:
- Orientation to the 16PF Questionnaire
- General life-style for coping with personal and work environments
- Sources of major gratification and satisfactions in life
- Work setting and structure preferences
- Leadership preferences and styles
- Problem-solving abilities and patterns
- Patterns for coping with stress conditions and experiences
- Preferred ways for coping with conflict and opposi tion from others

- Patterns of interaction with people
- Patterns of career, occupational, and vocational interests
- Considerations for personal career growth and development

In addition, a page of occupational comparisons about how a person's profile corresponds to the profile of others working in some 50 different occupations is provided. Finally, a separate page contains a graphic presentation of test scores and summary of vital broad patterns of behavior and clinical observations about the test-taker. *This last page of information is meant strictly for professional counselor use* (Walter, 1982).

Initially it was felt that through the use of Form E of the 16PF, the hearing-impaired students at the author's college, Golden West in Huntington Beach, California, could gain access to the (PCPD) Personal-Career Development Profile.

The author was concerned, however, that the Gallaudet norms may not be appropriate for use with Golden West College students. Gallaudet, a private institution, had established entrance requirements which permitted the screening of students for academic skills levels including reading comprehension. Golden West College, being a community college mandated to be an open-entry institution, thus was accessible to all individuals 18 years or older. The completion of high school was not mandated prior to admission to a California community college. For this reason the hearing-impaired student population at Golden West College could not be required to have as high an academic achievement level as students attending Gallaudet. Thus, the challenge was to provide appropriate vocational testing even though the student may have been functioning at a lower academic level than would be necessary to successfully respond to questionnaire items on the 16PF Form E or utilize normative data established at Gallaudet.

These concerns were confirmed on several occasions in which attempts were made to administer Form E. After those sessions in which students asked fundamental questions regarding test items, the author suspected that their cultural and environmental experiences as well as their reading comprehension may have distorted responses to the test items.

As with other bilingual populations who had been given tests in English rather than their native language, the question was raised: Were we just obtaining the information the test was designed to provide, or were we also testing their ability to read and comprehend English?

The problem of testing deaf persons has been a

continuing one. Levine (1974) reported on a national survey of psychologists who worked with the deaf. The highest percentage of returns came from psychologists who worked in either day or residential schools exclusively designed for the hearing-impaired. A total of 178 respondents serving a combined clientele of 24,224 in 48 states supplied data for the survey. A full 50% of these respondents reported no ability to use (or read back) sign language. In considering the skills of the other 50%, Levine inferred that about 90% of the respondent group were unable to communicate effectively in sign language with a manually oriented clientele.

Gerweck and Ysseldyke (1974) responded to Levine's study by questioning the appropriateness of the tests which were reportedly being used with the hearing-impaired. They stated of nine (9) devices for assessing intellectual capacity reportedly being used by 20 or more respondents in the Levine survey, only the Hiskey-Nebraska Test of Learning Aptitude had separate norms obtained through standardization on hearing-impaired persons.

No information was specifically given regarding the use of personality tests for the deaf. However, in the Levine study (1974) three institutions were reportedly using the 16PF. Although Jensema (1975) raised serious questions regarding the validity of at least two factors (M and N) for Form E for the hearing-impaired, he admitted the 16PF was one of the better personality tests currently in use with the deaf population. He did, however, cite a clear need for tests which were *designed* or *revised* specifically for the hearing-impaired.

The impetus of court actions (Diana vs. State Board of Education, 1970; Altman & Osborne for Stewart, et al. vs. Philips et al., 1970) was the initial effort to secure constitutional rights of minority group children to be intellectually assessed with due consideration to differing acculturation on intellectual development.

With the impact of PL 94-142 (1977) where all handicapped students gained access to a free and appropriate education, the issue of the appropriateness of psychological tests being used with deaf persons became even greater. There were stories of hearing-impaired students being placed in classes for the mentally retarded due to results on psychological tests standardized on non-deaf populations. This practice impacted not only deaf students but extended to many other bilingual populations as well.

Because of this need for testing despite the lack of appropriate tools, most psychologists who work with deaf college students resort to the use of a non-verbal test such as the Leiter International Performance Scale or one requiring very little verbal interaction such as Raven's Progressive Matrices or Coloured Progressive Matrices.

Additionally, very few vocational tests on the market are appropriate for the deaf college student. The Geist Picture Interest Inventory (Revised) Deaf Male Form is limited in its application as well as only assessing interests, as are the Picture Interest Exploration Survey, Strong-Campbell Interest Inventory and Wide Range Interest and Opinion Test-Revised. To this date no vocational assessment tool has been available for use with the hearing-impaired which integrates personality data and career information.

The advantage of such a tool is that it provides the user with information to assess the client in achieving accurate insights about themselves while eliminating the time consuming elements of the assessment, diagnosis, interpretation and report-writing. Of course, it is still necessary for the counselor to fill the critical role of interpreting and presenting the test results to the client in a meaningful way. The narrative report is not intended to replace the function of the professional in the interpretive process.

American Sign Language—A Language in its Own Right

Over the past decade linguistic research on American Sign Language (ASL) took place in research labs at Gallaudet College, Northeastern University and Salk Institute for Biological Studies as well as by numerous individuals across the United States.

Klima and Bellugi (1979) stated that linguistics had until recently limited the very concept of language to entail complex organizational properties intimately connected with vocally articulated sounds. They sought to address these fundamental premises and expand the idea of language to include sign language as an autonomous language.

As they pursued their studies they addressed these questions: What was fundamental to language as language, and what properties of language were determined by the mode on which it was produced? What sort of organization characterized a language developed in a visual-manual mode? Was that organization essentially different from that of spoken languages (Klima and Bellugi, 1979, p. 2)?

After seven years of intensive work with mostly native deaf signers (those who had learned the language first from deaf parents), Klima and Bellugi concluded American Sign Language was, in fact, a primary communication system developed and used by deaf people in the United States. It was a form with its own highly articulated means for expressing and relating concepts and with an underlying network of regularities connecting visual form with meaning. American Sign Language was for Klima and Bellugi a clearly separate language distinct from the spoken English of its surrounding community. Baker and Cokely (1980) concurred with Klima and Bellugi. In addition, they applied the following definition to language:

> A language is a system of relatively arbitrary symbols and grammatical signals that change across time and that members of a community share and use for several purposes; to interact with each other, to communicate their ideas, emotions, and intentions, and to transmit their culture from generation to generation.
>
> Baker and Cokely (1980, p. 31)

Utilizing this definition they described American Sign Language (also called ASL or Ameslan) to be a visual gestural language created by deaf people and used by approximately 250,000–500,000 Americans (and some Canadians) of all ages (Baker and Cokely, 1980, p. 47).

Translating the 16PF into a Form of American Sign Language (Pidgin Signed English)

Using the concept then that deaf people had a language which was indigenous to them, and further citing the serious problems encountered by attempting to secure comprehensive vocational and career inventories for assessing the deaf person, it was this author's opinion that efforts should be made to translate a test formerly administered in written English into American Sign Language. Great attention was given to securing a native ASL signer to assist with this project. In addition to being a child of deaf parents, the individual who was chosen was fully certified by the Registry of Interpreters for the Deaf. She was also an instructor in the college's certificate training program for interpreters of the deaf and functioned as the Interpreter Supervisor for the disabled Students Program at Golden West College.

It was determined a strict American Sign Language interpretation would be almost impossible to make and still preserve the integrity of the test items. Therefore, Pidgin Signed English (PSE), which is a form of American Sign Language, was used instead.

Form A of the 16PF was felt to be the form of choice due to its extensive research base. This decision was made in conjunction with research personnel at the Institute for Personality and ability Testing, the developer of the 16PF.

A grant was obtained from the Office of Educational Development at Golden West College to fully fund the project. A joint agreement was written between Golden West College and the Institute for Personality and Ability Testing in which IPAT granted permission for the translation of the 16PF Form A into American Sign Language (PSE) on videotape.

At this time the videotaped translation is being used by Golden West College, the Department of Rehabilitation in Westminster, California and a private psychologist in Laramie, Wyoming.

Additionally, a private Independent Living Center which serves the deaf in Garden Grove, California has indicated plans to purchase the translation and initiate its use within a Vocational Rehabilitation sponsored program by the time this book is in print.

Data to determine test-retest reliability of this translation is currently being collected by Golden West College.

The test takes approximately two hours to administer. The client has the option of stopping the tape or repeating questions as the test is not timed.

Scoring can be done by hand if the user only wishes to obtain the 16PF personality profile. The author uses the computer score sheets which then give access to a number of computer generated profiles including the Personal-Career Development Profile (PCPD), the Karson Clinical Report which is an easy-to-use report that features an in-depth analysis of underlying personality dynamics in the language of the clinician, and the Marriage Counseling Report (MCR) which examines individual and joint strengths and weaknesses in the personality organization of the individuals.

*It should be noted at this time there are no specific norms for the hearing-impaired on the PSE version of Form A. Depending on the client's age, college norms or adult norms are used. As more data is collected around the country Form A deaf norms can be established, thus increasing the validity of this instrument's use on the hearing-impaired population. However, it is still felt by this author the elimination of the bias of English reading comprehension is a significant step toward reducing discriminatory testing of deaf persons. Additionally, it increases access to sophisticated vocational and career assessments which are individualized for the client.

Summary

In summary, it appears that research has been generated for the past ten to fifteen years showing the negative impact of psychological tests which are not appropriate for the bilingual populations on which they were being used.

A strong effort took place to make certain this did not continue to occur with minority groups such as the Mexican-American population. Research also showed many deaf persons were equally affected by such testing methods. Most psychologists turned to non-verbal tests for that reason.

With the introduction of video recorders to the consumer and the common use of this equipment in educational settings, the feasibility of translating a written English test into American Sign Language for widespread use became much more of a reality. The first test of its kind to be translated onto videotape was the 16PF Form A into Pidgin Signed English.

It is hoped this translation and subsequent research will serve as a catalyst to review the possibility of attempting similar projects of this nature.

(See sample reports on the following pages)

This computer interpretation of the 16PF is intended only for properly qualified professionals and should be treated as a confidential report.

1/15/1983

Name-Sample	John	Age-29
ID Number		Sex-M

There is reason to suspect some distortion in his test responses. This is something that should be explored further.

Faking good/md (Sten) score is very low (2.0).
Faking bad (Sten) score is high (8.0).

16PF
Personality Profile

Scores				Low Meaning	1 2 3 4 5 6 7 8 9 10	High Meaning	%
R	U	C					
8	4	4	A	Reserved		Warm, Easygoing	23
10	8	8	B	Concrete Thinking		Abstract Thinking	89
10	2	3	C	Easily Upset		Calm, Stable	11
22	10	10	E	Not Assertive		Dominant	99
21	9	9	F	Sober, Serious		Happy-Go-Lucky	
							96
11	4	4	G	Expedient		Conscientious	23
19	7	7	H	Shy, Timid		Venturesome	77
9	6	6	I	Tough-Minded		Tender-Minded	60
11	8	8	L	Trusting		Suspicious	89
16	7	7	M	Practical		Imaginative	77
4	2	2	N	Forthright		Shrewd	4
15	8	7	O	Self-Assured		Apprehensive	77
15	9	9	Q1	Conservative		Experimenting	96
14	8	8	Q2	Group-oriented		Self-Sufficient	89
12	5	5	Q3	Undisciplined		Self-Disciplined	40
14	7	6	Q4	Relaxed		Tense, Driven	60

Note: "R" designates raw scores, "U" designates (Uncorrected) sten scores, and "C" designates sten scores corrected for distortion (if appropriate). The interpretation will proceed on the basis of corrected scores.

Personal Counseling Observations

Adequacy of adjustment is above average (6.5)
Acting-out of behavior tendencies are high (7.9)
Effectiveness of behavior controls is low (3.3)

Intervention Considerations

The influence of a controlled environment may help. Suggestions included—a graded series of success experiences to improve self-confidence.

Primary Personality Characteristics of Significance

Capacity for abstract skills is high.

Involvement in problems may evoke some emotional upset and instability.

In interpersonal relationships he leads, dominates, or is stubborn.

His style of expression is often lively, optimistic, and enthusiastic.

He tends to project inner tension by blaming others, and becomes jealous or suspicious easily.

In his dealings with others, he is emotionally natural and unpretentious, though somewhat naive.

He is experimenting, has an inquiring mind, likes new ideas, and tends to disparage traditional solutions to problems.

Being self-sufficient, he prefers tackling things resourcefully, alone.

Broad Influence Patterns

His personality orientation is extraverted. That is, his attention is directed out into the environment. This tendency is above average (7.5).

At the present time, he sees himself as somewhat more anxious than most people. His anxiety score is above average (6.6).

Tasks and problems are approached with emphasis upon rationality and getting things done. Less attention is paid to emotional relationships. This tendency is high (8.1).

His life-style is independent and self-directed leading to active attempts to achieve control of the environment. In this respect, he is extremely high (10.0).

Vocational Observations

At client's own level of abilities, potential for creative functioning is very high (9.0).

Potential for benefit from formal academic training, at client's own level of abilities, is high (7.6).

In a group of peers, potential for leadership is average (5.6).

Conditions of interpersonal contact or isolation are irrelevant, but extremes should be avoided.

Need for work that tolerates some undependability and inconsistent habits is very high (9.0).

Potentials for growth to meet increased job demands is below average (4.1).

The extent to which the client is accident prone is high (8.3).

Occupational Fitness Projections

In this segment of the report his 16PF results are compared with various occupational profiles. All projections should be considered with respect to other information about him, particularly his interests and abilities.

1. Artistic Professions

Artist	Above Average (7.1)
Musician	Extremely High (10.0)
Writer	Very High (8.9)

2. Community and Social Service

Employment Counselor	Average (5.7)
Firefighter	Below Average (3.8)
Nurse	Average (4.9)
Physician	High (8.1)
Police Officer	Very Low (1.9)
Priest (R.C.)	Low (3.3)
Service Station Dealer	Very Low (2.4)
Social Worker	Below Average (3.6)

3. Scientific Professions

Biologist	Above Average (6.9)
Chemist	Above Average (6.8)
Engineer	Below Average (4.3)
Geologist	High (7.9)
Physicist	Average (6.3)
Psychologist	High (7.7)

4. Technical Personnel

Accountant	Above Average (7.5)
Airline Flight Attendant	Above Average (7.0)
Airline Pilot	Very High (8.7)
Computer Programmer	Very High (8.7)
Editorial Worker	Average (6.0)
Electrician	Extremely Low (1.4)
Mechanic	Below Average (3.7)
Psychiatric Technician	Average (5.1)
Time/Motion Study Analyst	Average (6.4)

5. Industrial/Clerical Personnel

Janitor	Low (2.9)
Kitchen Worker	Extremely Low (1.2)
Machine Operator	Low (2.9)
Secretary-Clerk	Average (5.0)
Truck Driver	Very Low (1.6)

6. Sales Personnel

Real Estate Agent	Above Average (7.2)
Retail Counter Clerk	High (8.1)

7. Administrative and Supervisory Personnel

Bank Manager	High (7.6)
Business Executive	Very High (9.1)
Credit Union Manager	Average (5.1)
Middle Level Manager	Average (4.8)
Personnel Manager	High (8.4)

Production Manager	Extremely High (10.0)
Plant Foreman	Average (4.6)
Sales Supervisor	Average (5.8)
Store Manager	Low (2.8)

8. Academic Professions

Teacher-Elementary Level	Average (5.6)
Teacher-Junior High Level	Very High (8.6)
Teacher-Senior High Level	Very High (9.1)
University Professor	Average (6.0)
School Counselor	Above Average (6.6)
School Superintendent	Average (5.1)
University Administrator	Average (6.1)

This profile shows the 3233 pattern type. For additional interpretive information regarding this pattern, see "Interpreting 16PF Profile Patterns" by Dr. Samuel Krug. This publication is available through IPAT.

Personal-Career Development Profile

John Sample   ID Number _____
Sex M   Age 42   4/20/1984

Orientation to the 16PF Questionnaire

Mr. Sample appears to have answered most of the questions in the inventory realistically. He seems to have wanted to describe himself as accurately as possible. Even so, the information that follows in this report should be read in light of what is actually known about his personal career life-style patterns.

Problem-Solving Patterns

Mr. Sample functions quite comfortably with problems which involve abstract reasoning and conceptual thinking. He is quite able to integrate detail and specifics into meaningful, logical wholes. He is very alert mentally. He sees quickly how ideas fit together and is likely to be a fast learner. If Mr. Sample feels like doing it, he shows about average interest in the kind of controlled learning activities which formal university training offers.

Mr. Sample's approach to tasks is usually balanced between getting things done efficiently and having an awareness of the often hidden steps and outcomes that are part of the process of gettings things done. Mr. Sample is sometimes so sure that he can easily handle most any problem that comes up that he may not do enough planning and preparing for thoroughness. He is prone to act on the spur-of-the-moment without taking the needed time to prepare himself to decide and act on important issues. As a result, his decisions and actions tend to be rather riskseeking and with the expectation that somehow luck will intervene. He sticks mostly to practical methods as he deals with life and its problems. He usually pays attention to the everyday aspects and requirements of situations.

Patterns for Coping with Stressful Conditions

For the most part, Mr. Sample seems to be well-adjusted. He does not usually show signs of tension and worry, even when he is under a lot of pressure. He tries to be calm and even-tempered most of the time. He rarely allows his emotional needs to get in the way of what he does or tries to do in situations or relationships. He seems to be quite casual in the way he reacts to most circumstances and situations. He usually follows his own urges and feelings. He seldom gives much attention to controlling his behavior and sometimes finds it hard to consciously discipline himself. He feels confident in himself, and he has little need to explain his actions to himself or to other people. At the present time, he presents himself as a person who is relaxed and composed. He does not seem to be worried or frustrated. As a result, he probably does not really wish to change himself in any major way. He may come across to other people, though, as being too complacent and self-accepting. Generally, when Mr. Sample is faced with conflict or disagreement from others, he likes to challenge those who differ with him and to clearly state his views on the subject. However, if pushed far enough, he is likely to either give in or to break off the conversation—whichever seems to be best for him.

Patterns of Interpersonal Interaction

Most of the time, Mr. Sample tends to pay rather close attention to people around him and to their concerns and problems. He seldom spends a lot of effort and time being overly concerned about himself or his own problems. He likes to put forth a feeling of warmth and easygoingness when interacting with others. He is a good natured person and one who generally prefers participation in group activities. He is generally very forward and bold when meeting and talking with others. Mr. Sample may sometimes want to get others to do something so much that he may try too hard, and as a result, he could run the risk of coming across as overly pushy and demanding in such instances. Nevertheless, he appears to relate to most people with ease and comfort. He is normally inclined to state his desires and needs clearly and quite forcefully. He likes to have things his way most of the time and prefers freedom from other people's influence. Although Mr. Sample usually likes to be free from other people's influence, he can easily adjust his manner and he can be thoughtful of other people and their concerns or needs when it is important to do so. He normally feels closest to people who are competitive and who understand the importance of being in firm control of their lives and what they do to reach their goals. Sometimes, Mr. Sample may be in such a hurry to get things done that he tends to forget how others may be affected by his actions and how others may feel about matters that are important to them. Mr. Sample seems to have a sharp sense of what is socially necessary, and he is usually aware of the right thing to say and do in social get togethers with others. For the most part, he tries to be friendly and helpful to people since he tends to be trusting and accepting of himself and what he does in his life. Mr. Sample tends to gain his greatest satisfaction in life from being involved in activities that have chances for personal achievement while competing with others. When things are going well between himself and others, he likes to have influence over other people as he faces and meets difficult challenges.

Organizational Role and Work-Setting Patterns

Mr. Sample tends to experience considerable satisfaction when he is given the chance to be in a position of leadership in organizational settings. He likes to be in charge of others, particularly a group of friends or coworkers. He usually feels comfortable in situations which require him to provide direction over others. His group members, too, are likely to respond favorably to his leadership patterns. Mr. Sample generally attempts to influence others by directing, persuading and challenging them to get things done. He seems to truly enjoy talking and interacting with people to get them to agree with his points-of-view when it's important to him. If he were to take on a leadership role with others, he would probably strive to administer duties by focusing attention on the conditions which foster or hinder the performance of subordinates rather than on personnel problems which may be present. Being more solution-seeking than blame oriented, he strives to remove personality and power struggles from the work situation. Mr. Sample generally prefers to build feelings of mutual respect and interdependence among people. He usually likes to share with others whatever power may be necessary to accomplish assignments. He appears to value objective working relationships between superiors and subordinates.

Mr. Sample is likely to feel most at home when working in relaxed and flexible settings that are not boring or routine in nature. If some structure would be necessary, he likes to design it himself rather than having someone else impose it on him. He is basically quite flexible. He does not usually feel the need to follow rigid or long-established practices. He should enjoy and do a good job on trouble-shooting-type assignments in which he has chances to tackle and solve difficult problems. Mr. Sample seems to be a person who fits well into jobs which demand correct and quick decisions.

Patterns for Career Activity Interests

Mr. Sample's profile suggests that he is likely to enjoy career-oriented and/or vocational activities which entail:

- working out ways for accomplishing and doing things by convincing, directing or persuading others to attain organizational goals and/or economic gain—an activity pattern similar to people who express interest for one or more of the following career fields: administration, business management, consulting, law/politics, marketing, merchandising or sales.
- the use of verbal and numerical skills to organize information according to prescribed plans and well-established procedures required in administrative, data processing and office practice systems—an activity pattern similar to people who express interest in one or more of the following career fields: business data processing, clerking, finance or office practices.
- opportunity to be near or at the center of group endeavors and solving problems through discussions with others or by encouraging relationships between people so as to enlighten, serve or train them—an activity pattern similar to people who express interest for one or more of the following career fields: counseling, education, health care, religion, social service or training.

Mr. Sample's strongest interest themes are similar to those of people employed in some of the following occupations. In reviewing this list, he may find support for past or present career choices. Alternatively, he may find it helpful to review his interests, skills, and experience with respect to occupations he may not have considered. There are indications he may find it relatively easy to identify with and relate to people who are successfully pursuing careers in some of these occupations: Administrative Manager, Claim Manager, Credit Manager, Industrial Relations Manager, Insurance

Manager, Wholesaler. Additional occupations Mr. Sample may wish to consider include: Administrative Services Director, Chamber of Commerce Executive, Community Service Director, Compensation-Benefits Director, Consultant, Customer Service Manager, Food Service Manager, Public Relations Director, Retail Store Manager, Salesperson, and Advertising Account Manager, Art Center Director, Attorney, Buyer, Journalist/Reporter, Public Relations Specialist.

The occupational information reported here is based on career preferences suggested by Mr. Sample's general personality orientation. The occupational listings should not be treated as specific job suggestions. Some may not appeal to him. Others may not relate well to his training and experience. However, each represents an option open to Mr. Sample in his personal growth and career planning at this point in time. A careful review may bring to mind other alternatives that represent even more appealing career paths.

Personal Career Life-Style Effectiveness Considerations

Mr. Sample's life-style is typical of people who value self-directedness and independence. He generally strives to achieve control of and freedom of choice in his personal life and work-related situations. He shows a marked preference for activities and work which involve meeting and interacting with people. He generally gains much satisfaction when he is in a position of leadership and is able to direct the actions of others. He likes to be in charge of projects, to take on challenges, to accomplish things and to work in a business-like manner.

In terms of Mr. Sample's needs for performance effectiveness and self-growth, he could be urged to guard against: (*) his tendency, at times, to act with so much eagerness, energy and optimism that he may overlook important details; fail to prepare himself enough for what he undertakes; or sufficiently anticipate consequences of what he does; (*) the tendency to make spur-of-the-moment decisions, rather than preparing himself enough before making decisions and taking action or giving thoughtful consideration of possible consequences of such actions; (*) being overly confident about his ability to handle most any problems or situations that come up when more accurate thinking and more realistic planning may be required to accomplish what he most desires to do; (*) showing too much of his emotions or feelings in tense or stressful situations; (*) being in such a hurry to get things done that he does not see how others may feel about things that are important to them; (*) tendencies to avoid or to get out of his responsibilities because

of his need to build more effective work habits than he seems to have at this time; (*) urges to change from one career field or job to another or to not stay with one organization long enough to feel as if he belongs there; and (*) taking on activities or assignments which involve ordinary, routine tasks without much creative thought or tasks which may not fully challenge Mr. Sample's intelligence or curiosity.

In conclusion, Mr. Sample seems to place importance on making an honest and sincere impression when he presents himself to others. Mr. Sample's career and life-style appears to be well integrated and progressing with overall personal effectiveness.

This page of career activity interest theme, career field and occupational scores is intended for use by qualified professionals only. Any review of the scores for career planning should be used for explorative counsel only.

OCCUPATIONAL TITLE	SCORE*
Venturous-Influential (V)	
Occupations	9.8
Administrators: Mid-Level	8.9
Airline Pilots	8.7
Business Executives	4.8
Real Estate Agents	9.7
Sales: Wholesale	7.8
Creative-Self Expressive (C)	
Occupations	6.7
Artists	5.3
Elementary School Teachers	5.2
High School Teachers	3.1
School Counselors	9.3
University Administrators	7.2
Writers	6.7
Analytic-Scientific (A)	
Occupations	5.8
Biologists	6.1
Chemists	7.0
ComputerProgrammers	9.9
Engineers	3.0
Geologists	6.3
Physicians	2.2
Physicists	5.9
University Professors	1.7
Nurturing-Altruistic (N)	
Occupations	7.1
Employment Counselors	5.6
Psychologists	7.9
School Superintendents	7.3
Social Worker	10.0
Teaching: General	5.6
Procedural-Systematic (P)	
Occupations	7.2
Accountants	6.5
Bank Managers	8.7
Credit Union Managers	8.4
Department Store Managers	1.9
Personnel Managers	10.0
Sales Managers/Supervisors	8.5
Mechanical-Operative (M)	
Occupations	5.6
Firefighters	10.0
Plant Forepersons	7.3
Production Managers	9.1
Service Station Dealers	4.6
Urban Police Officers	10.0

This page of 16PF scores is intended for use by qualified professionals only. Data on this page should be treated with utmost confidentiality.

16PF Profile

		Low Meaning	1 2 3 4 5 6 7 8 9 10	High Meaning
A	8	Autonomous-Reserved	● (8)	Participating-Warm
B	9	Concrete Thinking	● (9)	Conceptual Thinking
C	9	Affected by Feelings	● (9)	Calm-Unruffled
E	10	Considerate-Humble	● (10)	Assertive-Competitive
F	7	Reflective-Serious	● (7)	Talkative-Impulsive
G	4	Changeable-Expedient	● (4)	Persistent-Conforming
H	8	Cautious-Shy	● (8)	Socially Bold
I	5	Tough-Minded	● (5)	Tender-Minded-Sensitive
L	3	Accepting-Trusting	● (3)	Mistrusting-Oppositional
M	6	Conventional-Practical	● (6)	Imaginative
N	8	Forthright-Unpretentious	● (8)	Sophisticated-Shrewd
O	3	Confident-Self-Assured	● (3)	Apprehensive-Concerned
Q1	5	Conservative-Traditional	● (5)	Experimenting-Liberal
Q2	6	Group-Oriented	● (6)	Self-Sufficient
Q3	3	Lax-Uncontrolled	● (3)	Disciplined-Conclusive
Q4	3	Composed-Relaxed	● (3)	Tense-Driven

References

Altman, M. L., and Osborn, W., Stewart, et al., vs. Philips, et al. (1970). Complaint filed in the U.S. District Court of the District of Massachusetts. No. 70-1199, F, 1–22.

Baker, C., & Cokely, D. (1980). *American sign language.* Maryland: T. J. Publishers, Inc.

Cattell, R. B., Eber, H. W., & Tatsuoka, M. M. (1970). *Handbook for the sixteen personality factor questionnaire (16PF).* Champaign, IL: Institute for Personality and Ability Testing.

Chandler, J. T., & Plakos, J. (1969). *Spanish-speaking pupils classified as educable mentally retarded.* Sacramento, CA: Mexican-American Education Research Project, Division of Instruction, California State Department of Education.

Diana vs. State Board of Education C-70 37 REP, California, 1970.

Eber, H. W., & Cattell, R. B. (1976). *Manual for form E of the 16PF.* Champaign, IL: Institute for Personality and Ability Testing.

Gerweck, S., & Ysseldyke, J. (1975). Limitations of current psychological practices for the intellectual assessment of the hearing-impaired: A response to the Levine study. *The Volta Review, 77,* 243–248.

Institute for Personality and Ability Testing. (1972). *Manual for the 16PF.* Champaign, IL: Institute for Personality and Ability Testing.

Institute for Personality and Ability Testing. (1970). *16PF handbook: Tabular supplement No. 1.* Champaign, IL: Institute for Personality and Ability Testing.

Jensema, C. (1975). A statistical investigation of the 16PF form E as applied to hearing-impaired college students. *Journal of Rehabilitation of the Deaf, 9*(1), 21–29.

Klima, E., & Bellugi, U. (1979). *The signs of language.* Massachusetts: Harvard University Press.

Levine, E. (1974). Psychological tests and practices with the deaf: A survey of the state of the art. *The Volta Review, 74,* 298–319.

Trybus, R. (1973). Personality assessment of entering hearing-impaired college students using the 16PF, form E. *Journal of Rehabilitation of the Deaf, 6*(3), 34–40.

Walter, V. A. (1982). *Personal career development profile manual.* Champaign, IL: Institute for Personality and Ability Testing.

Zieziula, F. (Ed). (1982). *Assessment of hearing-impaired people.* Kendall Green, Washington, D.C.: Gallaudet College Press.

GENERAL SUBJECT INDEX

Answers to assessment questions
  does client read the report, 4, 20, 32, 63
  what to tell the client
    after assessment, 20, 63–64
    before assessment, 20, 62–63, 97, 103–104
  when to make a referral, 1, 4, 19–20, 44, 59–60, 74, 87, 97, 104
  who discusses results
    with the client, 4, 20, 63–64
Assessment barriers, xii–xiii, 10
Assessment contents
  in forensic assessment, 75–76
  in neuropsychological assessment, 53–59
  in psychiatric assessment, 87–90
  in psychological assessment, 11–14, 28–31, 37–48
  in psychometric assessment, 2–3
  in vocational assessment, 95–97
Assessment outcomes
  and their evaluation, 111–118
  and their validity, 111–112, 114–116
  research, 111–112
Assessment process
  in forensic assessment, 74–76
  in neuropsychological assessment, 49–59
  in psychiatric assessment, 87–90
  in psychological assessment, 11–14, 28–31, 42–43
  in psychometric assessment, 3–4
  in vocational assessment, 97–100
Assessment purposes, 1, 9, 27, 37, 49, 71, 87, 95–96
Assessment recommendations, 18–19, 31–32, 43–44, 52–53, 89–90
Assessment report samples, 4–5, 21–25, 32–34, 45–48, 64–69, 79–85, 92–93
Assessment types, 9–10
Authors' backgrounds, vii–ix

Barriers to effective assessment, xii–xiii, 10
Behavior observation, 29, 42–43, 59–62, 75–76, 99, 103
  structure of, 29
Brain
  and behavior, 59–62
  impairment, 49
  impairment and behavioral assessment, 49–69
  impairment and personality, 58–59
Client background considerations, 2–3, 11, 14, 15–16, 28–31, 54–59, 75, 101–102
Clinical assessment
  importance of, xii
  definition of, xi
Clinical interview, 3, 11, 16, 28, 43, 54, 75, 88
Communication considerations, vi, 3, 10, 14, 27, 28, 52–53, 75, 77–78, 90–92
Computerized assessment reports, 100–101, 103
Consumer role and responsibility, v–vii, xi, xiv, 18–19

Deafness
  and brain dysfunction, 51–52
  and developmental tasks, 40
  and differences among clients, 9–10, 14–16, 28, 39–40, 42, 54, 90–91, 101–102
  and impact on assessment, 4, 14–19, 27, 52, 76–78, 90, 101–103
  and multiple handicaps, 15–16, 31–32, 39, 42, 51–52, 90
  and potential effects, 4, 10–14, 27, 51–52, 76, 90
Diagnosis
  and brain dysfunction, 49
  and classification, 18, 30
  considerations in, 14–15, 18, 29–30, 54–59, 71–74, 90–92, 101–103
  definition, 9
  differential d., 18, 41, 52
  importance of, v–vi, xi–xii, 10, 31
  issues in, 15, 17–18, 29–30, 62–63, 71–74, 90–92, 101–103
  problems in, 17–18
DSM-III, 18, 30, 31, 91–92
  inadequacy with deaf persons, 18, 31, 91–92
Dissembling, 75–76, 77–78

Ethical considerations, 32, 78
  and examiner qualifications, 32, 53, 74, 78, 90–92
Examiner competencies
  and ethical considerations, 32, 53, 74, 78, 90–92
  in professional discipline, 10–11, 27–28, 32, 53, 74, 90, 97
  with deaf clients, 4, 10, 27, 32, 53, 77–78, 90–92, 101
Exit interview, 99

Forensic psychological assessment, 71–85

General psychological assessment, 9–25, 27–35, 37–48

Interpreting during assessment, 2, 15, 27, 53, 77, 91–92, 104, 121–132

Malingering, 75–76, 77–78
Mental disorders, 27, 91–92

Neuropsychological assessment, 49–69

Personality
  disorders, 30–31
  features with brain dysfunction, 58–59
  style, 28
Projective hypothesis, 28
Psychological assessment, 9–25, 27–35, 37–48, 37–48, 71–85
Psychometric assessment, 1–8
Public laws and regulations
  Developmentally Disabled Assistance
    and Bill of Rights Act, xi
  P.L. 91–142, xi
  Rehabilitation Act of 1973, xi
  Psychiatric assessment, 87–94

Recommendations from assessments
   importance of, v, xiii
Referral criteria, 1–2, 19–20, 44, 49, 52–53, 59–60, 74, 87,
   97, 104
Referral information, xii, 2, 11, 28, 42, 44, 49, 52, 54, 74–75,
   87–88, 98
Referral questions, xii, 2, 20, 44, 54, 59–60, 75, 87–88, 98
Report contents, 2–3, 11–14, 31–35, 42–43, 53–59, 76,
   87–90, 100

Sample assessment reports, 4–5, 21–25, 32–34, 45–48,
   64–69, 79–85, 92–93, 104–109, 126–132
Sixteen Personality Factor Questionnaire
   description, 121–122
   use with American Sign Language interpreting, 123–124
   use with deaf persons, 122–123
Specialist clinical assessment
   and mental disorders, 27–35, 87–94
   forensic assessment, 71–85
   neuropsychological assessment, 49–69
   psychiatric assessment, 87–94
State of nature in forensic psychology, 72–74
Students in transition
   definition of, 37–38, 42
   evaluation of, 37–48
   services for, 39

Testing
   purpose of, 28, 55
   reliability and validity, 2, 17–18
   special norms for deaf persons, 2, 17
   (tests) used with deaf persons, 3, 17–18, 42, 55
   with deaf persons, 3, 16–18, 29–30, 52, 55–59, 76–78, 89,
   98–99
Transition
   evaluation of students in, 37–47
   services for students in, 39
   students in, defined, 37–38, 42

Videotaped test administration, 121–132
Vocational assessment, 95–109

AUTHORS' INDEX

Adams, R., 51
Allen, J., 29
Altman & Osborne for Stewart, et al. v. Phillips, et al., 123
Altshuler, K., 77
American Psychiatric Association, 18, 30, 78, 89
American Psychological Association, 32
Apprell, M., 111

Baker, C., 123
Battison, R., 55, 61
Benton, A., 55
Black, F., 49, 51
Brauer, B., 91
Braunwald, E., 51
Brier, N., 38
Brookings, J., 112, 116, 117
Bullis, M., vii, 111–118

Campbell, J., 112, 116
Cattell, R., 121–122
Chess, S., 90
Cheung, F., 103
Chiarello, C., 61
Cokely, D., 124
Coley, J., 77
Cook, D., 112, 116, 117
Corn, S., 90
Couch, R., 96
Craig, W., 3
Critchfield, B., vii, 1–8
Cronbach, L., 118

Davison, L., 55
DeJong, G., 51
DeMatteo, A., vii, 49–69
Demb, H., 38
Diana v. State Board of Education, 123

Eber, H., 121–122
Eisenberg, M., 10–11
Erickson, E., 38, 40

Farrugia, D., 102
Fernandez, P., 90
Fishell, K., 111
Florian, V., 55, 61
Frances, A., 31
Freeman, E., 96

Gannon, J., 40
Gellman, W., 111
Gerber, B., vii, 87–94
Gerwick, S., 123
Gill, M., 28
Gleser, G., 118

Goble, W., 55, 61
Golbert, J., 72
Golden, C., 55
Goldstein, K., 60
Goodglass, H., 55
Grzesiak, R., 11

Hammeke, T., 55
Hamsher, K., 55
Handelsman, R., 112
Heaton, R., 52
Hirsch, E., 29
Hoemann, H., 55, 61
Hoffman, P., 95, 96
Holt, M., 29, 31

Institute for Personality and Ability Testing, 121–122, 126
Isselbacher, K., 51

Jacobs, D., 11
Jansen, M., 11
Jenkins v. United States, 74
Jensema, C., 39, 122–123

Kaplan, E., 55
Keller, M., 89
Klima, E., 123
Knight, R., 61
Kolb, L., 88

LaBreche, T., 55, 61
Lane, H., 55, 61
LeBarre, A., 40
Lee, S.M., vii, 49–69
Levine, E., 3, 10, 18, 29, 31, 77, 123
Lezak, M., 49, 55

MacKinnon, R., 88, 91
Mandel, M., 61
Manning, A., 55, 61
Manschreck, T., 89
Markham, R., 55, 61
Marut, P., viii, 111–118
McGowan, J., xii, 9
McHugh, D., 102
McKeever, W., 55, 61
Meadow, K., 51, 90
Meyers, L., 77
Michels, R., 88, 91
Miranda v. Arizona, 77
Monahan, J., 72
Moores, D., 27, 39, 82
Mullens, C., 39

Nadolosky, J., 95
Naisbitt, J., 38
Nash, A., 91

Nash, J., 91
National Center for Law and the Deaf, 77

Orr, F., viii, 49–69
Ottinger, P., 77

Pascal, G., 28
Pendleton, M., 52
Petersdorf, R., 51
Poizner, H., 55, 61
Porter, T., xii
Pritchard, D., viii, 71–85

Rainer, J., 77
Rapin, I., 51
Rappaport, D., 28
Reitan, R., 55
Rieber, R., 72
Rodda, M., 44
Rosenberg, B., 111

Scanlon, J., 40
Scheerer, M., 60
Schlesinger, H., 51, 90
Shafer, R., 28
Shafqat L., viii
Shapiro, D., 28
Shiels, J., viii, 95–109
Siegel, S., 116
Smith, S., 27
Social Security Administration, 72
Stewart, L., iii, v–vi, viii–ix, xi–xiv, 9–25, 71–85, 118
Strub, R., 49, 51
Sullivan, P., 3, 37–48
Sussman, A., 91

Tatsuoka, M., 121–122
Thorne, F., xii
Trybus, R., 122

U.S. Bureau of the Census, 37
U.S. Commission on Civil Rights, 37
Usdane, W., 111

VanDenburg, V., 51
VanDeventer, A., 55, 61
Varney, N., 55
Vernon, M., 3, 39, 42, 51, 77, 90
Vetter, H., 72

Walter, V., 122, 130
Watson, D., i, 3, 100, 104
Weiss, S., 43
Wiggins, J., 11
Will, M., 38, 39
Williams, C., 111

Wilson, B., 51
Wilson, J., 51
Wisniewski, A., ix, 49–69
Woody, R., xi
Wurtz, R., 112

Yandell, D., ix, 27–35
Ysseldyke, J., 123

Zieziula, F., 3, 42
Ziskin, J., 74